SO MANY CHRISTIANS, SO FEW LIONS

SO MANY CHRISTIANS, SO FEW LIONS

Is There Christianophobia in the United States?

George Yancey and David A. Williamson

ROWMAN & LITTLEFIELD
Lanham • Boulder • New York • London

Published by Rowman & Littlefield
A wholly owned subsidary of The Rowman & Littlefield
Publishing Group, Inc.
4501 Forbes Boulevard, Suite 200, Lanham, Maryland 20706
www.rowman.com

Unit A, Whitacre Mews, 26-34 Stannery Street, London SE11 4AB,
United Kingdom

British Library Cataloguing in Publication Information Available

Library of Congress Cataloging-in-Publication Data
Yancey, George A., 1962–
So many Christians, so few lions : is there Christianophobia in the United States? / George Yancey
and David A. Williamson.
pages cm
Includes bibliographical references and index.
ISBN 978-1-4422-2406-3 (cloth : alk. paper) — ISBN 978-1-4422-2407-0 (electronic)
1. Christianity—United States. 2. Hostility (Psychology) 3. Religious discrimination—United
States. 4. Religious tolerance—United States. I. Title.
BR517.Y36 2014
305.6'773—dc23
2014027474

Printed in the United States of America

CONTENTS

I

INTRODUCTION

In 2013, from March 15 to 17, the Pioneer Valley Performing Arts Charter Public School performed a play titled *The Most Fabulous Story Ever Told*, described as "a satire on the Book of Genesis with gay characters."[1] It retells the story of Genesis from the perspective of Adam and Steve instead of Adam and Eve. The play reportedly contains a scene of Steve having sexual relations with an animal and depicts Mary, the mother of Jesus, as a lesbian. A social observer who predicted that this play would become a source of contention would be correct. For example, Rev. Timothy A. McDonnell, bishop of the Roman Catholic Diocese of Springfield, stated, "I didn't know it was the responsibility of charter schools to teach religious bigotry."[2] However, William Newman, director of the western Massachusetts office of the American Civil Liberties Union, said, "The highest function of art is to make people think and talk and consider and be challenged. This play seems to fill the aspirations and goals of art." Furthermore, the play's director stated, "It's not a play that bashes religion but it does make fun of some religious attitudes. . . . Although it's full of jokes—some of them at the expense of religious fundamentalism—the play is, at its heart, a thoughtful investigation of the meaning of faith and family."

This controversy is an extension of the recent argument in our society about the possible existence and nature of anti-Christian sentiment. Some, such as Steve Maltz, have argued that anti-Christian attitudes are such a problem that hating Christians may be considered the "last taboo" of acceptable bigotry in our society.[3] Others, such as Terry Sanderson, have argued that complaints by Christians about prejudice and discrimination are unfounded.[4] Few disagree that some individuals do not like Christians, but it is not clear whether hostility, which may be defined as "a feeling of antagonism and hate,"[5] toward Christians is similar to other types of hostility.[6] Furthermore, Christianity is the dominant religion in our society, and it is unclear whether Christians pay a price for others' hostile attitudes.

But while arguments about the nature of anti-Christian hostility abound, there is surprisingly little academic treatment of the topic. Our research begins to answer these questions about anti-Christian attitudes. We first reviewed the American National Election Survey (ANES), a national survey with 3,076 respondents, to look at hostility toward different religious groups, and we were surprised to find a relatively high level of animosity toward conservative Christians. In this book we use quantitative data to look at the extent of disaffection directed at conservative Christians and who tends to have such disaffection. We then collected qualitative data from open-ended questionnaires of 3,577 respondents from groups particularly likely to demonstrate anti-Christian attitudes to get more detailed information about the nature of this hostility. Our findings provide us with insight into previously undocumented social forces. Ultimately we argue that the term "Christianophobia" best explains the perceptions of some with anti-Christian hostility.

Although we rely on academic evidence to substantiate our arguments, we contend that these issues should be discussed beyond the walls of academia, with a wider range of readers concerned about attitudes toward religion and how they shape life in America. To this end, we strive to present this material in an accessible and, hopefully, engaging manner. We explain the basics of our research in the body of the book, but for readers interested in our methodology, appendix A provides much greater depth. The endnotes also provide more nuanced details that we omitted from the narrative for the sake of readability.

ANTIRELIGIOUS ATTITUDES

There is a significant amount of research on antireligious attitudes, such as work examining bigotry toward Jews[7] and Muslims.[8] Paradoxically there is also work exploring prejudice aimed at the irreligious.[9] The results of unreasonable religious intolerance can be particularly vexing for these groups since they do not have the power conferred by Christian membership. However, Christianity may also be the target of antireligious hostility—some research has indicated the presence of animosity toward some Christians.[10] Although Christianity is the largest religion in the United States, a small, but growing, body of work indicates that in certain social areas Christians face real discrimination.[11]

Some may argue that prejudice against conservative Christians does not have the same importance as the other antireligious prejudices, because Christians have a privileged status and enjoy many social benefits—from having holidays recognized nationally to being able to easily find items in stores that pertain to their religion. For example, most of us know people with prejudices against whites and men, and so we can talk about certain limited situations in which being white or a male can be a disadvantage. But it can be fairly argued that these groups still enjoy disproportionate power in almost all of our social institutions. People of color and women have nowhere near the economic and social power of whites and men. But while Christianity is clearly the most accepted religion in the United States, our previous research[12] suggests that those with an anti-Christian bias tend to have social power due to their education and income.[13] They likely have enough societal power to significantly affect the lives of Christians, particularly conservative Christians.[14] Furthermore, in certain areas in our society (e.g., media, academia), being identified as a conservative Christian may be a disadvantage. It is a mistake to ignore the potential barriers anti-Christian hostility creates for its targets.

WHICH CHRISTIANS ARE HATED

Discussing the potential presence of anti-Christian animosity suggests that all Christians are equally vulnerable to such a bias. As our quantitative data will demonstrate, this simply is not the case. We will show that fundamentalist Christians are generating a great deal of animosity among other members of society. Although that data does not tell us how individuals define what they mean by "fundamentalist," it is relatively safe to say that most people think of fundamentalist Christians as

Christians who are very conservative. Our qualitative sample comprises individuals who define themselves as opponents of the Christian Right—that is, of the types of groups that would attack conservative Christians. The nature of our qualitative sample does not allow us to explore animosity toward more moderate Christians. We do not see this as a problem because our quantitative findings indicate that moderate Christians are less likely to experience disaffection. Therefore our qualitative sample will allow us to examine the strongest source of anti-Christian sentiment.

Our attempt to merge our quantitative and qualitative data comes with some costs. For example, our qualitative data comes from a questionnaire about the Christian Right, while the quantitative data comes from a survey of attitudes toward fundamentalist Christians. It is fair to argue that our qualitative respondents' attitudes toward the Christian Right may differ from their responses toward conservative Christians in general. However, a merger of Christianity and politics makes it difficult for some of our respondents to disentangle the two. The following two representative comments indicate the propensity of several respondents to conflate Christians with Republicans:

> Well, first of all I don't think there is such a thing as a Republican who is not a Christian. (Female, aged 46–55 with bachelor's degree)
> Republicans and Christians are the same people. (Male, over 75 with some college)

For respondents like these, Christianity is a conservative political ideology. They fail to comprehend the diversity among Christians and develop a tenacious stereotype. A fear of conservative Christians colors the perceptions of individuals who have animosity toward Christians. As we will show in chapter 3 when discussing the quantitative data, our research suggests that anti-Christian hostility in the United States is primarily animosity directed toward conservative Christians or the image of Christians as conservatives.

As we discuss anti-Christian animosity or hostility in this work, it is clear that not all Christians experience the results of that hostility equally. It may be more accurate to talk about anti-conservative-Christian hostility than anti-Christian hostility. But we see little value in ignoring the simpler term of anti-Christian as long as the reader remembers that, generally, the animosity documented in this work is more likely to be felt by conservative, as opposed to moderate or progressive, Christians. It may be that the threat of conservative Christians to the political, cultural, and social goals of those with this type of religious hostility generates the latters' animosity. It is difficult to know just how "conservative" a Christian must be in order to suffer from the animosity documented in this research. If conservative Christians become fully disempowered and marginalized in the larger society, moderate and progressive Christians may well experience the type of animosity now directed at their conservative peers to the degree that they offer a challenge to the political, cultural, and social goals of those with anti-Christian animosity. So while we ask readers to interpret the phrase "anti-Christian hostility" as referring to an animosity directed at conservative Christians, we do not rule out the possibility that more moderate Christians may also experience limited versions of this phenomenon from time to time.

THE DEGREE OF HATRED TOWARD CONSERVATIVE CHRISTIANS

We have talked about anti-Christian hostility without looking at the type of fear and hatred that such animosity generates. In chapters 4 through 6, we will take a deeper, more nuanced look at how this animosity can manifest itself. But for now we want to show that our research has revealed attitudes of real hatred and fear, which we take seriously. We collected our sample using short-answer questions given through an online survey. The link to this survey was sent to individuals who identified themselves as members of organizations that oppose the Christian Right. It is quite difficult to measure intensity of emotion with survey data or even with open-ended questions that allow the respondent to fully express him- or herself. Had we interviewed these respondents, we might have been able to elicit more fully their emotional state as it concerned conservative Christians.

Our data do, however, provide important clues to the nature of the animosity of some respondents. For example, seven respondents referred to lions as they wrote out answers to various questions.

> My favorite bumpersticker, "So many Christians, so few lions."
> (Female, aged 46–55 with bachelor's degree)
> Bring back the Lions. (Female, aged 65–75 with master's degree)
> Not enough lions. They have abandoned their Christian views for
> a political position. (Male, aged 36–45 with doctorate)
> I wish we could start feeding them to lions again, or burn them at
> the stake. (Male, aged 36–45 with doctorate)
> FEED THE LIONS. (Male, aged 56–65 with some college)
> Feed them to the lions. (Male, aged 46–55 with some college)
> So many Christians, so few lions. (Male, aged 46–55 with some
> college)

Of course, use of the word "lions" refers to the practice during the Roman Empire of feeding Christians to lions. That is the only reasonable association of Christians with these animals. Do we believe that these respondents actually want lions to eat Christians? That seems farfetched, and even if it were the case, such attitudes would not become popular in modern society. Some can reasonably argue that focusing on a few unfortunate statements exaggerates the possibility that conservative Christians face hatred or fear in the United States,[15] an assertion strengthened by the fact that these are only seven responses from the 2,483 respondents who filled out the short-answer questions. Finally, it should be recognized that individuals answering online surveys enjoy an anonymity that allows them to say things they would not dream of saying publically. So rather than capturing real attitudes, we may be recording comments made for fun, or there may just have been a few troublemakers in the group. At this point we might be accused of mining the data to find false evidence in order to enable conservative Christians to claim to be victims.

So to make our point, let us change the wording of these statements. Imagine that we surveyed about twenty-five hundred individuals who attended a particular Christian church and received the following seven responses:

> My favorite bumpersticker, "So many Jews, so few ovens."
> Bring back the Ovens.
> Not enough ovens. They have abandoned their Jewish views for a
> political position.
> I wish we could start putting them in ovens again, or burn them
> at the stake.

> FILL THE OVENS.
> Put them in the ovens.
> So many Jews, so few ovens.

Of course, use of the word "ovens" refers to the practice during the Holocaust of cremating murdered Jews. Would we seriously believe that the church members actually wanted to put Jews in ovens? Probably as much as we would that the respondents of our survey wanted to feed Christians to lions. Furthermore, no one seriously thinks that the policies of the Holocaust will become popular in contemporary society. Yet such survey results would indicate to researchers serious anti-Semitism within this church. The fact that these comments were made online would not excuse them in the minds of academics, who would rather interpret the anonymous nature of the survey method as allowing anti-Semites to be truthful. Even these few anti-Semitic comments would have to be taken seriously, and hardly anyone would consider such concern merely a case of Jews pretending to false victimhood. No responsible researcher would imply that all members of this church were anti-Semitic on the basis of these seven responses, but seven respondents indicated more than one or two unbalanced individuals. Such a congregation, at best, does not challenge anti-Semitic thinking and, at worse, promotes anti-Semitism. If congregational leaders were overly hostile to anti-Semitism, then it is hard to believe that seven individuals would freely express such ugly sentiments.

We are comparing a single congregation to a loose group of associations, but it is likewise plausible that a tolerance of hostility toward Christians condones such sentiments within those associations. The ugly sentiments expressed in the statements about lions do not occur in a social vacuum. They occur with a certain degree of tacit approval found in these individuals' social networks. It is unfair to think that all of the respondents in those networks hold such distasteful sentiments, but the numbers are sufficient to show that they are not held by merely one or two unbalanced individuals. There is a hostility toward Christians and Christianity at least as irrational as any anti-Semitism. In fact, recently in the United States overt hostility toward certain Christians has been far greater than overt hostility toward Jews.[16]

We contend that these seven statements alone produce a level of concern about anti-Christian animosity that should be taken seriously.

Others may argue that seven statements, in and of themselves, do not warrant much attention. But these seven statements are not the only ones we found in our work to indicate an unreasonable hatred or fear of Christians. They are merely the only ones in which the word "lions" appears. Many other respondents promoted a hatred or fear that is difficult to stomach. To illustrate this, we will provide some of these statements. We understand that it may be tiring to read so many statements in support of a single point, and for most of this book, we limit ourselves to relatively few comments from our respondents to make our argument. Doing so opens us up to the criticism that we are cherry-picking the statements to make our respondents look bad.[17] This is not our intention, as we found strong themes within our data. So here, we provide a range of comments to illustrate that we are not writing about an outlier or two in our large sample and instead have a sample that clearly illustrates the potentially ugly nature of anti-Christian hostility. We will do this with a rather long, but not exhaustive, list of the quotes from our sample that can be considered hateful. If the reader tires of these comments and concedes that we are not cherry-picking a few statements of unreasonable hatred, then he or she can move on to the next section of the chapter. We want to establish clearly that in our future chapters we could add many more quotes from our sample but choose not to in order to keep this book to a reasonable length and make it more readable.

> Have pondered a suicide bombing attack to take out as many as possible. (Male, aged 46–55 with some college)
> Churches and houses of religion should be designated as nuclear test zones. (Male, aged 66–75 with high school diploma)
> They are well organized and highly motivated, kind of like a serial killer. (Female, aged 46–55 with bachelor's degree)
> Kill them all, let their god sort them out. (Male, aged 56–65 with some graduate school)
> I abhor them and I wish we could do away with them. (Female, aged 46–55 with master's degree)
> A torturous death would be too good for them. (Male, aged 36–45 with bachelor's degree)
> Scum, with apologies to scum everywhere. (Sex, age, and education unknown)

They are so arrogant and obnoxious and refuse to take NO for an answer. I'd probably end up shooting one of them out of frustration. (Female, aged 56–65 with some graduate school)

Would like to give them all a frontal lobotomy. (Male, over 75 with master's degree)

I'd be a bit giddy, certainly grateful, if everyone who saw himself or herself in that category were snatched permanently from our societal peripheries, whether by holocaust or rapture or plague. (Male, aged 66–75 with doctorate)

Line 'em up and shoot 'em. (Male, aged 36–45 with some college)

They're not dying fast enough . . . and they reproduce like rabbits! (Male, aged 46–55 with some graduate school)

I would not live in a neighborhood that was almost all Christian Right. I would probably kill some of them. (Male, aged 66–75 with some graduate school)

I want them all to die in a fire. (Male, aged 26–35 with doctorate)

I am only too well aware of their horrific attitudes and beliefs—and those are enough to make me see them as subhuman. (Female, aged 66–75 with some graduate school)

I would banish them to some continent all on their own. (Male, aged 56–65 with some college)

(Christianity) is a disease that must be kept in check. (Male, aged 56–65 with master's degree)

They should be eradicated without hesitation or remorse. Their only purpose is to damage and inflict their fundamentalist virus onto everyone they come in contact with. (Female, aged 66–75 with master's degree)

They make me a believer in eugenics. . . . They pollute good air. . . . I would be in favor of establishing a state for them. . . . If not, then sterilize them so they can't breed more. (Male, aged 46–55 with master's degree)

May they come to an unhappy end. (Female, aged 66–75 with master's degree)

The only good Christian is a dead Christian. (Male, aged 36–45 with doctorate)

We could go on but believe our point has been made. Many of these comments are clearly hyperbole. We do not actually believe that all of the above respondents actually want to see Christians die. But these comments are disturbing nonetheless. It is clear that anti-Christian hostility exists in some respondents.

We asked our respondents questions through an anonymous online survey. This confidentiality may have contributed to the hostility evident in such comments. Research by Frank Mungeam has suggested that Internet correspondence is often vicious since individuals need not reveal their identities.[18] However, Selma Vonderwell suggests that this anonymity allows individuals to display more honesty about their perspectives.[19] Other research suggests that online communication gives individuals time to process their thoughts at a high level.[20] Our respondents' relatively high level of education likely made them more careful to present themselves in a socially acceptable manner, and this online medium is at least as likely to produce honest answers as impolite comments. We argue that this method is likely to produce both honest and hostile answers from individuals who possess anti-Christian animosity.[21]

As shown later in the book, those with anti-Christian animosity have a relatively high degree of social power in our society. This particular type of antireligious perspective manifests itself differently from other types (e.g., Islamophobia, anti-Semitism). For example, given the relative social power of those with anti-Christian animosity, it may be somewhat easier to find open public quotes that exhibit anti-Christian hostility than to find quotes betraying other types of antireligious animosity. In chapter 7 we will point out some of those quotes. If we are concerned about the anonymous nature of our respondents' comments, these public quotes indicate that some of the attitudes we document in this book are stated openly and without the problems associated with confidential surveys.

We have given you a taste of some of the potential results of our qualitative research. Before fully exploring our data, we will discuss the historical and sociological framework for these antireligious attitudes. But first we here outline our plans for this book.

OUTLINE OF BOOK

In chapter 2 we look at historical reasons for the development of anti-Christian hostility in the United States. We first discuss the development of hostility toward religion during the Enlightenment period and how the religion/science battle has moved into the United States. The conflict between science and religion shaped a growing societal split

that eventually resulted in the emergence of individuals with an irrational fear and hatred of Christianity—particularly conservative Christianity. We then discuss how desire for social control explains why the
combatants on the side of science can develop extremely negative views
about Christianity, the dominant religion in the United States. To gain
and maintain social control, certain cultural progressives legitimate animosity toward and contempt for conservative Christians and Christianity, sentiments that become the basis for anti-Christian thought.

In chapter 3 we explain our research more fully. We used the
American National Election Survey to document the degree of relative
hostility conservative Christians face and who tends to have that hostility. That survey utilizes a set of what can be called "thermometer questions," which we can use to illustrate who tends to have disaffection
toward conservative Christians. Our quantitative research shows that
those with anti-Christian sentiments tend to be more educated, have
higher socioeconomic status (SES), be more politically progressive, and
be less religious than other Americans. Our qualitative research further
explores the demographics and characteristics of people with anti-
Christian hostility at least among cultural progressive activists.

In chapter 4 we look at the perceptions those with anti-Christian
hostility have of Christians. This chapter allows us to address the issue
of why well-educated individuals are capable of this animosity. We do
this by comparing them to other cultural progressives. Generally anti-
Christian attitudes are more likely to occur among cultural progressives
who fear that Christians are infiltrating our society and attempting to
take it over. Those with this disaffection are also more likely to complain about homophobia and intolerance than other cultural progressives. These differences may help to explain why some cultural progressives develop such anger toward and/or fear of conservative Christians.

Chapter 5 explores the possibility that those with animosity toward
conservative Christians engage in a process of dehumanization. We first
explore Nick Haslam's[22] model of dehumanization, which focuses on
incivility, coarseness, amorality, irrationality, and childlikeness. We then
see if that model applies to the hostility many of our respondents have
for conservative Christians. We find elements of dehumanization, indicating that under the right circumstances anti-Christian hostility can
lead to not perceiving conservative Christians as fully human. We then

explore the possibility that this type of hostility is an example of hatred, prejudice, and/or intolerance.

In chapter 6 we look at what those with anti-Christian attitudes want. Generally, they oppose overt laws against Christians. But while most do not directly advocate political measures aimed at inhibiting Christians, some individuals with this hostility do not mind laws with a disparate impact on conservative Christians. For the most part, the societal alterations they desire are based on their desire to remove the influence of Christianity from those in their personal lives and political realities. However, political activism is not the only solution generated by anti-Christian animosity. Individuals with that hostility are concerned about the religious socialization that they perceive to be the source of conservative Christianity. Therefore they also advocate use of our educational system to reverse the effects of this socialization.

In chapter 7 we argue that the term "Christianophobia" best illustrates the characteristics exhibited by the respondents. This term refers to an unreasonable hatred toward and fear of conservative Christians. We explore the potential influence Christianophobia has in our larger society. Those with Christianophobia comprise a group with a great deal of social control due to their racial status, gender, and education. Even though they often envision themselves as victims, they are in a position to influence society and punish those they disagree with. We are unable to determine with complete certainty if individuals in certain situations suffer from Christianophobia, but we look at a few of those situations to illustrate how Christianophobic attitudes possibly shape social events. Understanding the phenomenon helps us understand some of the larger conflicts and social processes in the United States.

In chapter 8 we discuss how individuals with Christianophobic tendencies differ from those with other types of intolerances. Their higher social position allows them the opportunity to affect the lives of their out-group targets in ways unavailable to those possessing other types of intolerances. To this end, we next discuss possible ways for dealing with Christianophobic animosity in the United States. We especially look at how education may exacerbate this type of intolerance but can be redirected to create global respect for individuals in a variety of social groups. Ideally, future research will build on this work and allow us to further define the contours and extent of Christianophobic thought.

By the end of this book, we hope to have stimulated more interest in fully exploring animosity toward conservative Christians. We are very comfortable asserting that this research illustrates the existence of anti-Christian hostility in a way that no previous academic work has done. However, we admit that given the current limitations of the data we have available, we are less confident about asserting the relative prevalence of this hostility. Thus, we do not see our work as the final word on this subject. In fact, in many ways, we see our work as the starting point for a long, fruitful empirical and theoretical discussion on an important topic. If this work stimulates such a discussion and future research to shape it, we believe that it will be of great value to readers, even if they do not agree with our conclusions.

Finally, when it came to presenting the respondents' quotes, we erred on the side of presenting them in their original form as much as possible. We corrected obvious misspellings and typos but did not do a rigorous proofing for grammatical accuracy. Furthermore we retained the use of all caps and parentheses as the respondents chose to use them. Unless we explicitly state otherwise, the reader can assume that any such uses are in the original quote and not added by us. We personally make no comments as to the meaning of all caps or wording put in parentheses. But we believe that keeping the quotes as close to the original form as possible will put the reader in the best position to assess the intent of the respondents.

2

A HISTORY OF ANTI-CHRISTIAN HOSTILITY IN THE UNITED STATES

A local controversy recently captured the headlines. The Christmas season was upon us, and in the face of the holiday's ubiquitous religious references, at least one atheist organization posted billboards and placed advertisements on city buses declaring, "You KNOW it's a Myth. This season, celebrate REASON!" and "Millions of Americans Are Good Without God." Reactions were mixed, although conservative Christians were quick to denounce the campaign, some publicly calling for bus boycotts and other strikes against this perceived egregious attempt to squelch the religious spirit of the season. Anonymous donors sponsored minivans to follow each bus that carried an antireligious slogan with countermessages: "2.1 billion people are good with God" and "I still love you. —God."

As surprising as these events may seem to unsuspecting American Christians who have inherited a sense of ownership of this time of year, the conflict is actually centuries old. This is just the most recent local manifestation of voices that have whispered, muttered, and eventually boldly spoken against the hegemony of Christian authority and its perceived abuses. Now those voices, riding the wave of once closeted causes recently finding emancipation, have become emboldened to speak more publicly for their concerns and against the institutional and cultural forces that they believe act against their right—in fact, everyone's right—to exist openly in a free society. Peter Berger points out obvious historical examples of that abuse in inquisitions, financial exploitation of uneducated masses, and conspiratorial alliances between political and religious authorities.[1] Interdenominational abuses in the early Protestant world gave further demonstration of religious abuse and intolerance, such as the ransacking of Catholic churches, threats against and murder of Anabaptists preaching baptism by immersion, and the persecution and murder of some who, like William Tyndale, introduced new translations of the Bible. More recent evidence has included sexual exploitation of children by religious authorities, the financial exploitation of vulnerable populations by televangelists, and, most threatening of all to some cultural progressives, efforts from the Christian Right to influence political processes.

The roots of animosity toward conservative Christians in the United States extend back to the social and political dialogue of seventeenth- and eighteenth-century Europe, well before the birth of this nation. From the Middle Ages until that time, a relative harmony between science (reason) and religion had existed, based largely on Thomas Aquinas's marriage of Christian theology and Aristotelian philosophy. During much of that time, science was simply a branch of philosophy. Ian Barbour points out that human reason was deemed capable of grasping the nature of the world and cosmos, the essence of which was believed to be moral (i.e., ordered and subject to law).[2] The source of that morality was to be found in Aquinas's *Prima causa*, based on Aristotle's *Unmoved Mover*, which served as the basis for his natural theology, according to which humans may understand, through reason, the nature of a universe ordered by God.

Over the centuries, as human observation of the physical universe became empirical, biblical literalism came into question, eventually giving rise to biblical higher criticism or the treatment of biblical texts as pieces of literature to be studied in the context of their times, authors, and cultures of origin. Although many point to Charles Darwin as the scientist who provided the final evidence that religion, as emperor, had no clothes, some in the Western world had reached that watershed at least by the seventeenth century. Social sciences in general and sociology in particular emerged in a world that was trying to answer the question of who controls the universe and human societies if God does not. Some early sociologists, such as Auguste Comte, presumed to answer that call, envisioning sociologists as a new breed of social priests. More broadly, though, there was a growing sense of individual liberty, a human right proclaimed to be sovereign. Biblical literalism as we experience it today was in part a reaction to a fundamental questioning of the authority of the Bible and, more importantly, the church.

By the end of the seventeenth century, a full-blown battle had emerged in Western Europe: the "Battle of the Books" or the debate between the ancients and the moderns. Charles Perrault's *Quarrel of the Ancients and Moderns* argues that human society was upwardly bound and that the age of Louis XIV was its pinnacle. Rather than looking to the authors, artists, and ideas of antiquity, we should look to the present and future to see the heights to which humanity might climb. Compared to the misery of the Dark Ages and medieval Europe, Perrault's view may seem rather obvious. However, according to church doctrine and biblical accounts (important sources of authority for conservatives), humanity was born into perfection, only to spoil its purity by searching for knowledge—or, literally, by partaking of the fruit of the tree of the knowledge of good and evil. Since then the human race has been sliding down a path that will, according to traditionalists, lead us to final destruction. However, the moderns, or progressives, glowing in the Enlightenment (insinuating that society had been living in darkness, largely caused by a dominant Catholic Church), championed a disdain for religion fueled by a confidence that not only does humanity not need God, but those who claim to speak for God are impediments to a rational, purposeful development of human potential.

The basic battle lines had been drawn, with progressives on one side, idealizing enlightenment, liberation, and the realization of human society free from the shackles of religion, and Christian conservatives on the other, espousing a return to traditional order based on biblical literalism. For progressives, to go back literally meant to devolve and digress. For Christian conservatives, to progress into a godless world without consideration for the moral structure of traditional religion was no progress at all.

Of course, the debate was not so simple. Progressives came in many forms; some were antireligious and materialistic, whereas others, such as Jean-Jacques Rousseau, led the age of romanticism in seeing a way forward for humanity that embraced a natural theology. Rousseau's natural theology was deistic, expecting not an acting God who intervenes in human history but an ordered world in which humans may access the goodness in themselves and others through rational observation and exercise of civil religion in order that human life may become ordered as well. Christianity, according to Rousseau, was destructive of human life and society, but not because it was a religion. It was destructive because it proposed a false hope in an acting God and established forms of control over human society that distorted it and limited its progress toward civility and liberty. Progress is made possible not by merely depending on cold rationality, as the materialists proposed, or by clinging to ancient religious ideas and forms, as the traditionalists believed, but by going beyond reason to understand one's feelings.[3] Those feelings, according to romantics like Rousseau, come from the innate goodness of humans and often lead us in directions counter to either stark rationality or blind allegiance to the past.

Enlightenment thinkers of the eighteenth century believed deeply in human reason's capacity to perfect humanity. Indeed, it was imperfect and even abusive social institutions that impeded such progress. The important point is that the confusion and distortions of human experiences are caused by society and its institutions—especially religious ones—not by humanity's evil nature. Barbour noted that by engineering society through a mastery of its laws we could, as physical scientists had begun to do, open the door to human liberation and to the goodness that was innately present.[4]

Conservatives, religious or not, were no more monolithic than progressives. Some were religious fundamentalists who eschewed progressive ideas and metaphorical reading of scriptures. Some, while politically and socially conservative, were religious moderates or even progressive. They valued the life of the mind and were open to more interpretive readings of scripture. However, because progressive ideas tend to permeate all dimensions of the worldview, it seems unlikely that those in this category maintained this dichotomous position for long. Most often, if inclined to value the life of the mind and embrace abstractions, we would argue, they would soon find the company of the fundamentalists uncomfortable. Thus the lines were being drawn between religious conservatives and all others who opposed traditionalism (i.e., progressives), whether religious or not.

We see from this evolution of thought not only two camps in diametric opposition but multiple camps with varying allegiances to the life of the mind and religion. Two of these camps are central to this research:

- Materialist and romantic progressives who believe in the potential for rational social development devoid of religion—at least traditional religion and its oppressive structures
- Religious fundamentalists who are pragmatists, opposed to intellectualism, and committed to a society ordered by literal interpretation of scripture and what they believe are traditional values

DARWIN, THE FUNDAMENTALS, AND THE AMERICAN CULTURE WARS

At its inception American life was dominated by faith traditions, although there always have been those who profess attachment to no official religion. That religiosity was, however, diverse. While many who came to the New World sought religious liberty, they were by no means guided by principles of pluralism and the separation of church and state. Colonies aligned and developed in concert with specific denominations. Religious intolerance was the rule of the day. Only over time and with the exigencies of protection from a common enemy and the need to build a strong American economy did tolerance develop. James Hunter has argued that a Protestantism emerged in which denominations worked together to create a vision that would direct all the major public institutions.[5]

The waves of Catholic and Jewish immigration in the later nineteenth and early twentieth centuries brought new problems, testing the limits of Americans' religious tolerance. But none challenged the basic beliefs and values that bridged the overwhelmingly conservative, literalist views of established denominations. The greater challenge was the encroachment of ideas that originated with progressives, from the French philosophes to Darwin and Thomas Huxley. Rather than challenging forms of worship or soteriology, their thinking threatened the very foundation of widely held belief systems.

The progressive threat to traditional religion in America was intensified when Darwin's ideas of natural selection and evolution hit the United States in the mid-nineteenth century. Theologians, even conservatives, grappled with the implications of these ideas and their supporting evidence. A famous illustrative case is that of James Woodrow, uncle of President Woodrow Wilson. An ordained Presbyterian minister and a scientist, Woodrow was selected in 1861, just prior to the Civil War, as the first Perkins Professor of Natural Science in Connexion with Revealed Religion at Presbyterian Columbia Theological Seminary in South Carolina (now in Decatur, Georgia). Initially a biblical literalist, Woodrow was influenced by scientific evidence that supported evolution and began to publish articles rationalizing it as divinely guided, although positing the human soul as immediately created.[6] His ideas were hotly debated and rejected four times by General Assemblies of the Presbyterian Church, U.S. (Southern) before finally being upheld in 1969.[7] This parallels broader progressive shifts in Presbyterianism.

Woodrow and Alexander Winchell were pioneers in religious progressivism, which became more than simply the irreligious and intellectual versus the religious. Progressivism strongly affected the mainstream American denominations, primarily through their seminaries. Ronald Numbers contends that even Methodism, which began as a very conservative offshoot of Anglicanism, evolved into a progressive leader in American Christianity, primarily through its seminaries.[8] The conservative reaction to this progressive and intellectual drift of mainstream Christian seminaries led to the coining of a new word: cemeteries.

Despite the growing influence of progressive thinkers, religious fundamentalism (although the moniker would not be used until the early twentieth century) maintained a dominant hand in shaping popular ideology in American thought, despite the rhetoric of materialists and romantics. It was energized by defenses structured and reinforced in reaction to challenges to the literal validity of the Bible and the authority of the church. However, even conservative Protestantism in some ways was made more vulnerable to the attacks of progressives by borrowing from the latter's championing of individual liberties and disdain for abusive authority. Using their detractors' own techniques made it all the more difficult to justify their own intellectual contributions.

By the twentieth century religion had been tamed in Europe and became an unthreatening vestige of an age of religious domination. Rodney Stark and Roger Finke[9] have argued that the separation of church and state and religion's diminished role in establishing social and behavioral standards reveal that the populations of Europe were never as religious as they appeared. No longer forced to participate in religious services, pay taxes supporting the church, and concede individual liberties, as they had been when membership in the state implied membership in the church, people became irreligious. For the last century, Europe has been the poster child for those who support the controversial secularization theory.

The American experience has been quite different. More than a mere tool for controlling the masses, religion has just as often been seen as a tool in the hands of the masses, giving them meaning and motive, comfort, and a theodicy that rationalizes the life of the working man and woman. The independent, pragmatic, working-class ethos at the heart of building this country was largely shaped by religious forces.[10] Richard Hofstadter contends that the masses' religion also tended to be anti-intellectual, a sentiment that has risen in sequential waves with surges in business, science, and war.[11] With industrialization and western/southern development, American society relied on courage, character, endurance, and cunning but was not seen as producing poets, artists, or intellectuals. It was also a society whose values had little need for the intellectual or, for that matter, the highly educated. Intellectuals are people interested in the life of the mind, not life on the land or in the factory. Who needs critics who sit on the sidelines and abstract everything, including—most importantly—the highly valued history and morality of the Bible?

Christian progressives tended to side with those, religious or not, who championed the life of the mind. When interviewing Christian liberals in the Pacific Northwest, James Wellman repeatedly heard that God wanted us to think for ourselves.[12] For conservatives God provided the infallible Word that you could trust over fallible humans. However, when the work of intellectuals is deemed pragmatic, anti-intellectualism has waned. Few Americans have questioned science and intellectual pursuits when threatened by war or disease.

It can be asked how the relations of intellectuals to progressives, both religious and irreligious, who oppose the religious Right matters to the task at hand. We are not suggesting that all progressives are intellectual or that all conservatives are anti-intellectual. However, there appears to be a clear connection. As Hofstadter[13] has powerfully argued, Christian fundamentalism developed into its current form in reaction to the innovations of science (e.g., Darwin) and the abstraction that is part and parcel of modernity. Intellectuals, including Christian intellectuals, demonstrated a proclivity for abstraction and critical thinking, skills dearly valued and taught in institutions of higher education. Whereas some of our nation's most prestigious universities started primarily as conservative seminaries, most have taken a clearly progressive track, championing biblical higher criticism, moral relativism, and the embrace of pluralism. Central to this movement is the progress to a more civil society in which boundaries are diminished and conflict is avoided. No individual group has the right to stand in judgment of another or to issue moral edicts or prescribe laws that inhibit the actions of others, as long as those actions to not injure or impede the freedoms of others.

In reaction to this liberalization and the perceived threat of Darwinism to conservatives' foundation of biblical literalism and inerrancy, a movement was born to reinforce the fundamental beliefs of conservative Christians. A series of publications, *The Fundamentals*, produced between 1910 and 1915 and funded by conservative and wealthy elites, gave name to the new movement. The energy of this movement was fueled by both the existing and cyclically renewed anti-intellectualism already present and the fear that Darwinism and biblical higher criticism were undermining traditional religion, which was, adherents believed, the bedrock of American society. Intellectualism and progressivism as applied to Christian teachings (e.g., James Woodrow) yielded, in their opinion, an emasculated religion that stripped Christianity of its most substantive beliefs and took down the moral barriers by which America had, in their perception, obtained the blessings of God and held back the floodwaters of materialism and immorality. Evolution and other perceived threats to traditional Christian beliefs and values came from the world of academia, even influencing Christian seminaries in that world. *The Fundamentals* were an attempt to counter that intellectual front with well-reasoned, conservative, statements of their Christian fundamental beliefs.[14]

FORMALIZING AND INSTITUTIONALIZING THE PROGRESSIVE MOVEMENT

Whereas *The Fundamentals* marked the beginning of a countermovement in reaction to the perception of a progressive infiltration of American higher education and public life, the progressive movement became more institutionally visible and active after World War I and the Bolshevik revolution. Fearing that communist sympathies might be brewing in the United States, Attorney General Mitchell Palmer began rounding up and deporting suspected radicals in 1919 and 1920. These became known as the Palmer Raids, which outraged progressives open to alternative forms of government and ways of thinking about economics and human rights. Legal efforts to defend and protect the targets of Palmer's raids resulted in what was to become the American Civil Liberties Union (ACLU), which shortly thereafter partnered with Clarence Darrow in the famous Scopes Trial of 1925. Concerned that the Tennessee General Assembly had passed legislation banning the teaching of evolution in public schools, the ACLU recruited John Scopes to do just that in order to test the law. Despite the organization's efforts, Scopes was found guilty (although the verdict was later overturned); still, the story made national headlines and brought into public consciousness the apparent standoff between religion and science, at least with regard to evolution.

Subsequent causes added to the ACLU's image and activity, including opposition to Japanese internment camps during World War II, the 1954 joint victory with the National Association for the Advancement of Colored People in the *Brown v. Board of Education* case, and perhaps its most famous win in the 1973 *Roe v. Wade* case. According to its website, the ACLU currently has around one hundred staff attorneys who work with approximately two thousand volunteer attorneys handling almost six thousand cases every year. The ACLU is funded by foundation and individual charitable gifts. No government funds support its efforts. Its mission is to defend the constitutional rights of every American, primarily the rights to freedom of speech, equal protection under the law, due process, and privacy. It particularly works to protect the underserved, including people of color, women, lesbians, gay men, bisexuals, transgender people, prisoners, and people with disabilities (http://www.aclu.org).

In 1947 Americans United for the Separation of Church and State (now Americans United) formed in response to a public action viewed as unconstitutional: the proposition that federal funds should be used to support private, religiously based schools. The founding principle was the absolute separation of church and state, and the organization's subsequent history clearly demonstrates that it has held to this principle. It has fought school vouchers, prayer in schools, and the reading of the Bible in public schools. Throughout its development, Americans United has expressly invited the participation of "Christians, Jews, Muslims, Buddhists, Hindus, Humanists and those who profess other religious beliefs or no belief" (http://www.au.org). Although we have no data to support our position, we assume most religious members of Americans United would also be cultural progressives. However, those from minority religions might be conservative and desire that Christians not impose Christian values and beliefs on otherwise neutral schools and political bodies.

Conservative Christians countered during the 1970s and 1980s with Jerry Falwell's Moral Majority and Pat Robertson's Christian Coalition, engendering a new wave in the "culture war"—and in fact coining that term—and bringing it front and center in American consciousness. Americans United responded with increased publicity advocating complete separation of church and state in attempts to invalidate the efforts of the Christian Right to influence political processes and policies. Patrick Buchanan's use of religious justification for political action in his speech at the 1992 Republican National Convention indelibly linked conservative politics with conservative religion, marking the high point in the most recent round of the progressive/conservative struggle. Hofstadter points out that although this link had been made much earlier, with this move it was made clear.[15] John Redekop argues that the fit was a comfortable one, with both religious and political conservatives tending to vilify the enemy, see only in black and white, and emphasize individual salvation.[16]

During Americans United's nascent years, other organizations with similar missions also sprang up. In 1963 Madalyn Murray O'Hair started American Atheists, which also worked for the absolute separation of church and state. However, unlike Americans United, it took as one of its primary purposes the defense of atheists, at the time a quite controversial position, considering the conservative spirit of the day. The Freedom from Religion Foundation (FFRF) began in 1978 with similar sympathies for atheists and today is the largest free thought organization in the United States. The FFRF fights for freedom from the undue influence of religion and the liberty to live and act without the cultural or institutional restrictions of traditional religion. This position puts it squarely in the tradition of the French philosophers, who, centuries before, had advocated human progress without the impediments of religious influence.

Although the public voice of the Moral Majority and Christian Coalition has subsided somewhat since the Ronald Reagan administration, interest and membership in cultural progressive organizations has not. In 2005 FFRF membership was approximately 6,000; by 2007 that number had almost doubled, reaching 11,600; in 2009, the FFRF reported a membership of 14,084, an astounding 235 percent increase since 2005. From a mere three members in its first year, FFRF has grown into a national group with representation in all fifty states and Canada.

CONTROL AND THE FORMALIZATION OF PROGRESSIVISM IN THE UNITED STATES

Jack Gibbs has proposed that, diverse as it is, the discipline of sociology has one central notion: control.[17] Regardless of theoretical orientation, the discipline views human behavior and organization, at their root, as efforts to establish and maintain order. From social psychology's idea that all behavior is adaptive (controlling) to conflict theorists' idea that all social organization is a manifestation of control and exploitation, the notion of control is the common theme. Even the functionalist Émile Durkheim believed that human behavior is destructive without appropriate integration and regulation, which in most cases, historically, had been provided by and through religion. We view this history and the current tension between cultural progressives and the Christian Right in this light. In this work we are primarily interested in looking at the beliefs and actions of those who value the life of the mind and individual liberty, as they combat the undue influence of Christians in a pluralistic society. For them, Christian conservatives threaten human potential to grow out of enslavement to tradition and constraint on individual liberties into a truly free society. The brief history outlined here may be best viewed as a struggle for control. Conservatives believe that social order is and should be rooted in the traditional structures and belief systems that established this country and gave birth to its greatness. To stray from those structures and belief systems means to evolve in the wrong direction. The concreteness and certainty of revealed truth and historical fact give order and certainty to a world that otherwise may be chaotic and meaningless.

Almost a century ago, in his famous exploration of religion in its simplest, most elementary form, Durkheim argued that one characteristic of religion is its emphasis on submission as a means of living at peace with God or a supreme being.[18] Whereas magic has to do with the manipulation of the spiritual, religion is about subjecting ourselves to that supreme being's will. Durkheim also proposed that the very existence of God emanates from our veneration of the society into which we are born, in which we are constrained (controlled), and which lives on after we die. The eternal is immortal; we are mortal. In that context, to subject ourselves to the control of the eternal puts us in contact with immortality. And in a community of believers, it provides a common conscience that unifies and orders. To threaten the existence of that belief is to threaten our community and our only contact with immortality.

In the Christian tradition submission is a means of attaining blessing. However, neither Durkheim's ideas nor the ideals of submission leading to blessings translate well in pluralistic societies in which some, rightfully, do not want to subject themselves to others' gods and morals. At least as the American colonies merged into our modern union, there did emerge some common religious ground that allowed us to go our separate ways denominationally, as long as we kept to those common values and morals. It was an uncomfortable but livable pluralism. But when modern ideas, especially atheistic and evolutionary ones, challenged that common system of beliefs and values, battle lines were drawn between the conservative Christian and progressive camps. Here we are talking primarily about those at the extreme ends of the spectrum, because they are the most active and it is they who are really fighting the culture war.

Anxiety about the control exerted by conservative Christians in a religiously dominated society can legitimate the concerns of those who fear those Christians. To negate the chances that such fears will be realized, antagonists of Christianity naturally seek to maintain societal control. If their perceived enemies have the social mechanism of control (i.e., political and educational institutions), then those mechanisms cannot be used against them. Opponents of conservative Christians may seek control in society as a way to defend themselves against real and imagined threats—real in that we have historical examples of the misuse of Christian power, but imagined in that, as we will see, some of our respondents have hyped-up and unrealistic expectations in the power of contemporary Christians to impose their beliefs on the rest of society.

Of course, it is not just conservative Christians who provide examples of excesses stemming from the need to control. The former Soviet Union provides evidence that the desire for control can lead to oppression by those with secular aims. Many religious individuals died in gulags so that Stalin could maintain control over any supernaturalist impulses that developed within the Soviet Union. To a lesser extent, we observe contemporary attempts to control religion through laws in France banning the wearing of burkas and the display of other religious symbols in public. It is quite possible that such actions are self-preservative, intended to protect cultural progressives from being controlled by religious conservatives. However, the desire for control itself offers its own rewards. The cultural progressives' desire to possess control over out-groups may not differ greatly from the desire of conservative Christians. Stephen Carter argues that many on the left seek to trivialize the political ideas of religious individuals, simply because they are religious, rather than intellectually challenging those ideas.[19] He contends that such intellectual challenges do not take seriously the ideas of religious conservatives, and those on the left merely write off their religious counterparts. In so doing, they deny religionists a voice in dealing with our society's problems. If he is correct, Carter illustrates an important mechanism by which cultural progressives take control away from religious conservatives, which helps them to maintain control for themselves.

Competing groups desiring control are ultimately the crux of the culture war. These groups seek to wrest influence from the hands of their mortal enemies. For both groups, opposition takes a form and force proportionate to the perceived level of threat. The thought that rationalism and evolution might tear apart what is believed to be the very fabric of society seriously threatens the conservative Christian. The legislation of morality and continued control by conservative Christianity undermines the core values of individual liberty and rational social development held so dear by today's cultural progressives.

Previous research has focused on the emotional energy generated by Christian conservatives as they fight the culture war.[20] This energy can be conceptualized as generating passion and even hatred toward non-conservatives and/or non-Christians. Some of the cultural progressive activists also feel passionately about the threats that they perceive from Christian conservatives. Those passions lead to seemingly extreme assessments of those conservatives. "They are THE MOST DANGEROUS ENEMY of America today. They are Enemy #1 of all of humanity," wrote one male respondent (aged 56–65 with some graduate school) in our study. Assessments of religious motivations and threats were also captured by statements such as "anti-woman agenda . . . policies should not be driven by the 2,000 year old beliefs of cattle-sacrificing primitives" (male, aged 26–35 with some college).

The history of the American culture war is one of struggle for control of a culture in which hyperpluralism exists and many value free thought. We do not hear of many concerns about progressivism in Europe or fundamentalism in Latin America because we do not share a common culture, a common legal system, or frequent personal interactions. It is an American war fought by and between people who must share the same space, media, law, and language.

3

WHO ARE THOSE WITH ANTI-CHRISTIAN ANIMOSITY?

In chapter 1 we documented the potential vitriol of anti-Christian antipathy. The coming chapters provide a more nuanced understanding of anti-Christian perspectives in our society. But what is the extent of this hostility? Where is it most prevalent? Who is most likely to develop negative attitudes toward Christians? Which general characteristics, real or imagined, of Christianity and conservative Christians do such individuals react to? To start answering these questions, this chapter assesses the social and demographic characteristics of those with anti-Christian animosity.

We start with an improved replication of a past study conducted by one of us,[1] which showed that among religious groups, only atheists are rejected more than conservative Christians. The original study only compared religious groups to each other, whereas here we compare the level of animosity toward religious groups with that of animosity toward different racial groups. We also compare the level of animosity toward conservative Christians with that of animosity toward other religious groups and look at the different subcultures connected to contrasting religious hostilities. This will put us in a better position to show the degree of animosity toward conservative Christians in our society and the characteristics of those with this animosity. But this quantitative analysis does not ask the questions that would tell us why people have these attitudes. So in the latter part of this chapter, we discuss our qualitative sample and use it to explore the nature of anti-Christian perspectives.

EXPLORING ANTIRELIGIOUS ATTITUDES

As noted in the first chapter, a variety of different religious groups experience animosity in our society. One of us previously utilized data from the 2010 American National Election Survey (ANES) to assess the relative level of disaffinity directed toward different religious groups. Respondents were asked to rate their level of affection toward eight religious or nonreligious (i.e., atheists) groups. They rated them on a scale of zero to one hundred, with higher numbers indicating more positive affection toward that particular group. Those ratings were averaged. If the respondent rated any group a standard deviation lower than the overall average of all eight groups, then the respondent was documented as having relative animosity toward that group.[2] Using this measure it was found that atheists experienced the highest level of animosity, but Christian fundamentalists were the second most rejected group, followed by Muslims.

Of course, religion is not the only characteristic based on which a person feels animosity toward others. A lot of sociological analysis has examined prejudice and bias,[3] and much of this work has focused on prejudice directed at racial groups.[4] When scholars discuss hostility toward out-group members, they often, although certainly not always, discuss animosity toward racial minorities. Assessing the level of antipathy toward racial groups enables a comparison to the potential hostility directed toward religious groups.[5] We have not only used the more up-to-date 2012 data but improved on the earlier attempt to use the ANES data, which did not employ religious/racial comparisons, by including racial groups in our scale. This allows ten groups—Asians, Atheists, blacks, Catholics, Christians, fundamentalists, Hispanics, Mormons, Muslims, and whites—to serve as reference groups in determining relative animosity.

We calculated an average of the zero-to-one-hundred ratings for these ten groups and were interested in whether a respondent would rank any of these groups well below that average. For example, if a respondent ranked all of the groups except Muslims at eighty, but then ranked Muslims at fifty, we think this is important information. On the surface it may not seem that this person has animosity toward Muslims, but one has to ask why he or she ranks Muslims so much lower than all the other groups. Relative, rather than absolute, rankings provide us with important information. Yet it may not be clear if a lower-than-average ranking is really that important. If the average of all ten rankings is eighty-five, then is it really a big deal if atheists are ranked at eighty? To ensure that when we found a ranking below the average it was far enough below to reflect a distinctly lower level of affection toward that particular group, we used a statistical concept called the standard deviation, and we took a lower ranking seriously only if it was at least one standard deviation lower than the average.

Previous research has shown that racial animosity toward people of color is more common among individuals who are white, less educated,[6] politically conservative,[7] Southern,[8] and older.[9] Many of the same factors predicting racial animosity also predict religious animosity. Previous research suggests that lower education,[10] higher religiosity,[11] greater political conservatism,[12] and older age[13] are correlated with rejection of those of minority or no religious faith. However, education, political progressiveness, and nontheist beliefs are positively correlated with rejection of conservative Christians.[14] Even though similar factors drive religious and racial animosity toward minority groups (e.g., age, political conservatism), critical differences may account for differing levels of each type of animosity. For example, while lower levels of education correlate with animosity toward both the racial and religious minority groups, higher education may contribute to rejection of conservative Christians. Furthermore, political conservatism tends to correlate with rejection of minority racial and religious groups; however, political progressiveness may correlate with anti-Christian rejection.

PATTERNS OF ANIMOSITY TOWARD CONSERVATIVE CHRISTIANS

We explore relative hostility by constructing a measurement that compares a racial/religious group against other groups. One may wonder why we do not simply take the rankings of different groups at face value. The answer is that doing so may obscure the nature of the respondents' animosity. For example, a respondent may have a propensity to rank all groups high regardless of his or her feelings about them. Such a respondent may possess hatred toward conservative Christians, but because of a tendency to rank all groups high, he or she may not rank them low in absolute terms. By comparing the respondent's ranking of one group to his or her other rankings, we capture the reality that this respondent does not think as highly of conservative Christians as he or she does of other racial/religious groups. Such comparisons are superior to absolute values since certain types of individuals, based on their social and demographic characteristics, may have differing propensities to rank all groups high or low. Absolute measures may hide the tendency to reject certain groups if respondents tend to rank all groups fairly high.[15]

Since the questions in the ANES ask respondents to self-rank their affection toward certain social groups, it is fair to assert that ranking social groups a standard deviation lower than other social groups indicates the opposite of affection, which would be animosity or hostility. We have previously defined hostility as antagonism or hate. Affection, which can be envisioned as warmth and love, would be the opposite of hostility. Thus groups rated dramatically lower than others on a scale of affection can be seen as experiencing the opposite of affection, which would be relative hostility, or animosity. We are comfortable discussing the results of our research as measuring the level of relative hostility individuals feel toward certain racial and religious groups.

The ranking of conservative Christians lower than other social groups does not necessarily mean that respondents have unreasonable hostility toward Christians. However, those with unreasonable hostility should perceive conservative Christians with less affection than they do of other racial/religious groups. The tendency to rank conservative Christians relatively low is a necessary component of, but not a sufficient explanation for, the hostility documented in the first chapter. Our quantitative assessment allows us to see demographic and social patterns of this animosity, indicating who is most likely to exhibit the emotions discussed in chapter 1. Our analysis also enables us to compare the level of animosity toward conservative Christians in relation to that toward other racial/religious groups. While not designed to measure the specific social attitudes noted in the first and subsequent chapters, this quantitative analysis documents the level of general animosity that makes such attitudes possible.

Table 3.1 lists the weighted[16] percentages of respondents who ranked a given group at least a standard deviation lower than the other groups. The lowest percentage (1.5 percent) of individuals express relative animosity toward the generic white group. But the group with the second lowest level of animosity has the basic Christian label (2.0 percent). This reflects our assertion that great animosity is not directed toward a generalized Christian identity. However, when we contextualize the question to ask about Christian fundamentalists, we find that almost a third of the respondents (32.3 percent) have relative animosity. As argued in chapter 1, anti-Christian hostility is a phenomenon that conservative Christians have to deal with, but Christians in general usually escape this level of animosity. The only group that experiences more animosity is atheists (45.5 percent), a finding that replicates that of the earlier study. Christian fundamentalists experience more relative animosity than most other social groups. Surprisingly, religious groups in general experience more animosity than racial groups.[17] Since the ANES used the term "Christian fundamentalists," it is safe to state that this term refers to conservative Protestants.[18] Thus animosity toward conservative Protestants is relatively higher than toward other religious

Table 3.1.   Percentage of Respondents Ranking the Racial or Religious Group a Standard Deviation Lower Than All Other Groups (N = 5,132)

Racial or Religious Group	Percentage of Respondents
Whites	1.5
Christians	2.0
Asians	3.7
Blacks	4.4
Hispanics	5.5
Catholics	10.9
Mormons	19.6
Muslims	31.2
Fundamentalists	32.2
Atheists	45.5

Note: Weighted for the full postelection sample.

Source: 2012 American National Election Survey.

groups, except for atheists and possibly Muslims, given how close those two scores are to each other (32.2 versus 31.2 percent).

But who holds this animosity? To tackle this question we divided the sample into those indicating apathy toward Christian fundamentalists relative to other racial and religious groups and those who did not. We ran t-tests to see if these two groups varied by their social and demographic characteristics. Table 3.2 shows the results of this comparison. There are clear differences between the population of those we can now label "anti-fundamentalist"[19] and the rest of the sample. The first line of the table informs us that the rest of the sample has a higher percentage of females than the sample of anti-fundamentalists (52.3 versus 48.2 percent; p < .01). This tells us that males are more likely to be anti-fundamentalist than females. In fact, as concerns other measures of social status, we find a common pattern. Anti-fundamentalists are more likely to be white, well educated, and wealthy compared to the rest of the sample. Our research confirms the finding of our 2010 study that people who harbor animosity toward conservative Christians hold relatively high levels of social power.

Other demographic and social findings are useful to note. For example, younger individuals are more likely to feel hostility toward conservative Christians, but the difference is not that great. Catholics are relatively more likely to be anti-fundamentalist, and other Christians (mostly Protestants) are less likely to be anti-fundamentalist. But among the non-Christian groups, those in other religions who see themselves as spiritual but not religious and atheists/agnostics are more likely to be anti-fundamentalist. Those who are not religious are not significantly more likely to reject fundamentalists. There are regional effects in that people in the South are relatively less likely to be anti-fundamentalist, whereas those who live in the Northeast and North-Central United States are more likely to be anti-fundamentalist. But the strongest predictor may be politics.[20] Nearly half of anti-fundamentalists in our sample were political progressives. On the other hand, among those who were not anti-fundamentalist, nearly half were political conservatives.

Based on the evidence in table 3.2, if we wanted to predict who would reject conservative Christians relative to other religious and racial groups, we would envision a white, well-educated, non-Protestant, wealthy, politically progressive male who does not live in the South. Yet this may not be the best way to describe such individuals. Some of these

Table 3.2. Comparisons of Respondents with Anti-fundamentalist Hostility to the Rest of the ANES Sample

Demographic or Social Variable	Anti-fundamentalists (%)	Rest of Sample (%)
Female	48.2	52.3[b]
Over age forty	61.6	65.5[b]
White	79.4	68.3[c]
Bachelor's degree	47.6	22.5[c]
Income over $50,000 per year	64.5	45.3[c]
Income over $100,000 per year	29.2	15.2[c]
Liberal	45.8	16.0[c]
Conservative	23.0	48.8[c]
Catholic	33.4	26.0[c]
Other Christian	34.9	58.0[c]
Other religion	6.6	.7[c]
Not religious	3.1	3.5
Spiritual	15.1	9.9[c]
Atheist/agnostic	7.0	1.8[c]
Located in North-Central region	24.0	22.4
Located in Northeast	19.6	15.6[c]
Located in West	27.0	20.7[c]
Located in South	29.4	41.4[c]

Note: Weighted for the full postelection sample.

[a] $p < .05$

[b] $p < .01$

[c] $p < .001$

characteristics tend to correlate with each other. For example, we know that people in the South tend to have less education than those in other parts of the country. It may be the case that the South has a high percentage of conservative Protestants, accounting for the relative lack of anti-fundamentalists. However, it is also possible that education is a major contributor to anti-fundamentalist attitudes and that Southerners' lower education level determines this regional effect. While it is not our intention to completely explain this animosity, we can eliminate some possible sources with a more sophisticated look at the data.

For readers interested in more detail about our data, appendix A shows logistic regression models, which control for all of the variables included in the model to see which are truly important. For example, if an educational effect is determining the regional effect, then the highly educated should be just about as likely to be anti-fundamentalist whether they live in the South or other regions of the country. If this is the case, then we will no longer see regional effects when we control for education. Indeed, once we control for all of the variables in table 3.2, our regional variables are no longer important. We contend that regional differences in the percentage of anti-Christians are due to the contrasting educational and other demographic and social variables among the populations rather than pure regional differences in the sample.

So, if region does not explain anti-fundamentalist attitudes, then what variables do? Race is still important as whites are more anti-fundamentalist in comparison to blacks. The difference between whites and Hispanics is not quite significant (p = .055), but when we consider the powerful differences between whites and blacks, it is safe to say that whites generally are more anti-fundamentalist than nonwhites.[21] Income and education also kept value as predictors of anti-fundamentalist attitudes as those with higher socioeconomic status (SES) and education were more likely to possess those attitudes.[22] Four of our variables (sex, race, income, and education) clearly help establish social status. Social scientists and thinkers generally contend that men, whites, the wealthier, and the more educated have higher-than-average social status. Although sex differences disappear once we control for other variables, the three other indicators of social status show that anti-fundamentalists tend to enjoy relatively high social status. The effects of religious preference remained somewhat weak, except that Protestants do not tend to be anti-fundamentalist, but the other religious identity variables do not matter except in the case of those who state that they are spiritual but not religious. However, we included two religiosity variables (belief that the Bible is the word of God[23] and religious service attendance), both of which are significant in the expected direction, which is that higher religiosity leads to less anti-fundamentalist attitudes. Finally, older individuals are more likely to have anti-fundamentalist animosity when we control for other social and demographic variables.

We now alter our expectation of who will possess anti-fundamental-ists attitudes to include those who are older, wealthy, well educated, progressive, and white, with low religiosity.[24] Region and sex do not appear to matter. In appendix A, we also include tables that explore what may be called anti-Muslim, anti-atheist, and anti-Mormon atti-tudes since these groups also had a significant number of individuals expressing relative disaffection toward them. These models indicate that those with relative hostility toward Muslims tend to be older, non-black, politically conservative males who do not live in the Northeast and who accept the Bible as the word of God. Those with relative hostility toward atheists are older, nonwhite, undereducated, Christian political conservatives who do not live in the Northeast and have high religiosity. Those with relative hostility toward Mormons are younger, nonwhite political progressives who regularly attend church and do not live in the Northeast. This book does not aim to conduct a deep explora-tion of who possesses relative hostility toward these groups, but clearly none of these groups possess the same per capita social power as the more educated, relatively wealthy whites who tend to have hostility toward fundamentalists.

Of course, the existence of relative hostility toward conservative Christians does not indicate the presence of the bigotry and hatred projected toward minority religious groups. Relative animosity does not have to lead to the anger and hatred we saw in chapter 1. How highly educated, wealthy whites manifest their disdain for rejected out-groups will likely differ from how others do so. For example, such individuals will likely have a lower tendency to resort to violence since they have more effective social resources to express their relative animosity. So while we have documented that relative rejection of conservative Prot-estants is fairly widespread and tends to exist among those with relative-ly high levels of social power, we still need to look at how this rejection manifests itself. Qualitative research provides us with valuable tools to explore these dynamics.

FINDING ANTI-CHRISTIAN ANIMOSITY

To better understand the attitudes and motivations of people hostile toward conservative Christians, it is helpful to research a group highly likely to take that stance. Because the data from ANES suggests that individuals who are politically progressive, highly educated, white, and not highly religious are more likely to have relative animosity toward conservative Christians, there is value in studying a group with these characteristics. In a previous study[25] of cultural progressive activists, we defined cultural conservatives as individuals who rely on a historical interpretation of their religion to define morality, which generally comprises a set of absolutes emerging from this traditional interpretation. We defined cultural progressives as individuals with a modern or postmodern understanding of morality that minimizes traditional religious justifications and is determined by what the individual decides is best for him- or herself. We concentrated on cultural progressive activists and found that they tend to value rationality, irreligiosity, and progressive political ideology. This sample of cultural progressive activists was also more likely to be more educated, wealthier, whiter, and less traditionally religious than the general population. Not surprisingly this group exhibited a strong antipathy for conservative Christians, indicating that its members are a potentially valuable source of anti-fundamentalist hostility.

We acknowledge that this sample is not an exact match for the group in the ANES that exhibited anti-Christian animosity, but its members do share many characteristics with those individuals. The purpose of the quantitative analysis was to discover patterns that can be generalized to the population. With our qualitative analysis, we aimed to look behind those patterns to see how at least some of those with anti-Christian antipathy express it. After we established the reality and extent of anti-Christian animosity in the United States, the qualitative sample consisting of individuals especially likely to have that attitude aided us in our qualitative exploration of anti-Christian antipathy. We cannot use our qualitative study to argue that all people with this antipathy will express it as our respondents did because our sample is limited to cultural progressive activists; however, we can still use this work to discover the cognitive constructs that some individuals use to legitimate their anti-Christian disaffinities. The fact that our sample tends to consist of individuals with the very characteristics tied to anti-Christian hostility (i.e., high education level, high SES, irreligiosity) helps us to see the phenomenon of anti-Christian hostility at its strongest among Americans. This can help make the nuances of this type of bias easier to detect. Ideally future quantitative work will assess the degree to which the characteristics documented can be generalized to common anti-Christian hostility.

In our original study we located several organizations that have as one of their primary missions to resist the Christian (or in some cases religious) Right. Members of such organizations are highly likely also to support this resistance and thus should have higher-than-normal hostility toward conservative Christians.[26] For the sake of privacy, the names of the organizations remain confidential; two of them are national in scope, and a third is located in a southern state. This latter organization skewed any attempts to assess the regional distribution of individuals who resist the Christian Right. A fourth source of respondents came from a contact with a small political organization who spread our survey to members of other smaller organizations. When we finished with our data collection, we had gathered 3,577 respondents and obtained a sufficiently large sample to reasonably locate patterns in the statements from our respondents. One final bias should be noted. One of the major organizations strives to resist religion in general, and its inclusion likely artificially increases the number of atheists and agnostics in our sample.

To conduct the research, we used the online tool Survey Monkey to send a link to the survey to leaders of the organizations. Those leaders then sent the link out to other members. We kept the link open for the smaller organizations as long as plausible. The organization focused on resisting religion in general contributed more than half of all respondents within two days of the link going out.[27] We shut down the link for that organization to limit its influence on the general results. However, the number of respondents was decreasing even after just two days, and we likely would not have gotten many more responses. Appendix B presents the survey we used; it combines closed and open-ended questions, allowing us to conduct both quantitative and qualitative analyses. Questions about respondents' demographics and social characteristics enabled us to explore if and how these individuals differ from the larger society. Open-ended questions were coded and then analyzed. Technical information about the coding is found in appendix A.

We used a similar version of the same instrument employed with the ANES data. We asked respondents to use "feeling thermometers" to assess their attitudes toward eight groups with different religious orientations: Mormons, atheists, Hindus, fundamentalists, non-fundamentalist Protestants, Jews, Muslims, Catholics, and agnostics.[28] They were instructed that higher scores on a one-to-one-hundred scale indicated more positive feelings toward a group, and a score of fifty indicated that they did not feel particularly warm or cold toward that particular group. The average thermometer score toward all eight groups was calculated and compared to the fundamentalist score for each respondent. If the fundamentalist score was more than one standard deviation lower than the average score, we determined that the respondent had a substantially lower evaluation of fundamentalists relative to other religious and nonreligious groups.[29] This indicates that the respondent is reacting not merely to religion but to the conservative Protestant orientation. We found that 72.5 percent of respondents scored fundamentalists at least one standard deviation lower than the average score for all groups, reflecting a higher degree of relative hostility toward conservative Christians than toward the general population.[30]

This is obviously not an exact match to the 32.2 percent of those expressing hostility toward Christian fundamentalists found in the ANES data since we are looking at a nonrandom group of individuals selected for their hostility toward the Christian Right and, in this sample, we used only religious, and not racial, groups to construct our index. Yet it is a good approximation of the type of individuals likely to make up a nontrivial segment of those who exhibit anti-Christian sentiment. Although not random, it is a sample in which whites, the highly educated, the wealthy, and the irreligious are overrepresented, which is in keeping with the general findings of the analysis of the ANES. Such demographics make this sample an excellent source for exploring the qualitative attitudes that buttress the general findings in our quantitative work. Once again, we make no claim that the attitudes documented here apply to all individuals who show disaffection toward conservative Christians; rather, this analysis produces findings of potential attitudes to consider as we investigate the possible effects of societal anti-Christian perspectives.

INDIVIDUALS WITH ANTI-CHRISTIAN ANIMOSITY IN COMPARISON TO OTHER CULTURAL PROGRESSIVE ACTIVISTS

It is not the case that cultural progressives automatically have anti-Christian sentiment or that all with such sentiment are cultural progressives. But characteristics of cultural progressives and individuals hostile to conservative Christians are similar. Table 3.3 compares those coded as exhibiting anti-Christian hostility with other cultural progressives in terms of selected social and demographic factors.

Those with anti-Christian hostility are similar to other cultural progressives as concerns age, race, education, and marital status. They are more likely to be highly educated, wealthy, and Christian and less likely to subscribe to no traditional religious belief (being either atheist or agnostic) than other cultural progressives. They are more likely to live

Table 3.3. Comparison of Anti-fundamentalist Cultural Progressives to Other Cultural Progressives on Selected Demographic and Social Variables

Demographic or Social Variable	Anti-fundamentalist Cultural Progressives (%)	Other Cultural Progressives (%)	N
Male	61.6	71.0[c]	2,307
White	94.3	92.5	2,092
Over age sixty-five	72.7	75.9	2,312
Graduate degree	45.9	37.6[c]	2,308
Income over 75K per year	53.9	49.6[a]	2,198
Married	53.5	51.1	2,304
Christian	10.0	6.2[b]	2,308
Atheist/agnostic	70.4	86.1[c]	2,308
Located in South	54.4	39.2[c]	2,304
Located in West	22.4	34.6[c]	2,304
Located in North-Central region	15.7	14.6	2,304
Located in Northeast	8.5	10.5	2,304

[a] p < .05

[b] p < .01

[c] p < .001

in the South but less likely to live on the West Coast. Some may have this animosity due to the political conservatism or Christian nature of the group. These individuals likely rate fundamentalist Christians lower than other religious groups simply because those Christians represent political conservatism or Christian religiosity. Others may resent the Christian Right due to the overall religious nature of the group, regardless of whether the group is dominated by Christians or not. The fact that Christians in this group were more likely to have anti-fundamentalist animosity, whereas atheists and agnostics were less likely to have this animosity, makes sense if we expect Christians to be less likely to reject religion as an institution while atheists and agnostics are more likely to do so.

We tested this possibility by including another question in our calculation: "Imagine that you choose who is going to be your neighbor. Please rate the desirability of having one of the following individuals as your neighbor—a vocal Republican who is not a Christian or a vocal Christian who is apolitical." To be marked as hostile toward Christians, a respondent had to indicate more antipathy for a Christian neighbor than a Republican neighbor and rank the fundamentalist Christian a standard deviation below the other religious groups. Even with this strict criterion, we found that 49.3 percent of our sample fell into a category of having hostility toward Christians. But using this measure we found that the percentage of respondents with anti-Christian hostility who were atheists or agnostic was higher than for the rest of the sample (80.4 versus 71.3 percent; p < .001), and the percentage who were Christian was lower than the rest of the sample (3.8 versus 13.9 percent; p < .001). For the balance of the book we use our less stringent standard to produce the best possible conceptual match to the measures used in the ANES when discussing the general findings of our qualitative sample, but since this standard may overinflate the number of respondents with anti-Christian hostility, we limit ourselves in providing comments from the sample to those from respondents who met our more rigorous standard, which includes the neighborhood measure.[31]

Interestingly, within this unique sample, women and those with higher levels of educational attainment were more likely to have animosity toward conservative Christians. In other situations those with more education are considered to be more tolerant, and women are generally considered more compassionate than men. However, within the confines of this particular subculture, those groups show lower levels of disaffection for a major out-group of cultural progressive activists. Whether characteristics such as education and gender predict sympathy for out-groups depends on the social context of these variables. Context may also matter as concerns potential regional effects. We found that those in the South were more likely to have anti-fundamentalist attitudes. This may be due to the fact that Christian religiosity is more common in the South than in other areas of the country.[32] It is plausible that cultural progressive activists who come into contact more often with conservative Christians are more likely to perceive them as a threat and thus more likely to develop animosity toward them. This possible explanation is reinforced by the result that disaffection toward conservative Christians is lower on the West Coast, an area not known for an abundance of Christian fundamentalists.

Given the unique nature of our sample, the qualitative findings are not automatically generalizable to all with anti-Christian hostility. Yet there is still great value in examining this data. First, it allows us to perceive what motivates an unknown degree of the hostility discovered by analyzing the ANES data. The ANES data merely demonstrates who tends to have disaffection toward conservative Christians and the degree to which that disaffection is prevalent in our society. Given the lack of previous research in this area, we have very little, if any, idea of what drives that alienation. Even if the trends in this qualitative research only reveal the motivation of a small percentage of those with anti-Christian fundamentalist perspectives, we will have more information than we previously possessed. Second, the nature of this sample likely brings out anti-Christian animosity at its worst. These comments may establish the boundaries of what those with that type of animosity are capable of conceptualizing. Future research using generalizable data can inform us as to the prevalence of the attitudes documented in the qualitative work; however, it is important to know what specific attitudes need to be measured.

DESCRIBING ANTI-CHRISTIAN ANIMOSITY

We asked respondents several open-ended questions about the Christian Right and coded the answers according to the substance of their responses. Specifically, we were interested in the issues they brought up in their description of the Christian Right. The vast majority of the time, there was no difference between those with anti-Christian animosity and other cultural progressives. But any difference that did arise indicated a possible contrast in how this hostility manifests itself among cultural progressive activists.

Since respondents were asked about the Christian Right, operationalizing these comments as antireligious presented a challenge. Clearly not all respondents were animated by hostility toward conservative Christians. Our operationalization separated out those who significantly assessed conservative Christianity lower than other religious and nonreligious beliefs. The comments made by such individuals were likely influenced by a more powerful hostility toward conservative Christianity than those of other cultural progressives. Understanding how comments made by people with this type of religious motivation provides insight into how this hostility manifests itself among some cultural progressives. At times it is clear that the respondent is discussing conservative Christians specifically and not the Christian Right. At other times respondents' comments are aimed at the Christian Right. But even in the latter case, it is reasonable to believe that these comments are highly motivated by animosity toward conservative Christians.

We previously showed a conflation of Christianity and political conservatism among some respondents. To the degree this conflating of religious and political conservatism takes place, it is fair to state that hostility toward the Christian Right is also directed at conservative Christians. Not all Christians face the ire of these respondents; instead, conservative Protestants are generally the target of anti-Christian attitudes. Given this reality, the negative comments made by those in our final sample can be conceptualized as negative comments directed at an image of conservative Protestants.

We examined the contrasting comments from the open-ended answers provided by respondents with anti-Christian animosity and other cultural progressives. We can see these contrasts in table 3.4. To keep this simple, we only explore important answers on which these two groups differed. The first four rows in the table show the average number of times a respondent mentioned a given quality as a characteristic of the Christian Right in his or her answers to the open-ended questions. The next two variables indicate the percentage of respondents who discussed the Christian Right being well organized or homophobic in one of their answers to our open-ended questions.[33] The last two characteristics refer to whether the respondent recounted never having had a personal encounter with a member of the Christian Right and whether we need to change our laws to deal with the Christian Right. We make two initial observations. We note that, in answering each of our questions, those with this hostility were likely to express similar attitudes as other cultural progressives. Only on a few variables did they provide answers at a significantly different level than other cultural progressives. Even where there were differences, the absolute distance between them tended to be quite small. In this sample, anti-Christian disaffection may be conceptualized as an important variation of the ideology of cultural progressive activists. Individuals with that hostility may not differ in kind from other cultural progressive activists but merely in the degree to which they emphasize their hostility toward conservative Christians.

The results in table 3.4 indicate that cultural progressive activists with anti-Christian animosity are more likely to mention concern about the Christian Right taking over society, being intolerant, and engaging in bad politics.[34] However, they also are less likely to mention that members of the Christian Right are crazy. They perceive the Christian Right as well organized and homophobic, yet are less willing to change the laws in the country to deal with the Christian Right.[35] They are cultural progressive activists disturbed by the possibility of a Christian takeover and express concerns about a coming theocracy that will oppress non-Christians. The concern about Christians' bad politics is not limited to agendas with mistaken and dysfunctional priorities but also includes the fear that this organization may succeed, an interpretation bolstered by the fact that when asked what is good about the Christian Right, those with anti-Christian disaffection were more likely to argue that it is well organized, indicating that they see in it a dangerous opponent who must be stopped instead of a bunch of crazy individuals. This reinforces the argument that part of what buttresses anti-Christian perspectives is the perceived struggle for societal control against conserva-

Table 3.4. Comparisons of Anti-fundamentalist Cultural Progressives to Other Cultural Progressives on Selected Measures of Attitudes toward the Christian Right

	Anti-fundamentalist Cultural Progressives	Other Cultural Progressives
Mentions of "takeover"	.577	.505[a]
	(2,034)	(752)
Mentions of "crazy"	.169	.289[b]
	(2,033)	(751)
Mentions of "intolerance"	1.037	.766[c]
	(2,033)	(752)
Mentions of "bad politics"	.566	.499[a]
	(2,034)	(752)
Assertions that the Christian Right is well organized	10.1%	7.0%[a]
	(2,045)	(748)
Assertions of homophobia	25.9%	19.6%[c]
	(2,056)	(762)
Absence of personal encounters with the Christian Right	12.3%	15.9%[a]
	(1,950)	(712)
Support for changing laws to deal with Christian Right	37.0%	43.6%[b]
	(1,776)	(668)

[a] p < .05
[b] p < .01
[c] p < .001

tive religious opponents. In the next chapter we illustrate these tendencies with quotes from our research.

Interestingly those with anti-Christian sentiments are less likely to state that they have had a personal encounter with a member of the Christian Right. The difference is small but noteworthy, given that we have already seen that people with this type of disaffection are more likely to live in regions of the country where conservative Christians live. It is likely that they avoid contact with conservative Christians. The combination of living close enough to conservative Christians to feel threatened by them, yet eschewing the sort of personal encounters that may humanize them, can play an important role in the generation of anti-Christian antipathy. Despite this antipathy these individuals are less willing than other cultural progressive activists to seek to use laws to control religious and political out-groups. We explore the implications of this in chapter 6.

Individuals with anti-Christian animosity in our sample can be understood as cultural progressives who place more emphasis on their hostility toward Christians than other cultural progressives. However, they do not seem to conceptualize their anger toward conservative Christians much differently from other cultural progressives. They are more concerned about theocracy, intolerance, and homophobia, more likely to admire the organizational skills of Christians, and less likely to desire to use laws against the Christian Right. Given that we have previously noted certain social and demographic differences between those with this antipathy and other cultural progressive activists, we used regression analysis to control for religious and regional differences in predicting whether a respondent had anti-Christian animosity. We found that the differences noted in table 3.4 basically remain even after these controls, with the exception of perceptions about bad politics and whether the respondent had had a personal encounter with a member of the Christian Right. The other attitudinal differences may be intrinsic to the possession of anti-Christian disaffection among cultural progressive activists.

CONCLUSION

Analysis of the ANES data indicates that relative hostility toward conservative Christians, but not Christians in general, is fairly common, especially among highly educated, relatively wealthy whites. We located a group of individuals with this hostility among cultural progressive activists. This group clearly does not represent all individuals with anti-fundamentalist sentiments, but it does possess the major characteristics of those with such orientations, providing an excellent opportunity to gain qualitative insight into the anti-fundamentalist mind-set. Documenting qualitative aspects of the individuals in this sample can provide potential testable measures for future research that assess how often those with an anti-fundamentalist perspective possess the attitudes documented in this book.

Anti-Christian attitudes may arise when an individual with culturally progressive ideas has had limited personal contact with conservative Christians, even if he or she lives in an area where many conservative Christians live. The combination of being near enough to those Christians to feel threatened but not having the personal contact that humanizes them may enable such individuals to develop a perspective that views conservative Christians and Christianity as the source of societal problems. Solutions emerging from this type of perspective would revolve around limiting Christian influence in society. Given our sample, our profile of who has anti-Christian hostility includes cultural progressive activists who reject Christian fundamentalists significantly more than they do those with other religious and nonreligious beliefs. Our analysis of the ANES data suggests that the number of individuals who possess such qualities is large enough to influence our society, given the education, wealth, and racial status they possess. Yet they clearly do not go unchallenged. The emergence of Christian conservatives gaining political and social power[36] serves as a warning to those with this hostility that their minority religious status may limit the degree to which they can use their SES, educational, racial, and gender power. It is not surprising that they perceive conservative Christians as an enemy whom they must defeat to secure their own social position.

Given their level of education, it can be insightful to comprehend how individuals justify anti-Christian attitudes. Although a solid percentage of the country has relative hostility toward conservative Christians, it is not a given that this is the same type of bigotry and intolerance linked to hostility toward minority religions or racial groups. The higher social status and educational attainment of those with animosity toward conservative Christians may lessen the negative dysfunctions connected to that animosity or alter how it manifests itself. To explore this possibility, we provided those with anti-Christian hostility the opportunity to express their animosity.

4

HOW ANTI-CHRISTIAN HOSTILITY SHAPES PERCEPTIONS OF CHRISTIANS

The mere perception of conservative Christians as political or social opponents is not sufficient to create individuals with an anti-Christian perspective. Individuals who perceive conservative Christians as opponents, but do not have such a sentiment, may work against the political aims of conservative Christians on issues of faith-based public support, homosexuality, and abortion or against their social aims as concerns traditional sexual mores. In this chapter we are not concerned with the general cultural progressive political critique of conservative Christians and Christianity. Instead we are interested in how cultural progressives possessing relatively high levels of animosity toward conservative Christians perceive those Christians. Cultural progressives without such animosity are our reference group. We are comparing those with anti-Christian hostility not to the rest of society but to other individuals who have political and social reasons to distrust conservative Christians but do not have the same level of relative hostility toward them. By making such a comparison, we can distinguish them from those who merely perceive Christians as general political or social opponents.

HOW INDIVIDUALS WITH ANTI-CHRISTIAN HOSTILITY VIEW CONSERVATIVE CHRISTIANS

Since our respondents with anti-Christian hostility are a subset of the larger group of cultural progressive activists, they share the same general values. This was advantageous for us since we know that individuals who are more educated, politically progressive, and less religious—common features among cultural progressives—are more likely to have relative animosity toward conservative Christians; thus our sample was highly likely to contain those with such hostility. In previous work we documented cultural progressive activist values as political progressiveness, irreligiosity, and rationality.[1] Adherence to these values alone is not enough to create anti-Christian hostility; however, these values may play an important role in why that animosity develops. The political aims of conservative Christians often run counter to the desires of political progressives. Irreligious individuals are relatively likely to have disdain for those with high levels of traditional religiosity. Cultural progressives often see rationality as the natural opposite of religious faith. Since cultural progressive activists are more likely to have relative hostility toward conservative Protestants, these basic values of cultural progressives may be a part of the value structure of those with anti-Christian hostility, which would be in keeping with our finding that religious and political progressives are more likely to have relative hostility toward conservative Christians.

Beyond these values, those with anti-Christian hostility differentiate themselves from other cultural progressives in specific ways. We identified these trends by comparing these groups, as seen in the analysis in table 3.4. Cultural progressive activists with anti-Christian hostility are less likely to make statements about the Christian Right being crazy. They are more likely to state that the Christian Right is intolerant and wants to take over our society. They are more likely to attribute homophobia to, and are less likely to have had personal encounters with, members of the Christian Right. In the following sections we take a qualitative look at these characteristics to see what they tell us about the differences between cultural progressive activists with anti-Christian hostility and the rest of the sample.

The Efficiency of the Conservative Christian Movement?

A question in our survey asks respondents about the most positive aspect of the Christian Right. One of the most common answers was that there is nothing good about it. Indeed, 28.7 percent of all respondents provided this answer. It is reasonable to expect that those with anti-Christian hostility will see nothing good in Christianity. However, they were slightly less likely to state as much than other respondents.

But those with anti-Christian hostility tended to elicit a legitimate compliment in the area of organizational power and structure. They admired the Christian Right's ability to get its message out and organize political institutions.

> They are excellent at marketing their position (both political and religious), including the use of standardized talking points. (Female, aged 26–35 with doctorate)
>
> They know how to promote their agenda. (Female, aged 36–45 with bachelor's degree)
>
> Great great ability to organize, gain and maintain followers. Potentially a strong voice for moral authority. (Male, aged 56–65 with bachelor's degree)
>
> That they have the ability of galvanizing broad swathes of their members into actions. (Male, aged 36–45 with some college)

Those with anti-Christian perspectives did not envision Christians as having more noble or profane personal qualities than others in our sample. They did, however, show a respect for the organizational abilities of conservative Christians. This type of "compliment" fit well with their fears concerning the imposition of a theocracy. Often they indicated that the ability of conservative Christians to organize and "brainwash" accounts for the political success of Christian Right organizations. Those with anti-Christian hostility do not have to recognize the legitimacy of the perspectives of conservative Christians or conceptualize the success of such organizations as due to the potential soundness of Christian ideas; rather they can blame conservative Christians' skill in organizing and manipulating for the political success of the Christian Right. The very legitimacy of conservative Christians possessing power is challenged as those who oppose those Christians gain justification for maintaining their own power.

In our previous work we documented how cultural progressive activists generally envisioned members of the Christian Right as simplistic followers. Individuals with anti-Christian antipathy see Christians as non–critical thinkers easily manipulated by Christian leaders, which makes it easier for Christians to organize social movements since these followers will follow blindly those organizing Christian organizations. Those with anti-Christian hostility can conceptualize the ease with which Christians follow their leaders as an advantage for Christians in the construction of their social movements. This feeds into their larger narrative of members of this group posing a threat to the enlightened society those with anti-Christian hostility desire to bring forth. Thus the focus on organization as an advantage does bring out an important implication of this research. Although the focus is on organizing, the Christian Right, as the name suggests, comprises conservative Christians. When we combine this observation with the earlier one that many of our respondents perceive Christians and Republicans as identical, we have even more confidence that the comments of our respondents are tied to their attitudes toward conservative Christians even though the questions were about the Christian Right.

Taking Over America

By attributing craziness to opponents, one implies that those individuals do not know what they are doing. But the information in table 3.4 indicates that respondents with anti-Christian animosity usually do not ascribe insanity to conservative Christians—especially those seen as leaders. If these respondents merely believed conservative Christians were mentally unbalanced, they might perceive them to be less of a threat. But, as discussed in the previous section, these respondents fear that Christians have fashioned a powerful movement. One important factor that may motivate antipathy toward conservative Christians is whether individual cultural progressives perceive them as either well organized, and thus a threat, or crazy, and thus relatively harmless.

Given that the respondents believed Christians to be very effective in shaping a social movement, there is value in assessing what the respondents perceived as the goals of that movement. Cultural progressive activists may use many issues that activate individuals in the culture war to motivate themselves in their fight against cultural conservatives.

Not all of these issues, however, may be important to those who have antipathy toward conservative Christians. Identifying which are important to cultural progressive activists with anti-Christian animosity is key to identifying the issues that may drive that orientation. To this end it is noteworthy that these respondents believed that conservative Christians seek removal of secular societal influences. They freely enunciated such concerns.

> I believe they seek to impose a theocracy on a secular nation, sort of a Christian Taliban. (Male, aged 66–75 with master's degree)
> I don't understand why our politicians re-interpret the constitution and get involved with religion anyway? No involvement whatsoever of the State and religion. Why do the two have to be connected? Why can't we have a strictly secular government? (Female, aged 46–55 with some graduate school)
> Intrusion of religion into secular matters, virulent and distressingly effective efforts to subvert political process to serve their agenda. (Female, aged 56–65 with doctorate)

These and many other comments indicate that individuals may possess anti-Christian animosity in part due to fear of Christians imposing religious values on society. These respondents discuss a world in which our society is either religious or secular. Like their religious and political opponents, such respondents may have a dichotomous view, in this case one that advocates for a secular rather than religious society.

These respondents resent more than conservative Christians' attempts to promote a social and political agenda. Some of them believe that Christians are not "fighting fair" in their activism. The notion of a hidden conspiracy came up from time to time.

> The training of CR lawyers in order to place them in high positions in govt. Training of teachers to push their ideas into public schools. Attempts to take over teacher boards in order to push religious ideas instead of science facts. (Female, aged 46–55 with some college)
> I have issues with the Christian Rights' actions in the sociopolitical arena—very underhanded and misleading actions and statements to mask their true agenda. Their actions and statements are very stylized to look like mainstream and reasonable values, but in fact their ideals are not the feelings of most middle-ground, everyday

people (Christian or otherwise). I am not supportive of stopping someone from campaigning for their ideals and beliefs, but what I AM against is that person hiding their real motives. (Female, aged 26–35 with bachelor's degree)

I am worried that they are more and more trying to get into the government so they can push their agenda on everyone. . . . Have heard they are home schooling to train their kids to get in to law and politics in order to do this. (Male, aged 26–35 with master's degree)

The propensity to see conservative Christians as not fighting fair is linked to the notion of Christians creating a formidable social movement. It allows the respondents to explain Christian political success without granting legitimacy to the causes those Christians advocate. Conservative Christians can be seen as posing a qualitatively different and more dangerous threat than other groups, one that demands extraordinary attention. Many respondents feared that Christians are plotting to take power illegally and dishonestly. They deeply dreaded a day when conservative Christians had fully infiltrated the government and ruled over the United States with an iron and intolerant fist. The data in table 3.4 indicates that cultural progressive activists with anti-Christian animosity are more scared of a Christian takeover than other cultural progressive activists. This fear can help them to conceptualize their own activism as a defense of society.

Complaints of Homophobia and Intolerance

Another key difference between those with anti-Christian animosity and other cultural progressives is the attention to homosexuality. Those with anti-Christian antipathy argue that Christians' homophobia buttresses an immoral intolerance and desire to force conformity to traditional sexual norms.

Homophobia, bigotry, and a general belief that personal freedom only exists when making personal decisions that are in line with their religious beliefs. (Male, aged 36–45 with doctorate)

The religious right does what it can to restrict the behavior of others to what they consider to be moral through political action. They are anti-choice, anti-gay, anti-science, and anti-sex. (Female, aged 18–25 with some graduate school)

Their extreme homophobia and disrespect for women as well as a lack of understanding & respect for pluralistic democracy. (Female, aged 56–65 with master's degree)

Specific issues I dislike: their activism to repress gays and lesbians. (Male, aged 46–55 with bachelor's degree)

Conservative Christians' rejection of homosexuals is seen as an indicator that conservative Protestants have an inferior morality. Given their high level of anti-Christian animosity, it is not surprising that our respondents made such claims.

The concern of those with animosity toward conservative Christians about homophobia also reveals itself in the ANES data. Our measure of anti-fundamentalism positively correlates with support for same-sex marriage,[2] support for homosexuals in the military,[3] and support for legislation to protect homosexuals from job discrimination.[4] This support holds even after we apply social, demographic, and religious controls.[5] It is not sufficient to argue that those with anti-Christian animosity support gay rights because they are politically progressive, not religious, or highly educated since they retain their support after we control for these and other important characteristics. Unless future research can show the relationship between anti-fundamentalism and support for gay rights to be spurious, it is plausible that an unknown degree of anti-Christian animosity is motivated by concerns about homophobia.

Previous research has confirmed a negative correlation between Christian religiosity and support for nontraditional sexual practices.[6] Concerns about Christians' nonsupport for homosexuals have merit. Other cultural progressive activists, however, are also likely to be aware of the support conservative Christians have for traditional sexuality, and yet they are less likely to state explicitly that homophobia is why they disfavor or mistrust the Christian Right. Whether the concerns of those with anti-Christian hostility have merit is less important than the fact that the issue of homophobia is of particular importance to them. Some may use it as a proxy to advocate for the sort of cultural and sexual mores they seek to promote. The traditional values promoted by Christians can be seen as interfering with the rights of others to practice new, progressive sexual freedoms.

Many respondents, whether they fit our definition of having anti-Christian hostility or not, expressed a general concern about conservative Christians holding society back. But there were also fears about retrogressive sexual attitudes.

> The Christian Right not only do this, but try and get the government to pass legislation based upon their own narrow view of morality and faith. (Female, aged 46–55 with master's degree)
>
> Antiabortion stance, yet offer broad based call to support those who carry the child to full term. They oppose any form of birth control, emphasizing abstinence for teens. They provide no real and true information about sexuality, problems or STDs. If you disagree or take a more moderate position, you are vilified. (Male, aged 56–65 with doctorate)

According to such individuals, conservative Christians' actions and attitudes inhibit other conservative Christians' ability to find fulfillment in their own lives. Some had lost all hope for the enlightenment of those Christians due to their adherence to regressive sexual norms and attitudes.

Some of this hostility to potential Christian homophobia is likely tied to larger issues of conflicting cultural and sexual values. Beyond mere anger at homophobia, a fear of the imposition of traditional notions of sexuality animates this antipathy. This concern may also be linked to the larger progressive/fundamentalist conflict described in chapter 2. Those with anti-Christian animosity want individuals to use the modern tools of science and rationality to determine their sexual attitudes. Thus they envision sexual experimentation and support for homosexuality as desirable since it reinforces the importance of individual rational choice over rules imposed by a supposed supernatural entity. Conservative Christians, relying on traditional religious interpretations of sexuality, decry sexual norms they perceive as dysfunctional and regressive.

Another key difference between the respondents with anti-Christian disaffection and other respondents provides possible insight into why these cultural progressive activists focus so much on issues of sexuality. That difference is the higher likelihood among these respondents to cite intolerance as a quality of conservative Christians or a reason to dislike them. The following are only a few of the many examples of this trend:

Religion belongs in church not at the ballot box. I dislike their condemnation of the plurality of religion in our country by their intolerance of gays, women's success, abortion rights, any religion but their own, and trying to pass laws and school policies that force their views on non-Christians. (Female, aged 46–55 with bachelor's degree)

They hide their intolerance and hate behind tradition and intangibles such as "the word of god." They use their faith and religion to end conversations, not to start or stimulate them. They use scripture from a ~2000 year old book to drive modern policy. (Male, aged 36–45 with master's degree)

Their general intolerance and their certainty that they know what's best for the rest of us based on a logically tenuous belief in a popular myth, for starters. Almost all publicly visible "spokespeople" for the Christian Right are in my opinion hypocrites who twist their own faith to suit their very worldly purposes. They pick and choose the parts of their religion that work for them while ignoring or rationalizing away many others. (Male, aged 26–35 with some college)

Naturally the idea of intolerance does not limit itself to ideas of sexuality. The image of an intolerant Christian is simply one in which that person consistently attempts to force his or her ideas and beliefs upon other individuals and attempts to force others to live their lives as he or she demands. This can be manifested in abuses related to proselytizing, passing laws that enforce the norms of a Christian theology, and demanding a "Christian" lifestyle. Obviously part of this fear of intolerance is tied to the notion that conservative Christians stand in the way of the promotion of gay rights. Ideas of intolerance likely mingle with concerns about homophobia to help create some of the antipathy felt by certain respondents toward conservative Christians.

Many of the respondents were less concerned about what conservative Christians actually believe and wanted them to stop attempting to influence others with their dysfunctional attitudes. They demand that conservative Christians keep their beliefs to themselves.

I think that Christians should butt out of other people's lives. Believe whatever religion you want, but shut the hell up about it. (Male, aged 56–65 with some college)

They can believe what they want as long as they do not use the political system to force that hate on me. (Male, aged 46–55 with master's degree)

It's ok to believe whatever you want, but don't try and force your beliefs onto others! (Male, aged 56–65 with some graduate school)

I dislike the Christian right because of their desire to impose their morality on the entire nation. Live and let live is not good enough for them. (Male, aged 56–65 with doctorate)

From such statements we gain more of an understanding of what those with anti-Christian perspectives mean when they talk about intolerance. Intolerance is not used to define identical thinking to the ideas of these cultural progressive activists; however, to openly state ideas contrary to the ideas of those activists is thought of as being intolerant. The ideas become intolerant when they are expressed in the public square and not if they stay in the head of the conservative Christian. This is likely connected to the belief of these activists that conservative Christians rely on an outdated, religiously based mode of thinking that should not be imposed on the rest of society.

CONCLUSION

So why do some individuals possess such hostility toward conservative Christians? In this chapter we see some reasons for this animosity. Our findings form a picture of some of the perceptions driving anti-Christian attitudes. Individuals with such attitudes fear a takeover of our society that will replace a scientific rational orientation with irrational Christian perspectives. Because of their concern about homophobia, they fear also that this takeover will lead to the imposition of more traditional cultural and sexual norms. The fear of a takeover is buttressed by the perception that conservative Christians have an efficient organization by which they cunningly infiltrate our government. Such stereotypes and fears are not erased by interaction with Christians, as those with anti-Christian sentiments are generally less likely to have personal contact with conservative Christians, even when they live in the same region. These findings indicate that they perceive themselves as waging a cultural war against a powerful, evil foe whom they dare not allow to win.

We have begun to understand cultural factors shaping anti-Christian hostility. Those with this hostility have relatively little contact with conservative Christians. As such they can latch on to images of Christians as homophobic, opposed to progress, and/or trying to take over society. Those with anti-Christian animosity have a cultural understanding of conservative Christians as conquerors who want to dominate them and take away their rights, which is why they struggle to find anything positive to say about the Christian Right, except that its members are efficient organizers and able to socialize others into accepting their traditional ideas. This paints a picture of conservative Christians as powerful enemies threatening our respondents' cherished values of democracy and rationality. This common image is reinforced in their social circles since they have relatively little contact with conservative Protestants. Those with anti-Christian hostility can use this picture to justify their efforts to exert social control to oppose conservative Christians and their institutions.

Often when individuals are at war, they dehumanize the enemy to make fighting easier.[7] This is true in physical war that results in death. Although we are not dealing with actual killing, in the first chapter we read disturbing comments in some of the respondents' answers. A similar process of dehumanization may pertain to hostile attitudes toward conservative Christians. This process may be connected to propensities toward hate, prejudice, and bigotry directed at conservative Christians. In the next chapter we more fully explore these possibilities.

5

DEHUMANIZING AND HATING CHRISTIANS

The responses thus far provide more than enough evidence that individuals with anti-Christian hostility have little respect for Christians, particularly conservative Protestants. But we want to go beyond the mere assertion of animosity toward conservative Christians to investigate whether dehumanization, bigotry, hatred, and prejudice also come into play.

We first wish to see if some respondents dehumanize conservative Christians. Dehumanization can be conceptualized as seeing an out-group as nonhuman. A lot of scholars have tied dehumanization to oppression of and violence toward out-group members.[1] Even in a society that outlaws oppression and violence, dehumanization can provide justification for indirect ways to mistreat out-group members. It is possible that those with anti-Christian sentiment possess antipathy toward conservative Christians but do not dehumanize them. They may perceive Christians as possessing full human qualities and merely have distaste for the beliefs and practices of conservative Christians. If so, then their perception of conservative Christians does not necessarily lead to the worst elements of prejudice, hatred, and bigotry. However, the animosity of those with anti-Christian sentiment could plausibly lead to the dehumanization of Christians.

DEFINING DEHUMANIZATION?

Dehumanization can lead to a willingness to oppress and exterminate unwanted groups.[2] Susan Opotow discusses the ability of certain individuals and groups to exclude out-groups perceived as outside the boundaries within which moral values, rules, and fairness apply.[3] Lasana Harris and Susan Fiske argue that while perceptions of low competence lead to pity and perceptions of low warmth lead to envy, combined perceptions of low competence and low warmth lead to disgust.[4] Extreme prejudice denies individuals their full humanity. But the best cognitive construction of dehumanization comes from Nick Haslam,[5] who notes that there are two different ways to look at "humanness." One considers what makes us different from animals—that is, the qualities that make us "uniquely human" (UH). The other tries to understand what we all have in common, or our "human nature" (HN). These concepts are not identical. For example, Haslam argues that HN is seen in an essentialist way that differentiates it from UH traits. Both HN and UH represent two distinctive ways to understand how humanness is defined.

Having established what humanness looks like, Haslam discusses the forms dehumanization can take. An individual denied UH qualities would be seen as lacking cultural refinement and intelligence and as no different from animals and lower life forms. A person seen as lacking HN characteristics would be deemed not to possess all of the human traits other individuals possess, such as warmth, emotion, or compassion. One way to distinguish between the two ways of dehumanizing is to see the image created in each dehumanization form. Those denied UH traits give rise to the image of an animal that is not quite human. Those denied HN traits engender the image of a robot lacking human warmth.

From this analysis Haslam constructs two different sets of stereotypes to apply to dehumanized populations, depending on whether they are denied UH or HN traits. Those dehumanized would be seen as lacking certain qualities, meaning that they were either not fully separate from animals or not endowed with essential human nature. The basic characteristics of those lacking UH traits would be lack of culture instead of civility, coarseness instead of refinement, amorality instead of moral sensibility, irrationality instead of logic, and childlikeness instead of maturity. The basic characteristics of those lacking HN traits are inertness instead of emotional responsiveness, coldness instead of interpersonal warmth, rigidity instead of cognitive openness, passivity instead of agency, and superficiality instead of depth. Few respondents characterized conservative Christians as cold, passive, or emotionless. If our respondents dehumanized them, then they did so by denying their UH traits and not fully distinguishing them from lower forms of life. We look to the five traits of UH dehumanization outlined by Haslam to see if they accurately reflect the perceptions of those with anti-Christian animosity.

Lack of Culture

The first trait Haslam identifies as part of animalistic dehumanization of out-group members is a lack of culture. Civility is seen as separating us from animals. Members of dehumanized groups are seen as lacking such civility and as uncultured. This stereotype plays into the idea that some humans are more evolved than others and have developed a more "human" culture than those with a great number of animalistic characteristics. Previous work has documented the tendency of some European Americans to perceive the cultures of people of color as less "civilized," allowing them to conceive of such individuals as more animalistic, or less human, and less evolved.[6]

This propensity can be fairly tied to how some individuals with anti-Christian animosity perceive conservative Christians. The theme of incivility and lack of culture is common in their comments. For example, many respondents argue that conservative Christians' backwardness is holding society back or even taking us back to a less civilized time.

Their agenda seems to include making America a theocracy, which frightens me, as it would take us back to the Dark Ages politically, culturally, educationally and morally. (Female, aged 46–55 with bachelor's degree)

The members are generally superstitious and share the same attitudes that led to the religious atrocities of medieval Europe. (Male, aged 46–55 with bachelor's degree)

It is to the disgrace of humanity that such ignorance, superstition and intolerance still persists in the modern age. It is a shame that in an age of enlightenment and scientific advancement, pre-medieval superstition is still so evident. (Male, aged 56–65 with some college)

In this sense those with anti-Christian sentiment envision conservative Christians as supporting a lower form of culture even as they strive for cultural and societal improvement. For such respondents, human advancement depends on controlling conservative Christians to prevent their uncivilized, backward ideas from influencing society.

Christianity's uncivilized nature, in this view, not only hampers positive political aspirations but is detrimental to the personal development of a society's individuals. Some of the characteristics those with anti-Christian hostility attach to conservative Christians illustrate that they see conservative Christians as lacking civility. For example, we have already seen that some respondents contend that conservative Christians have a backward sense of sexuality, which leads to sexual repression. Those with anti-Christian animosity see themselves as evolving toward sexual freedom and conservative Christians as a political barrier to that freedom. But in an even more basic sense, Christians are seen as denying themselves that freedom and thus unhealthily repressing themselves.

Those with anti-Christian perspectives perceive themselves as enjoying an enlightenment that has eluded conservative Christians. Consequently some discuss discovering a more enlightened path away from Christian beliefs. Statements from a couple of respondents represent this view quite well.

> I can't relate to you in words the severity of the continual state of conflict and guilt in which I lived. This was made especially intense by my level of education and belief in the scientific methodology. I was raised in a very religious house and it was a long and painful process for me to break off those chains and come to admit that I really do not believe in god or the supernatural. My life was almost instantly at peace and the conflict I felt for so long was completely resolved. I finally felt free to believe what I knew in my own heart and mind to be true and the measure of relief this brought me is beyond explanation. (Male, aged 46–55 with doctorate)
>
> As a teen I honestly didn't understand what was wrong with Christianity that everyone but me seemed to have issues with immorality and guilt. I found my answer when I dared to be open about my doubts. (Female, aged 26–35 with bachelor's degree)

Some respondents talked about the happiness Christians can find if they relinquish their religion and find enlightenment. For this reason they discussed ways to influence Christians to lose their faith or engaged in efforts to "de-convert" them. However, most with anti-Christian hostility did not engage in such efforts, likely because of an aversion to Christian proselytization. Such efforts might also conflict with their ideas about intolerance if they define it as pushing one's own ideas upon others. However, they generally had no problem enunciating the perception that they possessed an enlightenment lacking among conservative Christians. For instance, one female respondent, aged 36–45 with a master's degree, stated, "I am truly bothered by the fact that atheists are viewed as immoral in the US. I believe the Christian Right's propaganda has fueled this problem. There are MANY immoral Christians. But I guess they get a 'pass' because it is their belief that they will be forgiven. Their propaganda also stalls progress. Ignorance is bliss. I chose not to be ignorant."

Coarseness

Strongly related to the notion that Christians lack a developed culture is the perception that they are coarse. We touched upon some of the ideas tied to coarseness in the previous section when we discussed how those with anti-Christian animosity perceived Christianity as creating a culture whereby individuals develop characteristics tied to their uncivilized nature. The opposite of coarseness is refinement, which indicates adherence to higher forms of culture. A perception of coarseness aids in the development of animalistic dehumanization since members of the out-group can be seen as unrefined savages. Previous work has documented how such perceptions of minority groups have served to justify their oppression.[7]

Their perceived unrefined nature makes conservative Christians a danger as they threaten to poison society with their coarse nature. Some with anti-Christian animosity mentioned this coarseness in connection with previous experiences with Christians:

> I was leaving a music festival once. On the way out, there were Christians all over with signs that Jerry Garcia, Jimmy Hendrix and

others were in Hell, and so will you! It's a very typical situation with Christians. (Male, aged 26–35 with high school diploma)

When I went to my uncle's funeral. It was a fundamentalist church and instead of being able to grieve and pay my last respects I had to listen to lunacy. The preacher started by asking if anyone in the church was not born again. I couldn't believe that the question was asked. (Female, aged 56–65 with some graduate school)

I was surrounded and verbally blasted by girls in my dormitory room in college one night. It happened when one girl found out I was an atheist. I felt attacked but strong in my atheism and felt these girls were just repeating words they were taught in church or by their families and had never thought for themselves—mere puppets. I didn't know then how really dangerous their attitudes would eventually be. (Female, aged 66–75 with bachelor's degree)

These experiences lead to an expectation of coarseness, affecting the potential for personal relationships with Christians. However, as we saw in the chapter 3, those with anti-Christian animosity are less likely than other cultural progressive activists to have had personal encounters with individuals in the Christian Right. Thus it is not merely experience that leads to the idea that conservative Christians are coarse in nature.

Social distance can also generate these images. A lack of contact can reinforce stereotypes and minimize conservative Christians' humanness. Individuals who develop the perspective that conservative Christians are coarse and rude may create a social distance that embeds this stereotype into their belief system. After all, few people want to spend time with those they expect to be coarse and unrefined. Thus, their distaste can lead them to avoid contact with conservative Christians.

It made me want to avoid them. I got away from my hometown as soon as possible and moved to the most liberal and sinful place in the state. (Female, aged 26–35 with bachelor's degree)

I didn't used to think about religion much. Now avoiding others who seek to violate my rights, using religion, has started to absorb more and more of my time. (Male, aged 36–45 with master's degree)

When I find out someone is a right-winged Christian, I write them off as unreasonable and discount what they say heavily. I do not take them seriously and generally try to avoid them at all costs. (Female, aged 36–45 with some graduate school)

Perceived coarseness clearly has a significant effect on the willingness of those with anti-Christian hostility to enter into friendships and relationships with conservative Christians. Thus a vicious circle can develop in which individuals with anti-Christian perspectives stereotype Christians as coarse and thus avoid them, which prevents those individuals from having any pleasant experiences with conservative Christians and reinforces the stereotypes that led them to avoid Christians in the first place.

Amorality

It is tempting to link arguments about immorality to Christian traditionalists. Conservative Christians are generally conceptualized as attempting to enforce their morality regarding sexual and family issues, leading to a perception of intolerance. Cultural progressives often view this intolerance as immoral, and we know that intolerance is one of the major complaints those with anti-Christian sentiment have about Christians. The statement of one woman (aged 66–75 with a master's degree) represents the attitudes of many respondents as concerns fear of Christian intolerance: "Their dogmatism does not permit compromise; they are not tolerant of other religious views or the views of those who are not religious; they have the only correct answer to moral questions." She is reacting to the notion that conservative Christians have a moral ideal that they want to impose on everyone else. Many respondents find this imposition immoral. The statement carries an accusation of improper behavior generally linked to an understanding of morality. In this way intolerance is an offense against a different morality than that proposed by conservative Christians.

Others besides Christians have moral expectations. Those with anti-Christian hostility generally do not accept traditional sexual and family norms. However, they tend to endorse progressive political ideals, in keeping with the basic values of cultural progressive activists. Based on these values they have certain moral expectations of others and criticize conservative Christians for their failure to adhere to these expectations. For example, many argue that conservative Christians do not live up to a moral expectation to avoid being judgmental.

I do not like having someone try to force their religious beliefs on me, and disrespect my beliefs and values. . . . I find that hard core religious are much more judgmental and non-yielding in their beliefs and discussions. (Female, aged 46–55 with bachelor's degree)

I think they are a distasteful and judgmental lot of people who want to push their ideology on others. Religion should be an attraction, not a promotion and there is nothing attractive that I can see. (Male, aged 36–45 with bachelor's degree)

Christians are generally very judgmental of others measuring them to their imaginary friend's yard stick (even if they themselves don't measure well by their own biblical standards) and they can be vocal about it resulting in undesirable experiences with this neighbor or with experiences as a result of his doing. (Female, aged 46–55 with doctorate)

Those with hostility toward conservative Christians have constructed a morality distinct from traditional religious values. Part of this morality is a relativism that denounces judging the beliefs and actions of others; thus the judgmentalism of conservative Christians violates this morality.

Perhaps part of the anger toward conservative Christians stems from a perception of them as supporting an inferior moral system. It is not unlike the complaint Joshua Harris and other Christians[8] have enunciated about the toxic influences of modern sexual values and the threat they pose to the desired moral order. For those with anti-Christian animosity, the perpetuation of conservative political and religious values stands in the way of their desired moral order. The cultural war may in fact be a moral war with competing sets of moral values battling to establish societal and cultural norms.

An argument can be made that individuals with anti-Christian hostility exhibit an intolerance of conservative Christians and that this intolerance stems from their having moral values that differ from those espoused by Christians. Rather than attempting to control the sexual actions of other individuals, they build their moral ideas on expectations about religious beliefs and political activity. The failure of conservative Christians to adhere to these values produces a perception that they have a lesser set of values than progressives. Moral systems naturally attract comparisons to alternate moral systems and create some level of intolerance toward those alternatives, even in a moral system emphasizing tolerance.

Many respondents with anti-Christian hostility also argued that conservative Christians are often unable to live up to their own values. Accusations of hypocrisy were quite common.

> Simply pointing out the number of times a leader of the Christian Right has been found committing adultery or fraudulently obtaining monies from their followers, then claiming they were led by Satan, and should be forgiven for their "sins." Never accepting personal responsibility, instead placing the reason for their actions on an imaginary being. (Male, aged 36–45 with bachelor's degree)
>
> Hypocritical bible-literalists who are offended at the thought of anyone not exactly like them. . . . They preach morality and yet are some of the most immoral (Ted Haggard) people. (Female, aged 26–35 with master's degree)
>
> They are often hypocritical. They like to spout-out what the Good Book says, but they often don't follow it themselves. When they're confronted on their hypocrisy, they often respond with a "we are all sinners" and "Christians aren't perfect." Their holier than thou attitude is especially irritating. (Male, aged 36–45 with doctorate)

These charges of hypocrisy hold a great deal of weight for people with anti-Christian attitudes, providing them with important support in their moral war. If conservative Christians cannot adhere to their own moral values, then what right do they have to force those values on others? This can be seen as evidence that Christians' moral values are not based on what is best for our society but are tied to certain conservative Christian leaders' attempts to manipulate their followers. The inability of Christians to follow their own morality, combined with the idea that Christian leaders do not actually believe their own teaching, helps those with anti-Christian animosity to legitimate their own moral system while challenging the authenticity of a traditional Christian moral system.

Irrationality

A basic way to debase an out-group is to perceive its members as intellectually inferior to majority group members. Nick Haslam points to a trend in which the dehumanized group is seen as less motivated by cognitive reasoning and more driven by instincts and animalistic appetites. A common stereotype historically suffered by people of color brands them as intellectually inferior.[9] If mental abilities are linked to evolutionary and even cultural growth, then envisioning members of an out-group as unable to cope intellectually with contemporary reality is a useful way of implying their biological inferiority. Once biological inferiority has been assumed, it becomes easy to deny the humanness of out-group members. In Haslam's terminology, the perception of dehumanized groups as "irrational" presumes that their constituents lack sufficiently developed mental capacities to distinguish them from animals. Our respondents also often used the term.

> Christians, by nature of their belief show a level of irrationality beyond that of mere Republicans. (Male, aged 56–65 with doctorate)
>
> By their irrationality shall ye know them. . . . I fear irrational people they are not logical and they are very frustrating and a waste of time while they are brain washed like that. (Male, aged 56–65 with bachelor's degree)
>
> They impose ignorance and irrationality on a world desperately in need of reason. (Male, aged 66–75 with some graduate school)

Irrationality is commonly assumed to be a feature of Christianity. Some respondents seemed to enjoy making fun of the religious beliefs of the Christian Right by emphasizing what they deemed the irrational elements of such beliefs.

> I cannot intellectually engage vocal Christians in the same way because they believe in sky ghosts and other extreme improbabilities. (Male, aged 46–55 with bachelor's degree)
>
> Reinforced the idea I had that they were mostly stupid people pushing a program of militant ignorance, in the delusionary dream that a magic invisible skydaddy god and his offspring were guiding their every thought and action. (Sex undetermined, aged 66–75 with some graduate school)
>
> Advanced beyond Santa and the Easter Bunny, but still at juvenile intellectual stage. (Male, aged 56–65 with bachelor's degree)

Behind these jabs is contempt for religious fools who have latched on to an unsustainable belief system. Such perceptions can form an important part of a justification for dehumanizing out-groups.

Seeing conservative Christians as irrational suggests that they are incapable of thinking like "rational" humans. Individuals with anti-Christian hostility have a difficult time believing that conservative Christians use their full intellectual capabilities. The respondents with anti-Christian leanings would find this especially disturbing given that, like the rest of the cultural progressive activists, they tend to prioritize notions of rationality as a core value in society. Furthermore, many of those with anti-Christian animosity perceive conservative Christians as primarily driven by their emotions, impulses, and instincts.

A driving characteristic would be the fact they don't think for themselves. It's as if they were told what to believe as kids and now as adults are so emotionally tied to their beliefs it literally blinds them. I think this also hurts their ability to use . . . logic when deriving answers, not just with morals and politics, but also every day problem solving. (Male, aged 26–35 with some college)

Like anyone in any country who has little understanding of the world outside their immediate experience, they become aggressive in defense of their values, since they place all their identity there. The emotional psychology of this creates non-critical thinkers who are drawn to ideas which please them, rather than the truth. Thus they take the Bible literally, for example. (Male, aged 56–65 with master's degree)

Those associated with the Christian Right tend to polarize on issues based on obscure verses from the Bible. Ideas, taken out of context "drive" an attitude of righteous indignation. The characteristic that creates the polarization comes from lack of critical thinking coupled with mindless emotionalism. (Female, aged 66–75 with master's degree)

Such assertions paint a picture of conservative Christians unable to fully engage in rational thought or discourse. These conservative Christians can be conceptualized as an irrational obstacle to the rational future those with anti-Christian disaffection want to create. Such a conceptualization helps meet the need of these respondents to justify their struggle to wrest control from conservative Christians. They believe that they more clearly perceive social, political, and even religious reality than conservative Christians since they make the sort of rational assessments conservative Christians are not capable of. The image they project is that of rational, civilized individuals compared to animalistic, emotional fools.

Some respondents did not accept that an intelligent person can hold conservative Christian beliefs. However, occasionally they had encountered intelligent, capable Christians. Their intellectual expectations of conservative Christians were so low that some with anti-Christian hostility struggled to understand how individuals they respected could hold what they perceived as irrational religious beliefs.

> A woman who was part of a hiking group, who I consider a friend, was present when another hiker commented on my Darwin decal (on the car). She immediately ranted on about how she didn't believe in Darwin or evolution because she was Christian. I realized there were reasonably intelligent, high functioning people with a blind eye to any facts that differ from their world view. (Female, aged 56–65 with master's degree)

> A very energetic discussion involving new friends and their views based upon biblical stories and something about angels and a celestial war involving super-humans etc. These are people who are respected business owners in their community and are seemingly intelligent. However, they choose to believe a myth rather than using their brains to observe the world around them and come to their own conclusions. (Female, aged 46–55 with master's degree)

> My brother, a highly intelligent but troubled young man abandoned all reason and embraced fundamentalism. It is a tremendously depressing waste of his potential. (Male, aged 36–45 with some college)

These comments indicate respondents' expectation that conservative Christians will not have fully developed their intellectual capacities. An intelligent person with conservative Christian beliefs is a paradox they sometimes struggle to understand. Ultimately these respondents can perceive religious belief as a glaring anomaly in an otherwise orderly and rational mind. Sometimes irrationality is automatically attached to Christian beliefs even when those beliefs are held by a respectable and intelligent person. In this way Christian beliefs are deemed inherently irrational and incongruent with the use of one's full mental capacities.

For many with anti-Christian perspectives, Christianity is synonymous with irrationality. Some respondents suggested that as a result, full participation by conservative Christians in the political process might not be in the best interest of the country. Thus, Christians' irrationality can be used to justify excluding them from the political process.

> No one who actually believes in Armageddon or the biblical prophesies of the "End of Days" wars in Israel (i.e., the picture painted by the Left Behind series) should ever, ever be given the keys to power and control over the US's military and its weaponry. (Female, aged 46–55 with master's degree)
>
> Restrict their ability to become judges, senators, representatives, member of Cabinet, military chief of staff and other powerful members of government. (Male, over 75 with bachelor's degree)
>
> Should not be able to make decisions regarding the law, they should somehow have to be supervised if they are working with other people (drastic, I know). (Female, aged 36–45 with master's degree)

Among some with anti-Christian animosity, the perception of conservative Christians as irrational can be used to legitimate denying their "humanness" and even their human rights. The next chapter looks at the nuances of how those with anti-Christian perspectives deal with the rights of Christians.

Childlikeness

The final trait Haslam discusses is childlikeness. Out-group members are seen as not fully developed in terms of mature human qualities and as unable to take care of themselves. This attitude allows individuals to develop paternalistic attitudes toward out-groups and also justifies efforts by in-group members to protect society from the influence of the out-group at all costs. Out-group members are seen as like little children in need of guidance so that they do not hurt themselves or others. In-group members deny that the out-group has the full range of human abilities and intelligences and thereby validate dehumanizing actions taken toward them. Majority group members have often used the supposed intellectual inferiority of racial and ethnic minorities to justify attempts to control them.[10] Such controls deny the full humanity and agency of members of those groups.

Those with anti-Christian hostility have an image of conservative Christians as unable to think for themselves; as they see it, more powerful and manipulative leaders direct how their followers should act and vote. In chapter 4 we pointed out this tendency in our discussion of why those with anti-Christian antipathy believe that conservative Christians have been able to fashion a powerful social movement. Here we show you some of the quotes that helped us to see this propensity and why our respondents do not see this trait as a "compliment":

> I wish there was a way to discourage them from using people's misfortunes to advance their political agenda. . . . I believe their leaders are devious, unethical, immoral and hypocritical to use their followers so badly. (Female, aged 46–55 with bachelor's degree)
>
> The leaders are deceptive and power hungry individuals who invoke "God" in a political sense to rally their supporters. . . . They play to people's emotions, daily. (Female, aged 26–35 with bachelor's degree)
>
> Their movement's leaders are the worst type of manipulative authoritarian scum and their millions of followers are sad, weak people who are all too willing to give up their self-respect and liberty for a fantasy. (Male, aged 26–35 with bachelor's degree)
>
> The vocal leaders and public faces of this movement are capitalizing on the idiots who blindly follow and support them without thought to push private agendas. (Female, aged 26–35 with high school diploma)

Rank-and-file Christians are blamed less than those seen as manipulating them from behind the scenes. Some respondents exhibited a certain level of sympathy for the "followers" while disdaining their leaders. One woman (aged 46–55 with doctorate), stated, "Perhaps not the leaders, but most of the followers sincerely believe that they are on a mission to fix what is wrong in the world. (I am far more cynical about the motives of the leadership, for the most part.)" Such a comment reveals paternalistic attitudes some have toward conservative Christians, who are, as a group, unable to think for themselves and subject to manipulation by evil leaders. This perception justifies intervention so that followers will not be manipulated.

A few themes surfaced illustrating the notion that conservative Christians are immature and need guidance. Several respondents referred to brainwashing as an explanation for why conservative Christians have developed their beliefs:

EFFECTS OF DEHUMANIZATION

If Haslam is correct about the traits connected to dehumanization, then some with anti-Christian perspectives have developed dehumanizing attitudes toward conservative Christians. We are not asserting that they desire to oppress Christians. The association with sheep, rather than apes, likely alters the aim of their dehumanizing attitudes. There may be less desire to control conservative Christians legally, as they are not compared to vicious animals; rather, like passive "lemmings" or "sheep," they may require guidance. We look at the types of measures endorsed by those with anti-Christian animosity in the next chapter. Suffice it to say here, regardless of the animal referred to, these respondents evidently did not perceive conservative Christians as fully capable humans.

Dehumanizing attitudes can be an important component in efforts to oppress marginalized out-groups or to take away their constituents' human rights.[12] We have shown in previous work[13] that cultural progressive activists have high levels of education and a progressive political outlook. Our respondents also possess these qualities. No academic inquiry has investigated how individuals from a highly educated and politically progressive subculture may express attitudes that dehumanize out-groups. Because of their academic training, they may find overt oppression of groups dehumanized by those with anti-Christian attitudes distasteful. But they still may engage in some degree of hatred, bigotry, and prejudice against them.

Hatred and Anti-Christian Sentiment

Edward B. Royzman, Clark McCauley, and Paul Rosin[14] argue that there is no single and commonly accepted scientific definition of what constitutes hatred. Eran Halperin[15] argues that two dimensions of hatred are at the core of most definitions. The first includes the motives and nature of the hated object. Aaron Ben-Zeev[16] points out that hatred tends to incorporate an all-inclusive denunciation of the object. Jon Elster[17] contends that hatred is tied to the judgment of an object or person as evil. Thus hatred involves the idea of a total denunciation, rather than merely nonapproval of a minor aspect, of the targeted group or individual. The second dimension is linked to the intentions of the hater toward the hated. Ralph White[18] argues that hatred is tied to a desire to harm or even kill the hated object. Merging these two dimensions allows Halperin[19] to develop a definition of hatred as "a powerful, extreme, and persistent emotion that rejects the group toward which it is directed in a generalized and totalistic fashion."

It is often hard to pick up emotions through open-ended questionnaires, as some of what might be called hate may merely be disdain or contempt—which can be conceptualized as a more intellectual dismissal. Some respondents were quite open about their hatred. One male respondent (aged 56–65 with some college) remarked, "I hate their wanting to order other people around. Many of them are creepy and evil." Still, many respondents do not openly share their emotions in such a questionnaire. This is why Halperin's observation that "group-based hatred is related to a very specific emotional goal—to do evil to, remove, and even eliminate the out-group" is quite valuable.[20] If we recognize hatred as an emotion that devalues the target group to the point of its having no redeeming value and creates a strong desire to eliminate the target group, then we have a way of assessing whether respondents are exhibiting the natural outcomes of a hateful emotional state, regardless of whether we actually detect that emotion.

In chapter 1 we listed several respondents' comments indicating a desire to remove Christians from society. These can be seen as hateful, especially if they are tied to a tendency to perceive conservative Christians as evil and without any redeeming value. Indeed, many with anti-Christian animosity did have a propensity to perceive conservative Christians as evil.

> What a shame that these people know right from wrong but can't express it thanks to evil religion. (Male, aged 26–35 with bachelor's degree)
>
> I believe they are the definition of evil. (Female, aged 46–55 with master's degree)

This idea of Christians as evil comports well with the notion that they have no redeeming value. These types of comments do not leave open much possibility of anything good from conservative Christians and Christianity. The evil respondents feared led many to perceive their struggle with conservative Christians as a matter of saving civilization or humanity.

and atheists[24] and have little empirical backing; such assertions about Christians are also without merit. Although conservative Christians often seek political office, they are no more or less likely to conceal their religious and political ideals than other office seekers. No systematic information supports the assertion that they are more likely to run as "stealth" candidates. Individuals with anti-Christian animosity make such assertions based on their own prejudices.

More common than the notion that conservative Christians are infiltrating the government is the idea that they are attempting to install a theocracy. Beyond the fact that conservative Christians may obtain political office and have different political values, there is a perception that conservative Christians in power threaten the fundamental nature of government and society. These Christians are seen not as participating fairly in the game of politics but rather as seeking to institute oppressive social structures similar to those of the Nazis or the Taliban.

> They seemed like Nazis who KNEW they were right! (Male, over 75 with doctorate)

> They are America's Taliban. They will take whatever power they can get. The Catholic Church has a great record—look what they did in the middle ages. The Christian Right would put in a theocracy in a minute. (Male, aged 36–45 with some graduate school)

> They are dangerous and remind me very much of the Brown Shirts, straight out of Nazi Germany. (Male, aged 36–45 with bachelor's degree)

These quotes are instructive if we remember that the respondents were generally well educated. None of the respondents mentioned any research indicating that Christians who gain political power act differently than other individuals. It is reasonable to assert that regardless of their religious beliefs, most politicians seek to implement policies favoring the social groups that support them. There certainly is no reason to believe that Christian politicians are any more likely than other politicians to hope to set up an oppressive Nazi- or Taliban style of government.[25] Yet those with anti-Christian animosity cling to a stereotype that conservative Christians have an especially high propensity to misuse power and create oppressive social structures. Since they hold such beliefs without any real evidence, this overgeneralization reflects prejudice.

Stereotyping by those with anti-Christian disaffinity also occurs in interpersonal relationships. Individuals with anti-Christian sentiments made many disparaging comments about Christians as individuals. Many characterized Christians as intolerant, stupid, arrogant, sexist, judgmental, racist, sexually repressed, mendacious, hypocritical, violent, homophobic, complaining, immoral, and so forth. Such descriptions by themselves do not necessarily reflect prejudice as many or most may arise out of personal experience. However, some of the statements offered suggest that some with anti-Christian animosity hold on to these ideas so powerfully that they jump to conclusions supported by little or no evidence. For example, one male respondent (aged 46–55 with master's degree) commented, "They might burn me at the stake some day." There is no research suggesting that Christians are more likely than non-Christians either to be violent or to establish a violent regime. On the contrary empirical work suggests that religious individuals are more likely to obey the law.[26] Yet this respondent held to this unfounded prejudice. Even when Christians do not act in the dysfunctional ways expected of them, some respondents still apply negative stereotypes to them. Another male respondent (aged 36–45 with bachelor's degree) represents that particular tendency: "I have told Christian friends (not Christian Right) my beliefs and they don't say a whole lot. They seem respectful of my feelings to my face but probably talk about me behind my back, or if they are really faithful probably believe I am going to hell." This respondent sees in the silence of Christians a tendency toward judgment not evident in their actions. Clearly his prejudice has led to a stereotyping based on no rational evidence.

Finally, several respondents implied that racism is a feature of Christianity. For example, one male respondent (aged 18–25 with bachelor's degree) stated, "They are generally nice people but that might be because I'm white." This conflation of racism with Christianity reflects automatic acceptance of the worst stereotypes about conservative Christians. The relationship of Christianity to racism is complex. For this investigation, it suffices to note that most conservative Christians, like most other Americans, do not practice overt racism.[27] However, we should point out that those with anti-Christian animosity in this sample tended to be overwhelmingly white, yet commonly asserted that conservative Christians are overwhelming white because of racism. A typical representation of this attitude is found by a male respondent (aged

36–45 with master's degree) who described the Christian Right as follows: "Hate anyone that isn't EXACTLY like they are: white, Christian, heterosexual, small-minded bigots." Such statements are ironic considering the racial makeup of our sample. Furthermore, previous research[28] has documented that certain racial minority groups are more likely to hold the conservative Christian beliefs those with anti-Christian attitudes hate so much. These assertions demonstrate a prejudicial lack of critical reflection.

After describing a personal encounter with the Christian Right, 16.1 percent of respondents stated that the encounter confirmed their previous perception of Christians. But some respondents proactively looked for evidence to justify their stereotypes against Christians, which can thus become self-fulfilling prophecies. For example, some with anti-Christian hostility appeared to create conflict and then blame Christians for it. One male respondent (over 75 with master's degree) stated, "Asking for a copy of the Koran in a Christian bookstore resulted in lecture on the 'truth' of the bible." Note how the respondent had provoked this incident. Just as one does not expect an Italian restaurant to serve sushi, a reasonable person would not expect to find the Koran in a Christian bookstore. If the respondent did not want to hear someone defend the veracity of the Bible, then going into a Christian bookstore was not the way to avoid such a conversation. But this encounter likely was useful in helping the respondent maintain a stereotype of Christians as intolerant.

Some respondents strengthened their stereotypes by protesting Christian events:

> At a rally for "National Day of Prayer" when I was there to protest their being on the steps to the local city hall. The individual I spoke to sounded like a zombie. They seem like they have been brainwashed. It reminded me of the "Moonies" back in the sixties and seventies. I wondered if there is anyway these people will ever wake up to reality. (Female, aged 46–55 with bachelor's degree)

In this situation Christians were not invading the space of the cultural progressive; she was there to disrupt their event. Her provocation created a situation that reinforced her already low view of Christians. Christians did initiate conflict on several other occasions, and we are not arguing that conservative Christians did not at times live up to the stereotypes held by respondents. However, some respondents clearly sought confirmation of their worst fears about Christians.

Finally, it should be noted that some with anti-Christian animosity did not hesitate to attribute negative qualities to a person simply because he or she was a member of the Christian Right or a Christian in general.

> Desire the vocal Christian less, because I assume they are poorly informed. (Male, over 75 with some graduate school)
>
> My stereotype is that, as a group, the "Christian Right" is not Christian and that they, as a group, are neither ethical nor honest. While I know that the members of the "Christian Right" are not necessarily the embodiment of my stereotype, experience puts them in the camp of having to prove themselves to be different than my stereotype. (Male, aged 56–65 with bachelor's degree)

The power of the stereotyping is such that mere knowledge of an individual's religious beliefs was enough for some respondents to disregard that person's opinions. Previous research by one of us[29] indicates that a significant number of academics are less willing to hire a potential job candidate revealed to be either a fundamentalist or an evangelical. Some academics with anti-Christian perspectives may use the stereotypes exhibited here to judge such candidates even before learning about their qualifications. The current research endeavor cannot systematically document whether the stereotypes are so powerful that they overwhelm other factors in respondents' assessment of conservative Christians; however, some of their comments indicate that this phenomenon may be present.

Bigotry and Anti-Christian Sentiment

Bigotry is a characteristic tied to intolerance, although it has been studied less than hatred or prejudice. George Haggerty defines bigotry as the opposite of respect and tolerance.[30] His work suggests that bigotry on college campuses is problematic since it precludes the free exchange of ideas and entails dismissing the ideas of the target group without giving them serious consideration. This conception comports well with Ali Unsal's definition of bigotry as blind acceptance of an idea that results from intolerance and ignorance.[31] Discussions of bigotry often tie it to the rejection of individuals from a particular out-group and the unconditional acceptance of an idea that diminishes the worth of that group's members.[32] We attribute bigotry to the sentiments of those with anti-Christian hostility to the degree that they exhibit an unwillingness to entertain ideas about tolerating conservative Christians.

On an interpersonal level, many were willing to accept conservative Christians as friends. In fact some of them noted their friendship with Christians. For example, one male respondent (aged 56–65 with master's degree) stated, "I have had too many born again friends, and despite my revulsion at their beliefs, I get along well with them." However, it was quite common for others with anti-Christian perspectives to eliminate the possibility of friendship with a Christian because of that person's religious beliefs. We have seen some of this propensity to avoid conservative Christians due to perceptions of them as coarse. However, others also sought to avoid these individuals because they believed that conservative Christians are unable to engage with them intellectually and would thus make for poor friends.

> I would desire the vocal Christian less, because that is a person who is making decisions based on superstition and a cult-like mindset. I would never be able to have a real friendship with that person, and they would be trying to convert me. (Male, aged 46–55 with bachelor's degree)
>
> I would not have any one of them in my circle of friends, friends who tend to think, not just believe. (Male, aged 66–75 with bachelor's degree)
>
> I try to stay away from them. I do not trust their ability to listen to sound/logical debate. (Female, aged 46–55 with doctorate)

The inability to engage intellectually with conservative Christians was not the only reason given for avoiding friendship with them. Some respondents attributed other unfavorable qualities to this group and stated that, as a result, they did not want to have much interaction with Christians.

> Those who proclaim to be conservative Christians I tend to avoid. They tend to evangelize too much. (Male, aged 56–65 with some graduate school)

I try to avoid them as much as possible. They are so dead-set in
their ways it is difficult to have a conversation. (Male, aged 36–45
with bachelor's degree)

I would avoid the vocal Christian since they would be more likely
to be judgmental. (Male, aged 46–55 with master's degree)

Regardless of the reason given, many of our respondents avoided conservative Christians due to preconceptions about them. Many would
not seriously consider the idea of tolerating conservative Christians in
interpersonal relationships. They might have to interact with them on a
superficial level but were hesitant to allow conservative Christians into
their social networks. If bigotry represents distancing oneself from others based on group membership rather than individual characteristics,
we have evidence of bigotry among some with anti-Christian animosity.

Bigotry is closely related to prejudice. It is difficult to conceive of
how individuals would develop bigotry and a tendency to avoid certain
social groups if prejudice were not also present. Theoretically hatred is
not necessary to explain bigotry and prejudice, but it does complement
those two predispositions. Finding evidence of all three of these attitudes is relatively simple since the presence of one increases the
chances that the other two are present as well. Perhaps this is why we
can find elements of all of these concepts when we look at different
types of rejection of members of out-groups (racism, sexism, homophobia). In this, anti-Christian rejection is similar to other forms of rejection.

CONCLUSION

The manifestation of disaffectionate attitudes on the part of a politically
progressive, highly educated subculture and social and religious conservatives may differ. Previous research has documented the existence of
intolerance and bias among progressives.[33] We documented such attributes within some of our respondents. Some dehumanized conservative
Christians in such a way that the features of hatred, bigotry, and prejudice found among those with lower levels of education and higher levels
of political conservatism were also found among the highly progressive
and highly educated. If those with anti-Christian animosity are loath to
violate principles of religious equality through political measures, then

is the intolerance documented in this chapter merely an annoyance? The type of oppression normally linked to intolerance may be missing, meaning that it has no real consequences for the target group. With so little research on intolerance among progressives and the highly educated, there has been little speculation about how this intolerance impacts society. We look in chapter 6 at what those with anti-Christian sentiments say they want for our society. Then, in chapter 7, we speculate about the plausible social impact of these perspectives.

6

WHAT DO PEOPLE WITH
ANTI-CHRISTIAN ANIMOSITY WANT?

Some respondents express a fear of and desire to prevent a Christian takeover of society. For those with such beliefs, conservative Christians and their political ambitions are not merely annoyances. They pose a threat to the very fabric of the secular society those with anti-Christian animosity want to create or maintain. Conservative Protestants are seen as a social problem needing to be solved. Yet these individuals also tend to avoid using laws to control those Christians. Given this paradox, there is value in learning how cultural progressive activists with anti-Christian disaffection want to handle the problem they see created by conservative Christians.

How these respondents attempt to "solve" this problem can be instructive in understanding their values. Previous research has documented the potential effects of dehumanization on the rights, opportunities, and even genocide of target groups.[1] Yet highly educated individuals are generally socialized to reject overt inequality. Our respondents derive from a highly educated subculture not prone to violent or overly oppressive solutions. Despite their dehumanizing perceptions, it would be simplistic to assume that they seek political and legal mechanisms to oppress conservative Christians. Isolated respondents occasionally advocated overt oppression of Christians, but this was not the dominant theme. How dehumanization shapes the way a highly educated population treats a target group remains a topic for further research. In this chapter we start such an investigation with an assessment of the desire for social change among individuals with anti-Christian sentiment.

DO NOT CHANGE THE LAW

Toward the end of our questionnaire, we included a controversial question. We asked whether respondents saw legislation as useful in dealing with the Christian Right. We made this an exploratory question and did not suggest any particular legal changes. We were interested in what respondents would come up with in their evaluation. Because we did not suggest specific amendments to the law, many respondents did not know what to do with the question.

> Hmmm. This is too open-ended and generic a question. What kind of laws do you have in mind here? (Male, aged 36–45 with doctorate)
> I don't have a clue what sort of laws you might mean. (Female, aged 56–65 with doctorate)
> Too vague a question—what sort of laws? (Male, aged 56–65 with bachelor's degree)

This was an unfortunate side effect of keeping our question open-ended. With an opportunity to follow up, we could have crafted questions from suggestions offered by other respondents and observed the level of support for such reforms among individuals with anti-Christian hostility.

Despite these difficulties, we still collected a large number of responses that either supported or dismissed legal remedies. The majority (62.2 percent) of those with anti-Christian attitudes indicated that they did not support the imposition of laws to deal with the Christian Right or with Christians. The reason for this nonsupport varied. For many, the Constitution was too important to violate with laws against Christians.

> In our nation, as conceived by its founders, we can't pass laws suppressing religious beliefs. (Male, aged 66–75 with doctorate)
> No. There is a constitutional amendment prohibiting bills of attainder, and as a nation of laws, we cannot pass laws targeting spe-

cific groups; particularly religious groups. (Male, aged 26–35 with bachelor's degree)

We can't. "Congress shall make no laws respecting an establishment of religion." Hello? (Male, aged 46–55 with master's degree)

No. To me First Amendment rights are too important and should not be abridged for anyone, and that included those wishing to deny me those rights. (Male, aged 46–55 with some graduate school)

These respondents understood the question as asking whether we should have an explicit law punishing Christians. Many rejected this possibility as overt religious oppression. Laws targeting a religious group conflicted with their overarching values, which included the belief that conservative Christians have a right to believe what they want. Even though they considered Christian ideas foolish, they did not want to rob Christians of the right to believe in such "foolishness."

No. I do not favor infringing on people's rights to "believe" what they want. Being an imbecile is not a crime. (Male, aged 56–65 with bachelor's degree)

No. They have a right to their beliefs no matter how wacko I personally believe they are. (Female, aged 46–55 with master's degree)

This is America and you have the freedom to be an ass. (Female, aged 36–45 with bachelor's degree)

No, not really. Don't believe in targeting a group of people with a law designated to control behavior. As long as they leave me alone and stay out of influencing government and political activities, let them wallow in their stupidity. (Male, aged 56–65 with some college)

Some with anti-Christian hostility indicated that our current laws are sufficient for dealing with conservative Christians and merely need to be enforced. These respondents hoped the foolishness of Christianity would be exposed without the need to single out Christians. This outcome would allow them to avoid advocating new restrictions and contravening the values they support.

Some with anti-Christian sentiment did not advocate passing laws that directly affect Christians for practical reasons. Several used their fear of a Christian takeover to justify their reluctance. This question represented yet another opportunity to voice their disdain for Christian involvement in politics. Many indicated that they did not want to use laws against Christians because this was what conservative Christians would do.

> No! Legislating religious belief is what the extreme right would like to do. (Male, over 75 with some college)
> No. Why try and imitate their bad habits? (Male, aged 66–75 with some graduate school)
> I do not think it is ethical to pass laws restricting personal belief. If I would support laws restricting their free exercise, I would be the same as them. (Female, aged 26–35 with bachelor's degree)

Such comments allowed these respondents to take the moral high ground. Respondents' refusal to seek such laws served an important philosophical purpose. This allowed them to envision their concerns as superior to the concerns of their religious opponents since they, unlike those opponents, could argue that they were not seeking to force others to accept their beliefs. Some also believed that promoting anti-Christian laws would enable Christians to justify using legal means against non-Christians in the future. As one male respondent (aged 66–75 with master's degree) stated, "No. They have their freedom of religion and I want to preserve my freedom from religion." So in protecting Christians, these respondents believed that they were protecting themselves.

Some with anti-Christian sentiment exhibited irritation at Christian claims to victimhood. They perceived conservative Christians as seeking out victim status in order to push for special rights. In this light, they did not want Christians to be targeted in a way that provided justification for claims that their rights had been violated.

> No I don't. Laws passed affecting members of the Christian Right would only heighten the "persecution" complex that seems to be pervasive within that group today. People should be free to believe whatever they choose without interference, but the federal government need not grant any legitimacy for ideas that are not explicitly secular in nature. (Male, aged 26–35 with master's degree)
> No. Just because they favor discriminatory practices does not mean that they should be subjected to them. Free speech and free choice are founding principles of our country, and laws specifically affecting the Christian Right would go against everything that our country is supposed to stand for. Additionally, passing laws that

would result in discrimination against them would result in a martyr-like state for many of them, and would probably result in a strengthening of their message. (Female, aged 26–35 with some college)

Thus, a desire to neutralize conservative Christians' claims to victimhood also explains why those with anti-Christian perspectives avoid the passage of overtly anti-Christian laws. Not passing such legislation removes the potential for claims of injustice against conservative Christians. Therefore, those with anti-Christian antipathy see noninterference as the appropriate legal stance to take toward Christians, even as they also make sure that those Christians do not interfere with them.

Some answers to this question explicitly emphasized the need to keep conservative Christians in their proper place. Many with anti-Christian hostility highly valued separation of church and state. Some used this ideal to justify disengaging legal from religious matters. Although some discussed separation of church and state to indicate that government is not supposed to get involved with religion, the general emphasis was that Christians should not have an undue influence over public policy. In this particular anti-Christian interpretation of the separation of church and state, Christians do not become involved in the political and social sphere.

> Just enforce constitutional separation of church and state, allow all to believe or not as they wish without interference or support of government, don't allow them to force their religion into governing. (Male, aged 46–55 with master's degree)
>
> They should not be allowed to put a Christian Right spin on any legislation. Our country is made up of people of many beliefs and no beliefs. Let's keep government secular. (Female, aged 56–65 with some graduate school)
>
> I think we should not let religious belief that goes against scientific evidence be supported in any way by our government, at any level. In other words I believe there should be a stronger separation of religion and government. (Male, aged 46–55 with some graduate school)

The desire of those with anti-Christian animosity to avoid legislation is at least partially tied to their desire to protect themselves from a Christian takeover. This desire is possibly connected to the sheer number of Christians in the United States relative to those with anti-Christian hostility.[2] The perception of a high number of Christians may partially generate the fear some respondents have of a coming theocracy. In protecting conservative Christians, some respondents contended, they were protecting themselves.

In short, most of those with anti-Christian animosity did not advocate imposing laws against Christians for two powerful reasons. First, they had a philosophical problem with such laws. Some had experienced harassment and hatred due to their minority religious status, which may have helped them shape a philosophy of religious freedom that overrides any animosity toward conservative Christians in defense of the rights of people of all faiths and nonfaiths. This suggests a cognitive reason for resisting such laws. Second, they potentially resisted discriminatory laws as a way to protect themselves, conceptualizing laws that disadvantage Christians as a legal justification for conservative Christians to oppress them in turn or as a template that one day could be used against them. This suggests a more emotional or fear-based rationale for resisting such laws. These two reasons clearly overlap as emotional fears and concerns can buttress a cognitive rationale.

DON'T CHANGE THE LAW, BUT . . .

Most respondents indicated that they did not want to alter the law. However a subset started out indicating that they did not support anti-Christian laws, then went on to suggest possible legal changes. It is as if they wanted to adhere to a general principle of religious freedom, but the more they thought about it, the more willing they were to make certain legal alterations with a disparate impact on Christians. They may have wanted to retain the mantle of fairness but also to attend legally to their specific grievances against conservative Christians.

> I'd be opposed to any laws that target a group just because of membership. On the other hand, I think it's wise to target some of the behaviors that are at the root of this problem. Home Schooling— It's one thing to teach your kids your beliefs, but it's not OK to restrict their education. I'm in favor of stronger rules on the content of Home Schooling. Evidence Based Policy—Modern problems are complex and require complicated solutions and not faith or gut based. We should require policy be backed by evidence and increase

the non-bias/scientific review of government. It should be harder to disregard facts and cause harm, anti-vaccine movement comes to mind. (Male, aged 36–45 with master's degree)

No. I think we should maintain the separation laws we already have in affect. Actually, I'd like to see all churches be taxed like any money-making business. (Male, aged 36–45 with bachelor's degree)

I don't think we should pass laws against members of the Religious Right. . . . However, there are laws I would like to see passed that would affect members of the Religious Right. First of all, I would tax any churches that engage in outright politicking. Second, I would outlaw hate talk in broadcast media (i.e., the slandering of a group because of race or religion or ethnicity, and the outright calling for killing of anyone). I'm sure current laws prohibiting school prayer and religious displays on public property are considered anathema to the religious right. I would keep them. (Male, aged 56–65 with master's degree)

These respondents may feel conflicted about their general support for the separation of church and state and their hostility toward conservative Christians. Thus, despite initial assertions that they do not favor legal interference, emotional distaste for Christians still works its way into their answers. So they seek to maintain an image of religious neutrality but still propose legislation to control conservative Christians. These types of answers suggest a possible social desirability aspect to the answers respondents provide about legal interference.

The issue of social desirability as a component of attitudes toward an out-group is not new. Within the field of race/ethnicity, it is commonly acknowledged that looking at the old-fashioned, overt types of racism is no longer the best way to understand racial prejudice.[3] Modern forms of racism combine the need to maintain an image of racial tolerance with animosity toward or fear of racial out-groups.[4] Therefore it is important to look at political stances that contain racial and nonracial elements. Nonracial elements enable whites to take a stance on a certain issue that harms people of color and yet escape the charge of racism. For example, a white person who mistrusts Hispanics can favor tougher border legislation since there are nonracial reasons for doing so. The racist label is not socially desirable, and ascertaining whether individuals oppose illegal immigration due to mistrust of Hispanics or nonracial concerns about national security and economic stability is not easy.

Likewise, some with anti-Christian hostility may consider it socially desirable to maintain an attitude of religious fairness. The vast majority stated their nonsupport for overt discrimination against Christians as contravening their philosophy of church-state separation. However, some with anti-Christian animosity used the notion of church-state separation to justify reforms that would likely have disproportionate effects on Christians.

> I think we should pass laws that are fair. Keep church and state separate. No more tax breaks for churches. Crack down on right wing extremism just like we would on any other extremism. (Male, aged 26–35 with bachelor's degree)
>
> The constitution already prohibits unions of church and state. If we could elect an honest politician who would protect our rights as detailed by the constitution, would go a long way in affecting these Christian nut cases. To this day, we still see religious art and other mementos of their "beliefs" in State and Federal buildings which is prohibited by our constitution!!!!!! We should also abolish any tax advantage that Churches enjoy today. We should put in place mandatory extreme prison sentences for anyone or any group that attempts to take away civil liberties guaranteed by our constitution. (Male, aged 56–65 with master's degree)

Of interest here is not whether these are reasonable reforms that should be enacted. Individuals on both sides of the political spectrum will argue about the advisability of tax breaks for religious institutions or religious art on public property. The point is that these reforms would change the status quo in a way that affected Christian communities, and these respondents use church-state separation to justify these reforms, making it clear that this principle could be used to impact Christians. This is in keeping with the notions of modern racism in that those who do not like a particular out-group may express that antipathy on issues where the hatred can be hidden but applied in a religious rather than racial context. Using modern racism as a template for examining possible reforms offered by those with anti-Christian disaffection provides insight into how highly educated individuals may find socially acceptable ways to express their personal prejudices.

Is there a case study that might show us how highly educated individuals create justifications for rules or actions that disproportionately impact conservative Christians but do so with a rationalization that they are being religiously neutral? One possible example comes from the work of one of us revealing anti-Christian prejudice among academics.[5] The study relied on quantitative work demonstrating that academics are least willing to hire conservative Protestants as opposed to members of other social groups. Some of the responses to these findings were noteworthy. Whereas some individuals challenged the methodology and the data, others sought to justify the results. One example comes from the Even the Bravest . . . blog: "But why would there be, or seem to be, anti-Christian bias in the academy? For the same reason that there would seem to be an anti-educational bias in Christianity. The ideals of Christianity conflict with the ideals of humanistic or scientific inquiry."[6] According to this blogger's rationale, it is okay to discriminate against conservative Christians since they do not hold to scientific principles.[7] Thus the blogger suggests that conservative Christians can justifiably be treated differently than other individuals, even as she likely believes herself to be fair and religiously neutral. In a similar manner, we contend, some of our respondents want both to believe themselves to be religiously neutral and to put measures in place to control conservative Christians. This tension is reflected in answers that contain both elements of religious neutrality (such as appeals to church-state separation) and reference to measures that disproportionately impact conservative Christians.

YES, USE THE LAW

One group, albeit a minority of all with anti-Christian animosity, clearly supported laws to regulate the actions, especially the political actions, of conservative Christians. Respondents more overt about the type of legal remedies they desire may speak for those more hesitant to voice support for such legislation. The overt laws they advocate may have wider support among those who feel constrained by the need to take a public stance favoring religious equality.

The reform most supported by those with anti-Christian animosity concerns the tax status of churches. This was the reform most desired most among those not afraid to articulate the laws they wanted imposed on Christians.[8]

> Religion should not be privileged under the law. They should have to pay sales taxes and property taxes. The clergy should have to pay income and social security tax. Contributions to churches should not be deductible. Churches are like country clubs. They are a business and should be treated like a business. All of their employees should be covered by all the discrimination and payroll laws. (Male, aged 46–55 with bachelor's degree)
>
> I see no legal reason why churches/religions should not pay taxes just like any other business. As long as all are taxed the same it would not be favoring one religion over another. (Male, aged 56–65 with some graduate school)
>
> I think churches should lose their default tax exempt status and should go through the same procedures as any other organization. Some churches make extremely large profits yet don't have to give a dime to the government, while the nonprofit ones would not be effected. (Male, aged 18–25 with some college)

The advantages conservative Christians can gain through their tax status appear to drive these concerns in part. The desire of some with anti-Christian hostility for this reform is especially acute when churches engage in politics, as illustrated by one female respondent (aged 46–55 with master's degree): "They have started telling people how to vote from the pulpit, the tax exempt status of their churches should be revoked." Respondents perceived this reform as a way to level the playing field. They conceived of taxing churches as a way to produce equality between the religious and the nonreligious rather than as an attempt to punish Christians.

This fits into the general theme of the measures desired by those with anti-Christian animosity. They perceive their reforms as a way to produce equality between the religious and nonreligious. This perception can play on fears about losing control in their fight against conservative Christians. Reforms limiting the power and influence of conservative Christians can be justified as a way to keep Christians from gaining too much power. As previously noted, church-state separation could be used to justify possible reforms with a disparate impact on conservative Christians. In keeping with the theory of modern racism, church-state separation provides a viable way for individuals with anti-Christian hostility to endorse legal alterations without violating their stance of religious egalitarianism. Legitimate concerns about religious interference may intermix with the bias and animosity demonstrated in some respondents' comments (discussed further in chapter 7). Some used the principle of church-state separation to support measures that reduce religious influence. As one male respondent (aged 46–55 with bachelor's degree) stated, "We should pass laws that further limit the impact religion has on politics etc. We should more clearly define the separation of church and state and enforce that separation." Furthermore, calls to take tax exemptions away from the churches and uphold church-state separation were often linked, with the latter justifying the former.

> Yes. Strictly enforce the separation of church and state. Make churches pay use and property taxes and strip them of the most egregious privileges. (Male, over 75 with master's degree)
>
> Yes. We desperately need clarification and enforcement of the separation of church and state. All religious organizations should be taxed like any other profitable business. All charitable work should be tax deductible, though. (Male, aged 46–55 with bachelor's degree)

Ironically, government taxation of churches is conceptualized as a way of keeping church and state separate. This reinforces the tendency of those with anti-Christian attitudes to see church-state separation as keeping the church out of the government rather than the government out of the church. Both the removal of tax exemptions and church-state separation become means to support measures that disproportionately impact Christians and still allow respondents to claim religious neutrality.

Some respondents with anti-Christian animosity perceived the very concept of religious neutrality as a way to limit the influence of conservative Christians. They desired to hold on to the claim of egalitarianism but hoped that limiting the influence of conservative Christians would be a happy side effect of otherwise egalitarian measures.

> I don't think we should pass laws that are directed towards any particular group of people. However, if a particular °good° law happens to negatively affect practices or beliefs of the Christian Right, but protects the freedom of most Americans, then I would be in favor. (Female, aged 46–55 with bachelor's degree)

> I do not believe laws should be passed that affect any one religion
> over another. I do believe that existing laws should be enforced that
> could have a negative impact. (Male, aged 26–35 with some graduate
> school)

These statements make clear some respondents' understanding that legal reforms can be fashioned that have more of an effect on conservative Christians than on other religious groups. The intentions of some with anti-Christian sentiment are not as benign as their philosophy of religious egalitarianism suggests. They accept the notion of a culture war and enunciate a desire for a progressive victory. By linking their efforts to claims of religious neutrality, they justify seeking reforms that disproportionately impact Christians. These respondents provide some evidence that claims of religious egalitarianism may be exaggerated. If they are, then Stephen Carter's[9] observation that some progressives seek to eliminate religious influence, in this case Christian influence, from public consideration takes on more importance. He contends that many trivialize spiritual expression and seek to keep the ideas of religious individuals out of public discourse. Calls for church-state separation and taxation of churches can be tied to a desire to eliminate Christians' societal influence rather than to achieve religious neutrality. These issues serve as acceptable, symbolic ways to express that desire.

A few respondents did not care about religious neutrality and supported measures aimed distinctly at religious groups, especially conservative Christians. Some measures would overtly limit the ability of Christians to influence the larger society.

> Churches should be taxed, and all tax benefits to their employees
> should cease. They should be absolutely forbidden to have ANY role
> in politics, including collecting money and espousing platforms.
> Prayers at any civil ceremony outside the purview of their own
> churches should be forbidden, especially including at governmental
> meetings, oaths, etc. Churches should not be allowed to provide
> orphanages and adoption programs. (Male, aged 66–75 with docto-
> rate)
>
> [Members of the Christian Right should] not [be] allowed to hold
> political office, be police etc., serve in the armed forces. (Male, aged
> 56–65 with doctorate; text in brackets added)
>
> Yes, proselytizing should be outlawed entirely. People have a
> right to believe whatever they want to believe but should not be

permitted to impose their will on others, particularly the indigent in foreign countries. (Male, aged 46–55 with master's degree)

Although most with anti-Christian hostility stated that they did not support directly passing laws against Christians, those who did favor such legislation mentioned similar themes related to removing conservative Christians from influence, and they legitimated their stance with reference to the principle of church-state separation. Thus, although these respondents did not come to the same conclusion about using laws against conservative Christians, they did tap into the same value system as those who refused to support overtly discriminatory laws.

Some respondents went even farther, not wanting merely to limit the ability of Christians to influence political outcomes but desiring to inhibit their passing their religious beliefs to their own children thorough homeschooling.

> My law would be that they have to send their kids to public schools rather than homeschool because the isolation and fundamentalism breeds fear into many of their children that non Christians are of the devil, never to be trusted, etc. This does not bode well for the continuation of our country because an educated people is important to its success. They are not truly educated until they learn that non Christians are people too and that we die fighting for America too, and that we do not deserve to be treated like we are the plague of the devil. (Female, aged 46–55 with bachelor's degree)

> I am a great believer in Public education and feel that home schooling is simply a Madrasah with a Christian name, it should probably not be allowed. (Male, aged 66–75 with some college)

> They should not be allowed to homeschool their children unless they are qualified teachers and provide a balanced, reality-based education. (Male, aged 36–45 with master's degree)

These respondents were in the distinct minority. The vast majority did not endorse any overt attempt to limit the ability of Christians to practice their religion and spread their ideas. But the respondents supporting these overt measures differed from those who did not only in their proposed solution, not in their concern about the imposition of Christian values.

The question about whether those respondents with anti-Christian animosity would seek legal remedies in their effort to deal with the

Christian Right has provided important insight into how they attempt to address their concerns about conservative Christians. From their perspective, direct legal intervention is generally not acceptable, but laws with a disparate impact on conservative Christians are. However, these respondents did not just suggest legal solutions. Although hesitant to enunciate the use of overt legal means to combat Christians, they did indicate that lack of education is the problem behind Christians' influence in our society.

EDUCATION IS THE ANSWER

Reforming education makes sense to those with anti-Christian animosity since they believe that Christianity in its current form continues to flourish due to a lack of intellectual development. Thus, education, rather than direct legal intervention, becomes the acceptable instrument through which they seek to alter society. As mentioned previously, many respondents lament the type of religious socialization that has produced conservative Christians. Thus brainwashing was a common theme in the data. In fact, respondents used the word "brainwash" sixty-one times, always to indicate oppressive socialization in the creation of Christian belief. If brainwashing means forcing someone to believe something against his or her will, then modern scholarship reveals it to be a myth.[10] At some level individuals make a volitional choice to accept their beliefs. Perhaps those with anti-Christian animosity do not define the concept in such a way and rather use the term to refer to an undue influencing of children before they are able to make rational decisions.

> Yes. I think that we should restrict the indoctrination of children in religious dogma and ritual. . . . The religious freedom of children is being subverted by the only device that maintains the viability of faith-based ignorance. (Male, aged 46–55 with master's degree)
> I think that would most likely violate the 1st Amendment, but if something WERE able to be done, perhaps something making it so children would not be able to be indoctrinated into any particular religion until they have reached a certain age and proved they have achieved a certain level of critical reasoning in order to make up their own minds. (Male, aged 36–45 with some college)

> The only law that I could conceivably support that would affect the Christian Right (and all religions) would be a prohibition against the religious indoctrination of children, which I consider to be child abuse. (Male, aged 66–75 with some college)

Some respondents did not limit their concern about brainwashing to the socialization of children and conceived of it as occurring among adults. In chapter 5 we heard about manipulative and evil leaders with compliant followers. Those with anti-Christian sentiment may envision conservative Christian adults as ignorant and susceptible to the false religious claims. Their lack of education, in this view, enables the influence of a religion deemed harmful to our society.

Some with anti-Christian hostility hope that through education those who practice conservative forms of Christianity will gain the insight needed to escape their religion's harmful influence.

> Most of them are misinformed, and I'm willing to bet most of them don't know much about the bible beyond what their Preachers or Priests have told them. Most of them have been given a biased perspective their whole lives. A lot of them were not educated enough on how to evaluate evidence when they first accepted it, like when they were kids and they are too committed to it when they reach adult hood. (Male, aged 26–35 with some college)

Such an approach assumes the rational superiority of a nonreligious or non-Christian understanding of reality over a traditional Christian perspective. Using rationality to expose the shortcomings of Christianity is a common theme. Education is conceptualized as bringing enlightenment and enabling conservative Christians to escape their religious trap. Educated Christians are unexpected, which accounts in part for the surprised reaction of some respondents on encountering them. Those with anti-Christian animosity generally believe that education will reduce the number of conservative Christians, thereby creating a better society by abating the threat of a coming theocracy and other dysfunctions connected to conservative Christians. Those with anti-Christian disaffection envision education as more than a tool to create more productive workers; they see it as a means to reverse Christian indoctrination.

Even the best educational efforts, however, may not be of much value in altering the opinions of those already sufficiently indoctrinated. So education may be even more important as it concerns efforts to influence children. Many made it a point to discuss the importance of education in our school system. Their attitudes indicate that the educational system is an important front in the cultural war against conservative Christians. So there was frustration at the efforts of conservative Christians to influence our educational system.

> Heard Christian Right representatives speak on behalf of "Intelligent Design" in the science curriculum. It made my mind swirl in disbelief and gave me respect for how cleverly they presented their position. (Female, aged 56–65 with some graduate school)
>
> My biggest issue is their interference in public education, especially their insistence that biblically-based creation stories be given equal time with the teaching of evolution. (Female, aged 56–65 with doctorate)
>
> I find that their attempts to force religion into both politics and classrooms is disgusting. Promoting "Christian Science" through political movements instead of providing evidence in support of their "Theories" such as Intelligent Design, Abstinence only Sex Education, and School Prayer, which have been shown through actual scientific pursuit to be false at best. I also find the indoctrination of their own children to be an awful practice. (Male, aged 18–25 with some college)

Issues such as cultural diversity, evolution, and comprehensive sex education come up often in the comments of those with anti-Christian hostility. Battles over these matters likely extend beyond their particulars. They are larger symbolic issues concerning the socialization of children. They represent the clash of ideals regarding a desirable society, pitting those with anti-Christian animosity against conservative Christians. Fighting for reforms in the educational system becomes another way to reduce Christian influence while maintaining claims of neutrality.

We have already pointed out that most with anti-Christian hostility do not desire to personally "enlighten" Christians about the falsity of their religious beliefs, perhaps finding the similarity of such efforts to their perception of distasteful Christian proselytizing. Rather than persuasion, they tend to rely on altering educational, and perhaps political, institutions. The focus on structural, rather than individualistic, measures in altering society is an important cultural and ideological difference between conservative Christians and those with anti-Christian attitudes.

WHAT WORLD DO THOSE WITH ANTI-CHRISTIAN ANIMOSITY WANT?

What is the vision of those with anti-Christian animosity? If they managed to achieve their goals, what sort of society would we live in? The answers of some respondents reveal some of what such individuals want for a better society. Clearly they desire less Christian influence within the larger society. Those with the level of hatred that allows them to enunciate the elimination of Christianity may be in the minority, but they are not insignificant. However, many with anti-Christian animosity did not go this far in articulating their desire to manage Christianity. They accepted the presence of Christianity in churches and homes but did not want to see it in the political and educational spheres. Such a desire comports well with the principle of church-state separation. Rather than hoping to eliminate Christianity, they envision limiting it to individuals' private lives.

> Christian Right people can do what they want in their churches and homes, but not in the public arena. (Female, aged 66–75 with bachelor's degree)
>
> Yes. Mainly enforce separation of church and state. . . . Keep all religion in your church, in your home, out of the public square, and most of all, out of my face. (Male, aged 56–65 with some college)
>
> Keep your religion at home and in your church. Why oh why isn't that enough?!? (Male, aged 36–45 with some graduate school)
>
> If they want to be crazy in their own homes and not bother me, then I wouldn't mind. (Male, aged 26–35 with master's degree)

These respondents deemed private expression allowable as this would mean that Christian sentiment was hidden. In addition to the formal exclusion of Christianity from the political and educational spheres, some respondents desired limitations on Christian behavior (no proselytizing) so that they would be sheltered from the presence of Chris-

tians altogether. Thus notions of the degree to which Christian sentiment should be removed from the public square varied among respondents; however, the desire for its removal was fairly consistent in our
sample.

A few suggested a precedent limiting religious influences to the
private domain. They indicated desire to follow the norms of European
societies in which such attitudes toward religion are common.

> Europe recognizes them for the lunatic fringe they are. (Male,
> aged 46–55 with bachelor's degree)
> France banned all cross wearing, and Muslim headscarves, every-
> one is the same, no prejudices. We need to do somewhat the same,
> get rid of all bumper stickers, fishs, keep the Christ in Christmas,
> etc., it would calm everybody down. (Male, aged 56–65 with some
> graduate school)

That some with anti-Christian animosity held European societies up as
the ideal sheds light on their ultimate goal. They desire a secularized
society with limited Christian influence.[11] Christianity may exist but
must not be seen or heard about outside Christians' private lives. Such a
world would not automatically eliminate the presence of Christianity.
Direct measures banning Christianity are not desirable, given the cognitive dissonance they would create with values favoring religious neutrality. The privatizing of Christianity fits within the general framework
of indirect, rather than overt, efforts to limit Christianity. Christians'
inability to reproduce themselves in such a sterile environment would
clearly hamper the growth of the religion and perhaps hasten its de-
mise. Such a culture could relegate Christianity to irrelevance in the
larger context, as many European nations have done.

CONCLUSION

Certain patterns arise in the analysis of what those with anti-Christian
animosity desire for the larger society. We previously documented their
propensity toward dehumanizing thought patterns with regard to conservative Christians. Past research suggests that dehumanization tends
to lead to overt efforts at oppression of the dehumanized group. But our
respondents are a highly educated and politically progressive group that

generally rejects heavy-handed efforts. However, they still use their dehumanized perceptions of Christians to justify subtle and indirect limitations on Christian influence and power. In a zero-sum understanding of social power, these more nuanced attempts to limit the power of their Christian competitors can help them to maintain social control.

There is some disagreement among our respondents in this area. Some favor proactive laws and regulations more eagerly than others. The degree of their disagreement is difficult to determine without quantitative assessments. However, they all share reverence for the separation of church and state. No matter the possible direction those with anti-Christian sentiment want to take, they justify it with reference to that principle. Some use it to indicate hesitation to create explicit anti-Christians laws. Others see church-state separation as a way to rationalize such laws. In this way those with anti-Christian hostility may use common terms (e.g., "separation of church and state") but with differing meanings. Further research to study the distinct ways those with this hostility utilize such concepts is worth pursuing.

Their desired reforms and vision for an ideal society indicate a possible explanation of how a highly educated, politically and socially progressive group seeks to constrain a dehumanized group. Denial of efforts to mistreat Christians is important to maintaining a philosophical position of religious neutrality. Assertion of socialization that promotes egalitarian attitudes has often been linked to educational attainment,[12] although usually such assertions deal with issues of race, sex, and sexual preference. Michael Emerson and David Sikkink argue, however, that, rather than alter prejudices, education may enhance respondents' ability to hide them from researchers.[13] Since many have a visceral reaction to conservative Christians, a higher education level may help them to articulate a philosophy of religious egalitarianism while seeking out measures that disadvantage conservative Christians disproportionately. Research into symbolic racism has studied a phenomenon whereby subjects espouse racial egalitarianism while supporting efforts that work against the interests of racial minorities.[14] Whites with anti-Hispanic resentment may choose not to support immigration reform and offer nonracist reasons for their opposition. The lack of immigration reform is more likely to impact Hispanics relative to other racial groups and to have a disparate impact on Hispanics in the United States. Likewise, highly educated individuals with anti-Christian animosity may protect their image as supporting religious equality while supporting efforts that have a disparate impact on the lives of Christians. This type of symbolic expression can have consequential effects on conservative Christians.

We can further build on our understanding of how those with anti-Christian sentiment justify the actions and perspectives that increase their social control. We see the culturally appropriate means used to express opposition to conservative Christians and Christian institutions. They have little need to take into account any negative effects that "religiously neutral" rules and laws may have on conservative Christians. Such lack of concern may be one manifestation of the dehumanization of Christians. Furthermore, those with anti-Christian hostility also see education as a culturally acceptable tool for combatting the perceived misperceptions spread by conservative Christians. They may envision education as stifling Christianity by enlightening individuals and convincing them of the irrationality and danger of conservative Christianity. This makes individuals with an anti-Christian bent particularly vigilant against attempts to undermine their control of educational institutions.

So, what is the true nature of anti-Christian animosity in the United States? Is it merely an intellectual exercise? Or does this ideology have a real impact on the lives of those it rejects. In chapter 7 we dive fully into the nature of this perspective and argue that the concept of Christianophobia accurately encapsulates the results of our work. We also look at how Christianophobia may impact our larger society and at potential indirect practical consequences for its target group: conservative Christians.

7

CHRISTIANOPHOBIA IN THE UNITED STATES

Let us take stock of what we have learned thus far. An unknown percentage of individuals hate, mistrust, and/or fear conservative Christians to an extensive degree. We know from the information provided by the American National Election Survey (ANES) that their number is not likely minuscule since nearly a third of the country feels substantial relative hostility toward conservative Christians. The extent of relative hostility directed toward this group is at least as high as that directed at Muslims; thus those concerned about Islamophobia in the United States have as much reason to be concerned about this relative hostility toward conservative Christians—especially since those with this antipathy are more likely to be wealthy, educated, and white, thus to have greater per capita social power than the average American. Our deeper exploration through qualitative data indicates that at least some with relative hostility toward conservative Christians despise what they see as this group's intolerance and homophobia. They rely on stereotypes every bit as potent as those based on race, ethnicity, sex, or sexual preference. They show a personal mistrust of conservative Christians and consider them evil; as the opposite of respect or tolerance, this can be seen as bigotry. They fear Christians will take over our society and think of them as mindless sheep led by manipulative leaders. This dehumanization leaves some of them open to a societal rules that disparately impact conservative Christians. These qualities indicate an unreasonable level of hatred and fear of conservative Christians and together

make up what can be called Christianophobia. In this chapter we explore the definition of this term and how it can impact our society,
particularly since Christianophobic individuals are relatively likely to
hold positions of power.

WHAT IS CHRISTIANOPHOBIA?

Before discussing Christianophobia, we must first define this controversial term. We did not invent the word; Malcolm Evans and other
academics have used it, along with Islamophobia and anti-Semitism, to
describe a type of religious intolerance.[1] The *Macmillan Dictionary*
defines Christianophobia as "an irrational animosity towards or hatred
of Christians, or Christianity in general." Much of what has been
called Christianophobia concerns global oppression of Christians. For
example, the Against Christianophobia website (http://www.
againstchristianophobia.org) has called for a world day against Christianophobia and cites incidents of church burnings, mob attacks, and kid-
nappings in non-Western countries as examples of Christianophobia. In
Western countries, manifestations of Christianophobia include arson,
graffiti, anti-Christian protests, and destruction of church property. Rupert Shortt documents oppression of Christians, which he attributes to
Christianophobia, in several countries.[2] Christianophobia has led not
only to crimes but also to insults against Christianity and Christians. As
such, the Society of St. Pius X (http://www.sspx.org) labels as "Christianophobic" a play in which feces are spread over a picture of Christ.
Although there is little systematic evidence of violence against Christians in the United States, some incidents and attitudes that seek to
disregard or insult Christians result in a version of Christianophobia.
Clearly some of our respondents' comments indicate such animosity
and hatred. Because Christianity is the majority religion in the United
States, Christianophobia manifests differently here than it does global-
ly. However it is a social phenomenon that we should take into consideration to fully understand our culture.

   We have included statements that match the description of Christianophobia throughout the book. The overtly hateful and dehumanizing
comments introduced in the first chapters came from the same set of
individuals who made less overt statements of hatred in subsequent

chapters. Perhaps we should not view those later comments as Christianophobic, but given the desire of highly educated individuals to avoid charges of bigotry, it is difficult to dismiss the hostile statements in the first chapter as anomalies. We identified a subculture that feeds into the distasteful comments in the first chapters with the ideology expressed in the later chapters.

Of course, not all Christians face this hostility. Although some respondents indicated having little use for Christianity,[3] and at times religion in general, many indicated that theologically and politically conservative Christians drew their ire. Our respondents reacted to images tied to the Christian Right or intrusive Christians who rudely attempt to proselytize to everyone they meet. It may be more academically accurate talk of "conservative Christianophobia." It is also more accurate to use the term "radical Islamophobia" rather than "Islamophobia." Those who fear Muslims generally fear Muslim terrorists. That only some respondents fail to delink Christianity from conservative Christianity does not eliminate the fact that the image of conservative Christianity drives much of the Christianophobic perspective. The fact that many individuals with Islamophobic attitudes understand that not all Muslims are terrorists does not mean that Islamophobia is a myth. Like other names for antireligious orientations, Christianophobia is useful in illustrating for a wider audience than academics the particular social attitudes we have described. Even if not always academically precise, terms serve an important function in conceptualizing antireligious perspectives. We use "Christianophobia" in the hope that it will become a common term to describe the attitudes of the subset of individuals who direct unreasonable hatred, fear, and antipathy, for the most part, toward conservative Christians.

IS CHRISTIANOPHOBIA LIKE RACISM?

In many ways Christianophobia is like other types of irrational bigotry such as racism. Based on illogical fears and unrealistic stereotypes of some Christians, it leads to dehumanization of certain religious outgroups. If we want a society that minimizes intolerance and bigotry, then we have to comprehend their nature to combat these attitudes. But clearly there are also important differences between Christiano-

phobia and racism. Racism has historically singled out individuals perceived as biologically distinct. Furthermore groups that face racism are
minorities, with low power and status, whereas Christians have—with
notable exceptions pointed out later in this chapter—relative power in
the United States. We also contend that Christianophobia, at least in
the United States, is not likely to lead to the violence tied to racism.
Although we see similarities in the expression of prejudice, bigotry, and
hatred, the social position of Christianophobes engenders a phenomenon distinct from racism.

Although we can distinguish Christianophobia from racism, we can
use the concept of racism to illustrate the importance of discussing
Christianophobia. Imagine if we never acknowledged the concept of
racism? How would we understand the fact that people tend to live in
neighborhoods with same-race peers? Or the economic differences between racial groups? Or that people tend to marry others who are
racially similar? Some explanations are not based on racism. People can
prefer to live among those of a similar culture who happen to look like
them. Different racial groups have unique histories of arriving in our
country, and different paths can correspond to contrasting economic
outcomes. People may not be attracted to those who look vastly different from their own family members, accounting for a propensity to
marry within their own race. We can find nonracist reasons for all of
these social patterns. However, historical and contemporary racism offers us a significant degree of explanatory power, and these situations
are at least partially explained by the concept of racism.[4] Racism in our
criminal justice system helps explain black and Hispanic overrepresentation in our prisons. The effect of historical and contemporary racism
on our educational system helps explain differential educational outcomes. We cannot fully understand the dragging death of James Bird
and the controversy over Don Imus's comments about "nappy hoes"
unless we acknowledge the presence of racism. Without acknowledging
the role racism plays in our society, we lose some ability to understand
certain social facts. In the same vein, it is important to speculate about,
and eventually to research, how Christianophobia has influenced social
patterns and specific actions in our society.

It is fair to ask why, given the toxic nature of Christianophobia, there
has not been more research into this type of bigotry. Unlike other types
of bigotry, Christianophobia is more present among the well educated

and privileged. As such, individuals in a position to conduct such research are more likely to engage in Christianophobia than other types of bigotry, such as anti-Semitism, racism, sexism, and homophobia.[5] If it is important to battle the effects of unreasonable intolerance in society, then we must study this underinvestigated form of social bigotry more prevalent among groups not normally thought of as bigoted (i.e., the well educated and political progressives). Although the targets of Christianophobia are less likely to experience violence than the targets of other forms of bigotry, the social power of Christianophobes suggests that these victims may experience problems that victims of racism or sexism do not, such as neglect by the educational apparatus that usually attends to victims of prejudice and bigotry.

CHRISTIANOPHOBIA IN THE UNITED STATES

In our society certain well-educated, wealthy, white individuals feel animosity toward conservative Christians. This relatively powerful group is of unknown size, and no previous work documents its members' attitudes. Precious little academic research explores whether, or how, Christianophobia influences our society, and our failure to understand this phenomenon reduces our understanding of society. Actions attributed to other causes may also be explained by Christianophobia. Just as we must acknowledge that our society is racialized to understand it completely, so must we understand the potential influence of Christianophobia on social dynamics.

Because little has been done in this regard, it falls to us to begin a discussion of the potential ways Christianophobic sentiment may play itself out in the United States. It can be tempting to assert that Christianophobia manifests itself in the same exact way as anti-Semitism or Islamophobia. There are similarities, such as the fact that individuals in all of these faiths have been unfairly accused of wanting to take over society. But this assertion would likely be erroneous, since even though Christianophobia has similarities to other types of religiously intolerant behavior, Christianity's status as the largest religion and the social power possessed by Christianophobes likely create distinctive dynamics. The manifestation of Christianophobia in our society likely reflects modern forms of intolerance, with laws based on religious neutrality having a disparate impact on conservative Christians, rather than rank, overt bigotry.

POSSIBLE CHRISTIANOPHOBIA IN THE PUBLIC SPHERE

The attitudes discussed in chapter 6 suggest that individuals who do not like conservative Christians likely avoid efforts that seem overtly to punish Christians but still support finding indirect ways to control this religious out-group. Some respondents still enunciated their anger at conservative Christians quite openly. As they are likely to be politically progressive and highly educated, these are the same individuals who tend to document societal intolerance (i.e., academics, journalists). Such individuals do not want to consider themselves intolerant, which motivates them to rationalize Christianophobic attitudes. But the degree of stigma attached to other types of intolerant thought has not been attached to Christianophobic attitudes. As a result, it is relatively easy to find examples of Christianophobia in the public sphere.

We searched the Internet to see if public figures had made statements similar to those of our respondents. They were relatively easy to find. The following comments were documented by multiple Internet sources, and we found no claims about their being inaccurate.

> [Christian conservatives are like] a vengeful mob—revved up by rectitude—running around with torches and hatchets after heathens and pagans and infidels. (Maureen Dowd, columnist for *New York Times*)
> Christianity is a religion for losers. (Ted Turner, media mogul)
> From my point of view I would ban religion completely, even though there are some wonderful things about it. I love the idea of the teachings of Jesus Christ and the beautiful stories about it, which I loved in Sunday school and I collected all the little stickers and put them in my book. But the reality is that organised [*sic*] religion doesn't seem to work. It turns people into hateful lemmings and it's not really compassionate. (Elton John, singer)
> I'd barter with him [Megtron (*sic*), a fictional evil robot], and say instead of the entire planet, can you just take out all of the white trash, hillbilly, anti-gay, super bible-beating people in Middle America? (Megan Fox, movie celebrity)

> F*** Notre Dame, F*** Touchdown Jesus, F*** Jesus. (Dana
> Jacobson, ESPN personality)
>
> Radical Christianity is just as threatening as radical Islam in a
> country like America. (Rosie O'Donnell, TV personality)

Distasteful comments can be found about any well-known group. Locating comments that are racist, homophobic, sexist, Islamophobic, and so on, on the Internet is depressingly easy. However, the individuals making these Christianophobic comments are not little-known bloggers or anonymous commenters on an article. They are, for the most part, well-known public figures. These comments come from media personalities—not an accident since individuals in the media are generally more politically progressive than the general public,[6] and Christianophobia is tied to political progressivism.[7] These attitudes also show that anonymity does not explain the vitriol of the Christianophobic statements in the first chapter. The individuals quoted above made such comments freely and publically. Individuals with high levels of social, economic, and media power are not likely to make public comments expressing other types of intolerance (e.g., racism, sexism). Our assertion is easily proved wrong by anyone who chooses to look for overtly racist, homophobic, sexist, classist, and so forth, statements from such well-established, famous media personalities. But before we will stand corrected, such comments must be as overtly derogatory as the above comments are about Christians, not mere assertions of political policy, and they must be contemporary, not historical. We suspect widespread denunciation by other media figures would follow any such comments—something that generally did not happen with the above anti-Christian comments.[8]

Other comments we found reinforce the possibility of Christianophobia among public figures, some of whom also repeated the stereotypes and images of Christians our respondents mentioned.

> When people say to me, "You hate America," I don't hate America. I love America. I am just embarrassed that it has been taken over by people like evangelicals, by people who do not believe in science and rationality. (Bill Maher, comedian)
>
> There will always be the fundamentalism and the religious right, but I think there has been too much of it. I keep hoping that it is temporary foolishness. Some of it will always be around because

there will always be people who are so mean-spirited and such limited thinkers that their religious beliefs seem so logical: that there is a god, and so forth, that nothing else in their limited concept can explain what the existence of a god can. There's been a lot of it lately: Youth for Christ and that sort of thing. I'm hoping that this is just a bump in time. (Gene Roddenberry, TV producer, writer, and creator of *Star Trek*)

Conservatives in the heartland have persuaded themselves to vote against their own economic and social well-being because they consider hot-button issues more important than their incomes, economic chances, educations and the welfare of society at large. Their positions dovetail seamlessly with evangelical Christianity, and they accept hardship as the will of God when it seems more clearly to be the working of a top-loaded economy. (Roger Ebert, movie reviewer)

We have not asked these public figures to fill out a survey in which they substantially evaluate Christianity worse than other religious beliefs. Yet, some of our Christianophobic respondents could easily have made these statements. Even if these public figures are not themselves Christianophobic, their statements support public Christianophobia.

While the types of individuals with Christianophobic ideas are less likely to engage in overtly oppressive efforts, they also pay less of a social price for exhibiting Christianophobia than do racists for exhibiting racism, anti-Semites for exhibiting anti-Semitism, sexists for exhibiting sexism, and so forth. Keeping in mind these two critical factors— attempts at oppression are less overt, but less social stigma attaches to open Christianophobia compared to other types of intolerant thinking—helps us understand how Christianophobic attitudes influence social events in the United States. In the next section we speculate about the possibilities of Christianophobic influences in actual social events.

CHRISTIANOPHOBIA AS A POSSIBLE EXPLANATION FOR SOCIAL EVENTS

If there is a subgroup of Americans with a high degree of animosity toward conservative Christians and Christianity and with the educational power to affect society and social institutions, then we should be able to find social events shaped by Christianophobic perspectives.

Christianophobic individuals will hesitate to support overt religious discrimination but generally will not balk at enforcing rules that disproportionately affect conservative Christians. With this in mind, it may be instructive to seek out social events in which powerful individuals have an opportunity to act against the interests of conservative Christians but can justify such actions as nondiscriminatory. Thus, we are looking for social events in which a Christianophobic attitude helps account for an individual's actions. Due to general hesitation to show overt religious oppression, such events would not be obvious attempts to discriminate against conservative Protestants, and there would be some plausible explanation that did not entail anger or hatred toward Christians—as in the operation of symbolic racism.

One possibility is the situation faced by Jennifer Keeton, a counseling graduate student at Augusta State University who filed a civil rights action on July 21, 2010, claiming she was being discriminated against because of her Christian faith.[9] Keeton had expressed verbally and in written documents her adherence to traditional views on human sexuality and gender. The faculty mandated that she complete a "remediation plan." Keeton contends that this plan would require her to alter her religious beliefs. Augusta State University contends that her attitudes would make it difficult, if not impossible, for her to counsel individuals from the Gay, Lesbian, Bisexual, Transgender/Transsexual community.

Augusta State University provides a reasonable explanation for its desire to set up a remediation plan for Keeton. Some faculty members likely have an honest concern about her ability to counsel individuals from a variety of different communities. However, given the level of Christianophobic animosity prevalent among the highly educated, we would be remiss in ignoring the possibility that some of the sentiment Keeton is dealing with stems from a desire to marginalize traditional Christianity. This concern is heightened by the reality that it is not uncommon for counselors to refer patients whom they do not perceive a good fit for them to other counselors—an option not suggested for Keeton. Christianophobic individuals are more concerned about homophobia than other cultural progressives and can use this concern to legitimate regulations with a disparate impact on those expressing traditional notions of sexuality. Rules legitimated for combatting homophobia can be useful in weeding out individuals with conservative Christian beliefs without overt religious discrimination. Given the dehumanizing attitudes toward conservative Christians documented in this book, the faculty may well view eliminating those Christians from positions of influence as a desirable action.

This is speculation. None of the faculty members have stated Christianophobic motivations; nor would they do so publically. Given their educational level and likely political progressiveness, however, it is reasonable to believe that some are Christianophobic, and it would be naive to assume that such sentiments do not play a role in this controversy. The fear, hatred, and mistrust documented earlier in this book could inhibit faculty members from finding a solution that does not require a lawsuit and admits a conservative Christian to a position of influence. We cannot be certain about the role Christianophobia plays in this situation, but the answers of some of our respondents clearly evinced the type of emotional intolerance that makes it difficult to find solutions in contentious situations.

A more clear-cut case of how fears of homophobia can lead to Christianophobia can be seen in Dan Savage's speech at a high school journalism conference.[10] Savage heads up an antibullying organization that focuses on the bullying of homosexual kids, the issue that he was to speak to the high school kids about. Yet he also went on a diatribe criticizing the Bible and Christians. After several Christian kids walked out, he hurled insults at them. He later apologized for the insults but not for his attack on Christianity and Christians. Here we have a case in which a speaker clearly did not need to engage in a Christianophobic attack but did so anyway. Savage could rationalize this attack as a concern for the bullying of youth. Yet it seems that a more workable approach would have been to develop a rapport with those he saw as blind to his concerns. Given the dynamics documented in this book, it is logical to assume that Savage's anger at Christians led to his verbal assault. As further evidence of Christianophobia, much of his assault met with applause from individuals in the audience who greeted his Christianophobic statements with appreciation and not disapproval.

Christianophobia may also play a role in explaining conflict that occurs outside an educational setting. On October 22, 2010, the Fair Housing Center of West Michigan filed a complaint against a Christian woman for engaging in "an illegal preference for a Christian roommate."[11] There are fair arguments to be made concerning a person's right to choose whom she lives as well as the need to deal with housing discrimination. But the legal matter aside, Christianophobic attitudes may plausibly have been at play in this situation. Of the many complaints it likely received, the Fair Housing Center had to decide which to take action on. In this situation a person's Christian preference was challenged as a basis for selecting a roommate. If some respondents in our sample were in a position to decide which complaints to follow up on, might their fear and hatred toward conservative Christians not plausibly drive them to adjudicate this case? Can the principle of equal housing be used to hide Christianophobic bias? Given the results of this research, such questions should be asked.

Christianophobia may play an important role in other incidents. For example, Kandy Kyriacou and Ojoma Omaga lawsuit's against Peralta Community College concerned a professor who entered another professor's office to stop a prayer two students were saying for the professor in that office.[12] The professor they were praying for had not objected, but the other professor felt duty-bound to interrupt. Is it really difficult to imagine that the emotions exhibited by some of our respondents might be powerful enough to convince one professor to intervene in the interpersonal matters of a colleague? Such intervention is rare as professors generally do not enter other professors' offices to interrupt their conversations with students.[13] However, a desire to marginalize Christian action in an academic setting is a viable explanation for this action. At Eastern Michigan University, a Christian group's view on homosexuality was used to deny that group, rather than an individual, rights.[14] Whether a decision has been made to protect homosexuals or to marginalize the Christian perspective, these situations reveal that potential explanations include Christianophobia. We have demonstrated that Christianophobic attitudes exist. It is unrealistic to believe that the attitudes we have documented do not play a role in similar incidents with relatively powerful individuals seeking to hide expressions of direct religious discrimination.

Christianophobia can also help to explain some societal attitudes. Here we are operating from the same premise connected to notions of symbolic racism. Those with Christianophobia generally do not support overtly discriminatory measures against Christians as doing so could lead to charges of religious intolerance; they do, however, hold the cultural assumption that conservative Christians are enemies and Christian influence in society must be limited. Their emotional angst, combined with this demonization of conservative Christians and a desire to project an image of tolerance, creates conditions ripe for the expression of symbolic hostility toward Christians. If symbolic hostility is taken into account, then certain political issues take on additional meaning. For example, there is a general argument in our society about the use of vouchers to improve our education system. Some argue that vouchers would create an efficient way to help parents send their children to the school of their choice. Others argue that such a system would threaten our current public school system. On its face, the argument about whether we should use vouchers is about whether damage to the public school system is worth the greater choice and efficiency parents would gain.[15] Because Christian schools exist, however, we can consider the possibility of symbolic hostility.[16] If parents who received vouchers were to send their kids to Christian schools, some people argue, that would violate church-state separation. Some of these individuals may well be motivated by Christianophobia: they do not want Christians to be able to use vouchers to help them socialize others into their religion, even if such vouchers provided beneficial educational outcomes. Some of our respondents showed great concern over the ability of Christians to socialize children into their faith. Keeping Christians from amassing more control in society may provide strong motivation for opposing the use of vouchers. We are not sure if such vouchers will produce positive educational outcomes, but Christianophobia would lead to less concern about the utility of vouchers and more desire to end the program altogether to inhibit Christians' ability to socialize others. The program thus faces the opposition not only of those who want to maintain the public school system but of Christianophobes who wish to prevent Christians from gaining additional social and cultural resources and who can hide this desire behind symbolic opposition to vouchers.

This type of symbolic hostility can potentially play itself out in other social and political issues. We can imagine how this dynamic would be relevant to such issues as faith-based initiatives, hate crimes legislation, education curriculum reform, speech codes, public holiday displays, campaign finance reform, sex education, and so forth.[17] These issues cannot be completely understood unless we take into account the potential ways in which Christianophobic ideology shapes their resolution. Symbolic hostility can influence those with Christianophobia in ways that that can work to the disadvantage of conservative Christians socially and economically. Christianophobia may not be highly recognized by scholars and intellectuals, but the hidden nature of this intolerance heightens its ability to influence highly educated, progressive, secular individuals with social power. It is a force scholars should take into account in exploring issues with a disparate impact on Christians that are justified with a nonbiased rationale that allows for the expression of Christianophobic fear and anger. Space prevents us from analyzing several of the above issues in greater depth. Ideally future work will help explore ways that Christianophobia can influence other political issues debated in our society.

We have looked at social situations and political issues to see how they may be influenced by Christianophobia. These situations and issues are important for understanding how Christianophobic perspectives can shape the lives of Americans. The accumulated resolutions to these situations and issues can eventually shape social institutions. Changes to these institutions not only could affect the status and lives of conservative Protestants today but might also influence their experiences in the future. For this reason, it is important to speculate about how Christianophobia may shape current social institutions.

CHRISTIANOPHOBIA AS AN EXPLANATION FOR SHAPING SOCIAL INSTITUTIONS

We have suggested several isolated incidents and social attitudes where Christianophobic attitudes may help account for some of the actions of social actors. Because of the social desirability of not being labeled as biased, it is impossible to determine if our speculation in the last section is accurate and, if it is, the degree to which Christianophobia shaped the social events discussed. Nonetheless we want to expand our speculation to consider what the presence of Christianophobic ideology may mean for larger social institutions in the United States. Doing so brings us out of the realm of exploring isolated incidents and into an examination of how Christianophobia might influence social structures.

Ruy Teixeira and Alan Abramowitz posit the existence of a political movement in our society whereby wealthier and highly educated individuals have gravitated toward the Democratic Party.[18] Wealth was previously associated with political conservatism.[19] Thomas Frank argues that this change has often been linked to the relationship between socioeconomic status (SES) and progressive positions on cultural issues such as abortion and homosexuality.[20] That is a very viable explanation. However, a theory of the saliency of Christianophobia offers a complimentary but distinct explanation. The positive correlation of educational attainment with Christianophobic attitudes makes it plausible that the movement of the wealthy and highly educated into the Democratic political camp reflects, rather than mere acceptance of a progressive stance on cultural issues, animosity towards conservative Christians and Christianity.

This explanation may seem similar to that given for the culture war argument since Christian religiosity is correlated with rejection of abortion and homosexuality.[21] However, we cannot ignore the symbolic value of such issues. Many respondents discussed Christians' backwardness, ignorance, and hypocrisy and indicated their fear of a Christian "takeover," stereotypes and myths that engender fear and hatred. Respondents saw these social issues as symbols of Christian influence, which motivated them to resist cultural conservatism. The use of symbols to drive individuals from a given subculture into a political party is not unprecedented. It has been argued that Republicans used such symbolism on racial issues in their famous "Southern Strategy," which helped them solidify their hold on the Southern white vote.[22] Republicans may have used whites' fear of blacks to win their support against the Democrats. A similar process may also help to explain the movement of well-educated and higher-SES whites into the Democratic Party.[23] There is value in carefully crafted research to determine whether support for progressive cultural attitudes is a more or less powerful explanation than resentment or fear of fundamentalists and evangelicals for the movement of the wealthy into the Democratic Party.

Given the level of anger and mistrust documented in our research, our assertion that Christianophobia explains some of the political movement of the highly educated and wealthy into more progressive political organizations has merit.[24] Hostility toward conservative Christianity can be viewed as a way to advance civil liberties and individual freedom. Christianophobic desires to fight Christians may shape some of our society's political structures. If that is the case, then such attitudes may influence other social structures as well. One obvious possibility is our legal structure. The outcomes of political races have consequences. Individuals elected or appointed to office by people with Christianophobic attitudes are likely to incorporate those attitudes into lawmaking. Given the nature of who is Christianophobic, such actions are unlikely to be overtly discriminatory against Christians. Legal action can reflect Christianophobia in other ways. We have already pointed out how hesitation to use vouchers to repair our educational system might be partially motivated by Christianophobia. This possibility is realistic since we have noted that some respondents are bothered by other means Christians use to religiously socialize children, such as homeschooling. We can also consider how issues such as hate speech policies, sex education, same-sex marriage, fairness doctrine, taxation of churches, campaign finance reform, and so forth, are also affected by Christianophobia. In fact many respondents brought up these issues as they discussed Christians and the Christian Right.

An illustration can help demonstrate how such issues may play themselves out in the public arena. A current political controversy in our country concerns voter ID laws. Critics of these laws contend that their purpose is to limit the voting rights of racial minorities,[25] and some have even levied accusations of racism.[26] The stated purpose of these laws is to limit the possibility of voter fraud, the reality of which is evidenced by the conviction of individuals such as Melowese Richardson, Roderick Wright, Enrico "Jack" Villamaino, and Charles White. Whether voter ID laws would curb voter fraud is beyond the scope of this book. That the problem exists and thus warrants attention from public officials interests us here. It is not feasible to argue that all supporters of voter ID laws are attempting to stifle the vote of people of color. Racial animosity does motivate some individuals to desire such laws, but this is not likely to be the only reason for their passage. Still, because it has been documented that we live in a racialized society,[27] it is reasonable to argue that racial animosity plays some role in support for voter ID laws and raises support for such laws to a higher level than one would expect otherwise. As we have already seen in the ANES data that animosity toward Christians is more prevalent than animosity toward people of color, and as we have noted some of the dehumanizing attitudes that help to buttress this animosity, why is it so hard to believe that at least some of the issues in the preceding paragraph are influenced by antireligious hostility? We argue that it is naive not to expect this animosity to have played a role in shaping our political landscape.

Christianophobia possibly also affects our educational process. Education is seen as an important weapon in the war against conservative Christians. Leonard Dinnerstein argues that anti-Semites paid special attention to efforts at limiting Jewish influence in the educational realm since education might enhance Jews' ability to shape society.[28] There is reason to suspect that such fears are also operative among Christianophobes. Given this possibility, we can look at some of the battles over curriculum with new eyes. Some cultural progressives may advocate for certain revisions in educational curricula for more than logical and pedagogical reasons. They may be acting out of animosity toward Christians and more receptive to curricula that create negative as opposed to positive images of Christians. Given the fear of a Christian takeover, they may also welcome curricula that devalue the place of Christians in society and history and overvalue curricula critical of Christianity, particularly of the conservative Protestant variety. We should account for the possibility that emotional animosity, not just rationality, drives some advocates for progressive educational curricula.

Our educational system can be shaped by Christianophobia in other ways. One of us previously documented that fundamentalists and evangelicals pay a price if their religious beliefs become known while they are seeking academic employment.[29] It is not unreasonable to suspect that Christianophobia in academia makes it more difficult for conservative Protestants to find employment and positions of status within the educational system.[30] To the degree that there is a lack of religious diversity among those holding positions of power in the educational system, we can expect to find a system that lacks sensitivity toward conservative Protestants. It is also possible that Christianophobia plays a role in debates about the role of religious expression. The filtering of interpretations of church-state separation through a Christianophobic lens could result in decisions that support mistrust and fear of Christians. For example, teachers and administrators with Christianophobic sentiments may support indirect ways to disapprove of Christian expressions by students. Scholars[31] have talked about the "hidden messages" within our educational system. The evidence we have presented in the previous chapters, coupled with the fact that educators are well represented in our sample, suggests that an exploration of possible hidden Christianophobic messages is warranted.

Institutions dominated by wealthy and highly educated politically progressive individuals may be vulnerable to Christianophobia. For example, it is worth considering whether Christianophobia may shape different media outlets. Although news journalists strive to maintain objectivity in their reporting, it is plausible that Christianophobic animosity sneaks into some of the storylines of those with anti-Christian antipathy. Entertainment media may also express Christianophobia without fully realizing it. Governmental organizations are generally run by the well educated and politically progressive. Although some elected officials have to cater to conservative Christians to gain office, unelected officials, who often create government policies, can have more conspicuously Christianophobic motivations, which can possibly lead to policy decisions supporting Christianophobia. Indeed, there is some evidence of an anti-Christian bias in social work institutions,[32] which tend to be government controlled.

These last few paragraphs suggest several possible avenues by which Christianophobia may manifest itself in our culture. David R. Hodge has discussed what he perceives as "secular privilege." His lists of possible privileges outline other ways in which Christianophobia may be reflected in society.[33] Ideally, future research will confirm which of these avenues are accurate expressions of Christianophobia and which are false alarms.

We do not want to paint this picture with too broad a brush. While we have looked at possible institutions generally controlled by progressives and the highly educated, these intrusions do not happen in all institutions. A lot of businesses are run by individuals with traditional values, who are not highly vulnerable to Christianophobia. Certain conservative political organizations and media institutions, such as talk radio shows, are also unlikely to be Christianophobic. We live in a multifaceted society in which different political and religious entities dominate differing sectors. Christianophobia is not likely to be powerful in sectors controlled by cultural, political, and religious conservatives, whereas it may be fairly common in sectors controlled by cultural, political, and religious progressives. Nothing in our analysis should be read as a claim that conservative Christians are being persecuted, as they obviously do not operate at a disadvantage in all areas of our society. An accurate rendition of our findings is the acknowledgment that in some social places, being a conservative Christian is a disadvantage; in others, having traditional Christian faith is an advantage. The latter part of that statement has been well established in previous scholarship, while the former part is a natural consequence of our findings.

We fully accept the criticism that our argument in this and the previous section is speculative.[34] Until now, however, the presence of Christianophobia has not been documented. We are quite comfortable asserting that our current work reveals the existence of Christianophobia and at least some of the ways it can manifest in the United States. We are less confident as to the power and reach of anti-Christian sentiment. To gain such confidence we would need a large probability sample assessing some of the specific Christianophobic attitudes found in our qualitative sample. Nevertheless, accounting for Christianophobia provides possible explanations for some events, attitudes, and institutional aspects in our society. Although we cannot absolutely claim that Christianophobia has a powerful influence in our political, legal, educational, media, governmental, and/or economic spheres, it seems unlikely that at least some individuals with these attitudes would not allow them to shape decisions affecting conservative Christians.

CONCLUSION

Research[35] has illustrated how the attitudes of cultural conservatives contribute to the cultural war, and our previous work[36] has explored the attitudes of cultural progressive activists. Several scholars have asserted that prejudice and intolerance partially motivate cultural conservatives.[37] We have provided information indicating that cultural progressives are not immune to the lure of religious prejudice. To completely understand the culture conflict in our society, we have to account for the likelihood that emotionalism and unreasonable biases can be found in both cultural conservatives and cultural progressives. How this emotionalism manifests itself can differ among these two subcultures as the individuals they comprise come from different social sectors and bring with them distinct presuppositions about our society. However, they likely share an inability to accurately assess their ideological opponents due to their emotional disdain for them.

The presence of Christianophobia supplies potential explanatory power for some social events. We have provided information allowing us to speculate about the possible effects of irrational hatred and anger toward conservative Christians. Speculation is important in helping us conceive of ways Christianophobia can operate. Because so little previous research has been done on whether anti–conservative Christian prejudice has a real effect in our society, we are forced to speculate about what those effects may be. Other types of intolerance (racism, sexism, anti-Semitism, Islamophobia) have been explored in more depth, and their societal effects are well documented. But, except for possibly Islamophobia, other types of intolerances have been discussed and studied for a long time by academics. Our speculations have not been verified, but they cannot be dismissed until sufficient study has been done concerning the potential effects of Christianophobia.

8

CONCLUSION

We have demonstrated the existence of an unreasonable anger and hatred toward conservative Christians and theorized about whether this is consequential. We have seen evidence of antipathy toward conservative Christians among individuals with educational and economic-power majority status in race. We have shown dehumanizing and illiberal attitudes some cultural progressive activists have toward conservative Christians. Some of these individuals likely possess opportunities to express Christianophobic beliefs in ways that create problems for their conservative Christian targets. Because little previous work explores the possible existence and consequences of Christianophobia, we cannot conclusively document, in this initial elaboration of this phenomenon, the degree to which the ideas expressed by our respondents impact individuals in the larger society. However, the nature of this type of intolerance makes it important for us to consider the ways it can be managed in a culturally diverse society.

Individuals with Christianophobia are different from those with other types of intolerant attitudes. This makes Christianophobia both less and more harmful than other types of bias. Christianophobia may be less troublesome because individuals who possess it are less likely to be overtly prejudicial than those who are racist, Islamophobic, anti-Semitic, and so forth. Education produces a fear of being labeled as intolerant, and theoretically individuals with Christianophobia could go out of their way to treat Christians in a fair manner. Many respondents indicated a strong distaste for any laws that single out conservative

Christians, even as they also strongly indicated a visceral anger toward them. On the other hand, the desire to avoid being perceived as having prejudice can lead to a denial of the reality of Christianophobic bias. Individuals with Christianophobia can use their educational training to hide their biases from public view. Thus, Christianophobia may be more problematic to eradicate than other types of intolerance. If Christianophobia leads to "symbolic" actions that disadvantage conservative Christians, then we have a consequential prejudice difficult to remove.

Our respondents reacted to a series of cultural perceptions motivating their hostility. Understanding those perceptions is important for understanding the potential of Christianophobia to impact society. We have illustrated that many respondents have a perception of conservative Christians as enemies who seek to overturn the benefits gained from the cultural values of democracy and enlightenment. Because of their cultural values of civil rights and individual freedom, they sometimes feel discomfort with direct efforts to oppress conservative Christians. However, imposing laws or rules with negative disparate impact on Christians or using education to convince others of their subculture's values can help such respondents promote their goals. Like other purveyors of intolerant attitudes, those with Christianophobia can gain control at the expense of the out-group activating their fear and hatred, but they more likely to do so indirectly. Using rules disproportionally geared against Christians—such as Bowdoin's and Vanderbilt's regulation that all school student organizations cannot use religious criteria for leadership[1]—can minimize the influence of conservative Christians and maximize the promotion of the goals of those with Christianophobia. This perspective has explanatory power for many events characterized by conflict between cultural progressives and Christian conservatives.

Given the demographics of who tends to have Christianophobia, it is fair to assert that a person with political, social, and legal power is more likely to have Christianophobia than racism, sexism, homophobia, Islamophobia, and so forth. This person is more likely to be in a position to make decisions that reify his or her intolerance than individuals possessing other types of intolerances. One hypothetical example may suffice to help us understand the potential ramifications of this. When individuals look for redress because they have been mistreated, they often look to the judicial system. Since the highly educated are more likely to have Christianophobic than racist or xenophobic tendencies, well-educated judges, who make the final decision on whether a lawsuit or an appeal has merit, are more likely to be Christianophobic than racist or Islamophobic. It is one thing if an African American goes before the judge, who is not likely to have a hidden animosity toward African Americans, to gain justice in the face of racism. It is quite another for a person to look for redress due to Christianophobia when he or she has to go before a judge who may possess that prejudice him- or herself. Of course, conservative Christians can, and usually do, get fair hearings in our court system. But a judge with Christianophobia does not have to acknowledge having less sympathy for what may be a real case of religious bias. Discovering the degree to which such a bias may occur is nearly impossible, given the incentives such individuals have to hide their Christianophobia. However, given their social position and the types of attitudes we have documented, it is hard to argue that such bias never occurs in cases where Christianity is included as a factor in someone's actions.[2]

Even though the effects of this type of intolerance have not been fully established, because of the important ramifications of Christianophobia, we want to consider ways to combat it. If future research indicates that Christianophobia is not as troublesome as we originally feared, then little will be lost by considering how we can reduce the anger and fear some individuals possess. To this end, we next discuss possible ways for dealing with Christianophobia.

COMBATTING CHRISTIANOPHOBIA

Despite the arguments we have put forward, individuals still may not perceive Christianophobia as a problem that needs attention. Other forms of intolerance (e.g., racism, sexism, homophobia) are generally recognized as deviant and undesirable social attitudes. As long as Christianophobia is seen as acceptable, it will be very difficult to combat. The most basic initial way to deal with Christianophobia is to document the problems it creates and attach stigma to this type of intolerance. There will be strong resistance since individuals with Christianophobia tend to have the societal power to oppose these efforts. But fighting to create this stigmatization is important, not to punish those with Christianophobia but to provide the motivation to reduce its effects.

A common way social activists and theorists attempt to reduce intolerance is through education to socialize individuals about the harm of their intolerant attitudes. If ignorance is at the heart of intolerance, then educated individuals can gain the knowledge necessary to overcome their bigotry and bias. Several scholars argue that education can provide the critical thinking skills necessary to help people overcome simplistic dualistic thinking,[3] which stigmatizes out-group members. Researchers and scholars envision education as a general antidote to racism, sexism, homophobia, anti-Semitism, and the like.[4] Since education is an acceptable instrument for individuals likely to have Christianophobia, we should consider how it may be used to reduce Christianophobia. But education, in and of itself, is not a solution. In fact, our research suggests that education may exacerbate Christianophobia. Therefore we cannot merely look to higher levels of educational attainment as a solution. There is a need for a type of education that differs from the type that may help produce Christianophobia.

To consider how education may be used to reduce Christianophobia, we first have to consider why education may contribute to the development of Christianophobia. We question the assumption that education is a natural cure for intolerance. Work by Michael Emerson and David Sikkink[5] indicates that education may not be the solution to racism that many believe. They note that, after the application of proper statistical controls, while educational attainment is consistently connected to a stated willingness among whites to live in integrated neighborhoods and send their kids to integrated schools, education was positively correlated to whites living in racially segregated neighborhoods or sending their kids to segregated schools. Highly educated whites stated that they wanted to live among people of color, but when they purchased their homes, they were more likely than less educated whites to live among other whites. Highly educated whites stated that they wanted to send their children to schools with children of color, but they actually sent their kids to schools with higher-than-normal percentages of white children. Education seems to alter racial attitudes but not racial actions. The limit of the power of education to alter intolerant actions concerning race suggests that education may have limited power to create an overarching attitude of acceptance of out-group members.

If education has limited ability to alter intolerant attitudes, then why do studies consistently indicate that education is linked to more tolerant attitudes? We conceive of two possible reasons for this. The first is that the highly educated have learned how to respond to tools used by social scientists (i.e., surveys and interviews) in ways so that they appear more tolerant than they really are. The highly educated are in a better position to understand how such tools are used to evaluate bias and can avoid being stigmatized as having bigoted motivations. It is possible that education trains individuals in proper self-presentation without truly altering their attitudes. The highly educated know not to indicate racial animosity on surveys, but their actions concerning educational and residential segregation reflect their actual racial preferences.

However, there is a second reason why education may be linked to more tolerant attitudes. The target groups usually seen as "victims" of prejudice may be individuals toward which the highly educated already have sympathy. They may have this sympathy since many of the educated fit into these categories. For example, homosexuals and Muslims in the United States tend to be highly educated and to have highly educated friends.[6] These friendships provide intergroup contact to create sympathy for those groups. Even for groups without a lot of highly educated individuals, such as racial minorities, those with high levels of education are likely to be exposed to teaching about their cultures and challenges. Highly educated whites may gain intellectual sympathy due to this educational training. This may persuade them to indicate acceptance of people of color in surveys, even if they do not actually live out their sympathetic attitudes.

With either reason, education does not actually alter a person's overall tendency to accept members of out-groups. If education lacks the ability to heighten tolerance of outsiders, then we should not be surprised that higher levels of education are associated with Christianophobia. Conservative Christians are not a group with higher-than-normal levels of educational attainment; nor do they possess a culture often portrayed sympathetically within institutions of higher education. Highly educated individuals, as well as those who are politically progressive, have not learned the cues that bias against conservative Christians can be equated with bigotry, prejudice, and other socially undesirable traits. If the highly educated possessed high levels of global tolerance, then they would exhibit such tolerance even for groups they disagreed with, such as conservative Christians.

However, education may not produce such tolerance. For this reason, we are not looking for educational reforms that involve the development of a program that helps individuals to deal with their specific animosity toward conservative Christians. Such a program would likely only help the highly educated learn how to exhibit socially desirable attitudes in social surveys, even if they maintained their animosity toward conservative Christians. Rather we want to challenge educators to think about how to generate global attitudes of tolerance rather than tolerance toward specific groups. Such an approach would first help students identify groups they have animosity toward, then encourage them to learn more about these particular out-groups to overcome their stereotypes and negative images. This would allow individuals to engage in a level of introspection that would help them become more tolerant. We believe that, to varying degrees, almost all individuals struggle with prejudice against out-group members. Addressing the global tendency toward prejudice is a better approach than identifying certain groups and requesting tolerance for them. If only specific groups are seen as needing protection from bias and prejudice, some individuals will face greater challenges than others. An individual with a social network including several homosexual friends but few conservative Christian friends is not likely to be challenged by an educational program directed at ending homophobia. The individual with few homosexual friends and many conservative Christian friends, on the other hand, will be challenged. Yet the level of bigotry that each individual possesses may be similar, just directed at different social groups. Programs that teach people how to engage in introspection can help both individuals to develop more tolerant social attitudes.

Generating a program that assumes that nearly everybody has prejudice can help educators look for mechanisms that give students tools for managing their biases. The actual target of a person's prejudice is fairly irrelevant. Learning how to recognize one's own biases may be a skill transferred from one type of intolerance to another. Whether this is an accurate assessment of human nature needs to be validated with future research. If our assertion is correct, then it may be possible to use education less to focus on a particular type of intolerance (e.g., sexism, racism, Islamophobia) and more to help people develop the skills necessary to live a life in which acceptance of out-group members is normative. Because such a program is likely to be personally challenging to each person's distinct target of prejudice, it has the opportunity to alter not only attitudes but actions. We recommend the creation of educational tools that not only seek attitudinal alterations but encourage individuals to think about practical ways they can take actions combating their particular prejudices. This approach can help deal with the missing attitude-action connection documented in Emerson and Sikkink's research.

Such a change of emphasis does not have to be limited to programs in educational institutions. Diversity training in other types of institutions can focus on developing general tools for recognizing and combating bias within oneself. Eventually this may lead to finding holistic diversity tools to deal with issues of diversity and tolerance. Including Christianophobic bias may be important in helping progressive and highly educated individuals recognize their own biases and prejudices. But we are not looking for the development of Christianophobic diversity programs per se. We would rather see the development of diversity programs challenging individuals from all sectors of society to deal with the biases and intolerances they bring to social interactions.

We do not claim expertise in diversity or educational training, although we have seen enough of such training to recognize that the priorities just enunciated are generally not implemented. In part they may not be implemented because of the hidden assumptions developed with this training. We have already discussed the assumption that intolerance is due to a lack of education and sophisticated thinking. This leads to the presupposition that lack of education or nonacceptance of progressive political and social philosophy is the key to the existence of prejudice and bias. We suggest that this presupposition exists because most previous work looking at bias and prejudice has utilized groups already accepted by the highly educated and political progressives. When exploring how some highly educated and political progressives discuss social groups that they do not accept, such as conservative Protestants, we find that individuals in these groups also possess the ability to dehumanize and demean out-group members. Once we rid ourselves of the assumption that prejudice and bias are innately linked to the less educated and political conservatives, academia can engage in research into the general nature of intolerance. Comparing the commonalities between the types of intolerances less educated conservatives are more likely to engage in, such as sexism, and those that highly educated progressives are more likely to engage in, such as Christianophobia, allows us to see the similarities between different types of intolerances and understand this general condition in humankind.

FUTURE WORK

Comparing Christianophobia to other types of intolerance is clearly a potential extension of this work. But there is a need for more work that provides us with a better understanding of Christianophobia. For example, we have documented the presence of anti-Christian fundamentalist antipathy with the American National Election Survey (ANES), a national probability sample. But that survey does not allow us to look specifically at the types of attitudes buttressing that antipathy. We did use qualitative research to explore those attitudes. But because we did not gather a probability sample for our qualitative exploration, we are not in a position to document the extent of the specific attitudes our cultural progressive respondents have in the United States. Future work is needed that uses a probability sample to estimate not only the percentage of people with animosity toward conservative Protestants but also the extent of specific fears (such as the fear of theocracy), stereotypes (such as believing that Christians are unintelligent), or hatreds (such as seeing conservative Christians as evil) in the larger population. Such work can tell us whether Christianophobia is found among a relatively small or large percentage of Americans.

The attempt to measure the degree of Christianophobia in the United States brings up another important research extension. Our methods for documenting the existence of Christianophobia are experimental in nature. We have shown the existence of attitudes that can be defined as unreasonably biased or prejudiced against conservative Protestants. But this is a crude attempt to assess what Christianophobia looks like. Additional careful work can document the nature of Christianophobia and develop measures for it. Only after we have developed accurate ways of measuring Christianophobia can we fully understand how powerful a hold it has in our society. We suggest future qualitative work to more fully document the nature of Christianophobia. Once researchers can more fully enunciate the ideology Christianophobia espouses, then it will be possible to develop a list of statements to measure it. This will enable the establishment of an index of attitudes to predict the presence of Christianophobia and the degree to which an individual possesses it. We may also be able to use such an index to determine if there are different varieties of Christianophobia. This index will also place us in a better position to determine the characteristics of Christianophobia beyond the educational and political qualities we have already documented. Since the development of such an index would allow us to better comprehend the ideas animating Christianophobia, educators and activists will have more understanding about how to debunk Christianophobic stereotypes. Although we do not advocate specific programs to target Christianophobia as opposed to other types of intolerance, there still is a need to identify specific Christianophobic stereotypes and myths so that educators can effectively work with those with Christianophobia.

The creation of a Christianophobia index is not a one-time action. It will need to be refined and developed as more information about Christianophobia becomes known. So we do not expect the first indexes of Christianophobia to be the final word. However, as these indexes are tested and recalculated, we will gain a better understanding of the presuppositions driving animosity toward conservative Protestants. The development and reconfiguration of indexes measuring Christianophobia will take years, even decades, to complete, but the project promises to provide some of our most fruitful exploration of this phenomenon.[7]

We have provided potential examples of how Christianophobia may shape some of our current social and political events. Of course, our assertions are speculative and not easily tested with empirical data. Whether the actions of the social agents we have discussed are driven by Christianophobia is beyond the scope of researchers to fully determine.[8] But this does not prevent further theorization about the role of Christianophobia in our society. We do not need complete certainty of the presence of Christianophobia in a given situation to consider how this attitude potentially shapes social and political outcomes. The culture war has become a significant fixture in the United States. The presence of Christianophobia suggests that the persistence of this war is driven by the biases and fears not only of cultural conservatives but also of cultural progressives. Some actions taken by cultural progressive activists may be, instead of rational assessments of how to further their cause, emotional Christianophobic reactions. Exploring the actions of cultural progressives, while accounting for symbolic fear and hatred of conservative Protestants, can be theoretically fruitful for understanding certain social and political activism.

Acknowledging symbolic actions connected to intolerance is not a novel approach. The concept of modern, as well as symbolic, racism is a way some researchers understand the actions of whites who want to mask racial animosity. Likewise, some activists[9] have linked charges of homophobia to those who do not support political legislation they have deemed to be "gay-friendly." They argue that individuals attempting to hide their homophobia can still use nonhomophobic reasons for opposing such legislation. Likewise, legislation that Christianophobic individuals support may have a rationale not automatically hostile toward conservative Protestants. However, the existence of claims of nonintolerance does not invalidate the possibility that some support of certain social and political policies is tied to Christianophobia. Future work should theorize about what Christianophobia looks like and what sort of social and political policies are vulnerable to being shaped by Christianophobia.

IF ONLY

As we conclude this work, we want to be clear about what we claim. We claim that there is a degree of anti-Christian animosity called "Christianophobia" that has an unmeasured, but not insignificant, impact in our society. This animosity is generally directed at conservative Christians. We have shown that the level of anti-Christian animosity at least rivals that of the animosity aimed at Muslims and that at least some individuals with this animosity exhibit characteristics of dehumanization, prejudice, and bigotry. We have not claimed that all with anti-Christian animosity have those characteristics of intolerance; however, this research reveals that these characteristics exist, and future studies are needed to show whether they exist at nontrivial levels. We have supported our claims with quantitative work documenting the level of anti-Christian hostility in society as well as qualitative work looking at some attitudes buttressing that hostility.

Research such as this sometimes attracts individuals who make what can be called "if only" arguments. For example, some may argue that if

CONCLUSION   139

only we had documented with a probability sample a sufficient level of anti-Christian bigotry instead of merely a general anti-Christian animosity, then we might be onto something. Or if only we had showed that conservative Christians are subject to violence, then there might be a case for Christianophobia, just as we talk about Islamophobia. How about if only we had compared our qualitative sample to a reference group of conservative Christians talking about progressives. Finally, if only we had showed that the respondents were referring to conservative Christians in general and not to extremist groups such Westboro Baptist Church, then we could believe that the respondents were dehumanizing conservative Christians as a group and not some extreme elements within that larger religious group. At that point we could make the argument that anti-Christian perspectives are as intolerant as anti-Semitic or Islamophobic attitudes. Generally "if only" arguments demand perfect research before drawing conclusions, and research is never perfect. Nonetheless we will address each of these objections one at a time.

It would be fantastic to assess the level of support for some of the stereotypes and myths believed by many of our respondents. But the documentation of antireligious bigotry with a probability sample is not necessary to have sufficient concern about the existence of such bigotry. We have yet to find a study with a national probability sample documenting Islamophobic bigotry in the United States,[10] and yet this has not stopped individuals from showing concern about this problem. We have documented what Christianophobia can look like, and future work can attest to the frequency of what we have documented. Our research is not the final word, but it does open up possible social explanations for the actions and institutions we discussed in chapter 7. Given the types of intolerances expressed in our work, the relative social status of those with anti-Christian animosity, and the relative frequency of anti-fundamentalist animosity demonstrated by our quantitative sample, it simply is not sufficient to ignore the potential effects of Christianophobia until we have a national probability sample of individuals indicating the specific Christianophobic beliefs in our qualitative sample, unless we are willing to set the same standard for the value of studying Islamophobia. The empirical evidence we have demonstrated, incomplete though it may be, indicates that our argument's detractors have some burden of producing empirical evidence refuting our assertions rather than merely pointing out that more work needs to be done. The stakes of ignoring antireligious bigotry of any type are too high to simply avoid the implications of our work.

Our respondents did not discuss plans for violence against conservative Christians; nor do we argue that violence is a major concern for such individuals.[11] Furthermore, some may argue that conservative Christians are overrepersented in the political realm, and there is work documenting the relative power of conservative Christians.[12] But such arguments assume that antireligious bigotry, as well as other types of bigotries, have identical characteristics. Scholars of race and ethnicity understand that the type of racism faced by African Americans differs from that faced by Asian Americans. In the same manner we should not expect Christianophobia to have identical characteristics to those of anti-Semitism and Islamophobia. Given the relative social status of those with Christianophobia, it is not surprising that violence is less likely to originate with them. Such individuals possess alternate ways of expressing their animosity due to their social status. Previous work[13] indicating the willingness of academics to discriminate against conservative Christians reflects negative outcomes more likely to occur among conservative Christians than among other religious groups, as well as outcomes tied to the higher level of educational status those with Christianophobia possess. Indicating that conservative Christians do not suffer from the possible effects of Christianophobia in one dimension of society does not eliminate the possibility that they do in other social dimensions.

We like the idea of comparing antireligious intolerance between two distinctive social groups. Given our assertion that modes of antireligious bigotry vary, there is valuable information to be gained by making such a comparison. However, that was not the original research design of this particular study. Our intention was not to document differences among the religious intolerances of conservative Christians and other social groups. It was to examine anti-Christian sentiment in its own perspective and to explore the nature of this sentiment. This exploration possesses important scientific value since there has been little, if any, previous academic assessment of anti-Christian sentiment. Just as we do not need a probability sample to provide empirical information on a topic that has received little previous study, we do not need a comparison group to generate new data and research agendas concerning antireligious hatred. We encourage future work that includes comparison groups, but lack of a reference group does not diminish the value of this work.

It is possible that when respondents considered conservative Christians, they were considering extremist groups and not conservative Christians as a group. The most famous extremist group is Westboro Baptist Church. Yet the name of that group came up only once in the answers to the open-ended comments of the more than twenty-five hundred respondents who provided those answers. This was also true for the word "dominionists," referring to another fairly well-known extremist Christian group. It is hard to believe that the attitudes documented in this book are due to perceptions toward Christian extremist groups since those groups are mentioned so few times. Perhaps the term "Christian fundamentalist" primed respondents in the ANES to think about Westboro or dominionists when they responded to thermometer questions. Yet, because the demographic characteristics of anti-fundamentalist individuals in the ANES are very similar to those of respondents expressing Christianophobic attitudes in our qualitative sample, it is unlikely that extreme groups such as Westboro or dominionists are a major factor shaping the attitudes of the ANES sample either. We cannot show the degree of influence these extreme groups have on attitudes toward conservative Christian groups, but the influence seems minuscule. The most logical answer is that respondents are reacting to their ideas of conservative Christians in general rather than only to the most extremists segments of that religious population.

FINAL THOUGHT

Our study questions the very nature of tolerance itself. The value of tolerance is often advocated by those who are most likely to possess Christianophobia—highly educated political progressives. Real tolerance comes out in how we treat those with whom we totally disagree. For many political progressives and highly educated individuals, accepting individuals of different races and sexual preferences is relatively easy since they have an affinity with highly educated progressives of color and different sexual orientations. But accepting those they disagree with, such as conservative Protestants, is more difficult. Battling

Christianophobia provides these individuals with the opportunity to practice the type of tolerance they value. Failure to confront Christianophobia produces questions about whether tolerance is truly possible. The need to define oneself and one's culture through negative reference groups may make it socially impossible for any subculture to practice total tolerance. If subcultures containing political progressives and the highly educated can reduce Christianophobia in their midst, then we can hope that true tolerance can ultimately be developed within those subcultures. If they cannot reduce Christianophobia within their ranks, then scholars should consider whether intolerance is an unfortunate part of the human experience.

APPENDIX A

This book's arguments stand on their own, and we provide enough basic information for individuals not trained in methodology and statistics to understand them. Those with methodological and statistical training, however, may want more details. We use this appendix to discuss the methods by which we collected the data in this book and document the statistical tests used to make some of our assertions.

THE AMERICAN NATIONAL ELECTION SURVEY

In 2010 one of us published an article using the American National Election Survey (ANES) to assess the relative hostility Americans have toward certain religious and nonreligious groups. As we were completing our qualitative analysis, the 2012 ANES data became available. We decided to use this data to again assess the degree of hostility faced by certain religious groups. We included racial groups to anchor these measures of hostility with assessments of groups known to face animosity.

The 2012 ANES utilized a thermometer measure of affection toward those groups. Respondents were asked to rank their affection on a zero-to-one-hundred scale, with higher numbers indicating more positive feelings. Attitudes toward six religious groups (Christian fundamentalists, Catholics, Muslims, Christians, atheists, Mormons) and four racial groups (whites, blacks, Hispanics, Asians) were assessed. We calculated the average ranking of the ten religious and racial groups. If a respondent ranked a group a standard deviation or greater below that average, we noted that he or she had a negative affinity for that group. Those with negative affinities we labeled as having an "anti" attitude toward that group (i.e., anti-fundamentalist, anti-atheist).

We constructed regression models to assess the relative importance of the independent explanations of anti-fundamentalist, anti-Muslim, anti-atheist, and anti-Mormon attitudes. We chose to look at those four groups since they had the four highest percentages of rejection relative to the other religious/racial groups. Our independent variables included sex, age, race, socioeconomic status (SES), education, religious preference, political ideology, region, and religiosity. Sex was derived from a dummy variable, with female coded as 1 and male as 0. The age variable included thirteen categories (ranging from "17–20" to "75 or older"). Measurements of race came from a four-category variable (white, black, Hispanic, other). White was the reference group. SES was assessed with a twenty-eight-category measure of family income (ranging from "under $5,000" to "$250,000 or more"). Education was assessed with a five-category measure (less than high school, high school, some college, bachelor's degree, graduate degree). Religious preference was assessed by a series of dummy variables: other Christian, other religion, not religious, spiritual, and agnostic/atheist, with Catholic as the reference group. Region used the General Social Survey designations for North-Central, Northeast, and West. The South was the reference group. To assess religiosity, we used two variables. One was tied to a question about whether the Bible was the word of God. The respondents' choices were (1) the Bible is the actual word of God, (2) the Bible is the word of God but should not be taken literally, and (3) the Bible was written by men. Higher values indicate lower religiosity. The other religiosity variable was a six-category measure of religious service attendance whereby higher numbers indicated more attendance.

All variables measuring types of antireligious hostility were dichotomous. Respondents either did or did not rank a group at least one standard deviation below the mean of the other groups. We used logistic regression analysis. In these models (see table A.1), we eliminated any respondents who did not answer all of the religious and racial thermometer questions, but even with these deletions, we retained 3,076 respondents.[1]

We report the major findings in chapter 3, but these models show the rationale for our reporting. For the anti-fundamentalist model, age, race, education, SES, religious affiliation, political ideology, and religiosity were important predictors of anti-fundamentalist attitudes. Odds ratios indicate the power of these variables. For every increase into the next highest education category, the probability that a respondent would be anti-fundamentalist rose by 48.5 percent. Political ideology was also very powerful as every move toward political progressiveness on the one-to-seven scale resulted in a 39.3 percent increase in the chance of that respondent having anti-fundamentalist attitudes. Accepting conservative Protestant Christian beliefs negatively shapes one's propensity to accept anti-fundamental perspectives. Non-Catholic Christians were 36 percent less likely than Catholics to accept anti-fundamentalist perspectives, and every move away from accepting the Bible as the word of God in the three-category variable resulted in a 151 percent increase in the chance that the respondent would accept anti-fundamentalist attitudes.

The other three models indicate different factors in religious hostility. Males, older individuals, whites, political conservatives, those not living in the North-Central region, and those seeing the Bible as the word of God were more likely to have anti-Muslim perspectives. While whites and males are majority groups, it is important to note that education and income are insignificantly negatively related to anti-Muslim attitudes. Because these variables are not significant, it is a mistake to argue that individuals with higher education and higher SES support Muslims, but clearly those with income and education are not more likely to have anti-Muslim attitudes. Older individuals, nonwhites, less educated individuals, Christians, political conservatives, Southerners, and those with higher religiosity are more likely to have anti-atheist sentiments. There are more individuals with anti-atheist sentiments than with relative hostility toward any religious group, but those with anti-atheist animosity do not have the per capita social power of the white, educated, and wealthy individuals with anti-Christian attitudes. Finally, younger individuals, nonwhites, the nonreligious, political progressives, those not living in the Northeast, and high attenders of religious services are more likely to rank Mormons relatively low. Education and SES are not significant in predicting this type of animosity, and detractors of Mormonism do not seem to differ greatly in social power

Table A.1. Betas and Odds Ratios of Selected Variables for Animosity toward Certain Religious Groups (N = 3,076)

Variable	Anti-fundamentalist	Anti-Muslim	Anti-atheist	Anti-Mormon
Female	.032	−.294[c]	.014	.018
	(1.033)	(.745)	(1.014)	(1.018)
Age	.036[a]	.076[c]	.049[c]	−.071[c]
	(1.036)	(1.078)	(1.05)	(.931)
Black	−.475[b]	−1.078[c]	.588[c]	.963[c]
	(.622)	(.34)	(1.801)	(2.62)
Hispanic	−.278	−.002	372[b]	.593c
	(.757)	(.998)	(1.451)	(1.809)
Other race	−.301	−.299	.252	.674b
	(.74)	(.741)	(1.286)	(1.962)
Education	.395[c]	−.056	−.08[a]	.015
	(1.485)	(.945)	(.923)	(1.015)
Income	.028[c]	−.003	.005	−.007
	(1.029)	(.997)	(1.005)	(.993)
Other Christian	−.446[c]	−.013	−.007	.116
	(.64)	(.987)	(.993)	(1.123)
Other religion	.536	−.116	−1.218[c]	−.22
	(1.71)	(.891)	(.296)	(.803)
Not religious	−.182	−.459	−.973[a]	.922[b]
	(.834)	(.632)	(.378)	(2.515)
Spiritual	−.53[b]	−.158	−.491[b]	.235
	(.589)	(.854)	(.612)	(1.265)
Agnostic/atheist	−.259	−.328	−2.208[c]	.516
	(.772)	(.721)	(.11)	(1.675)
Political view	−.499[c]	.34[c]	.259[c]	−.184[c]
	(.607)	(1.405)	(1.296)	(.832)
North central	−.054	−.235[a]	−.255	−.316
	(.948)	(.791)	(1.179)	(1.172)
Northeast	.083	−.183	−.255[a]	−.316[a]
	(1.086)	(.833)	(.775)	(.729)
West	−.136	−.167	−.287[a]	−.044
	(.873)	(.846)	(.75)	(.957)

Bible as word of God	.921[c]	−.31[c]	−.672[c]	−.094
	(2.512)	(.734)	(.51)	(.911)
Religious attendance	−.127[c]	.000	.15[c]	.072[a]
	(.881)	(1.00)	(1.162)	(1.074)
Nagelkerke R²	.345	.165	.25	.103

Note: Betas are entries; odds ratios are given in parentheses.

[a] p < .05

[b] p < .01

[c] p < .001

than the rest of society. These regression models support our assertion that those who oppose fundamentalists tend to have more per capita social power than others in society.

Finally we note that the Nagelkerke R^2 for the anti-fundamentalist model is larger than for the other models. The independent variables have more explanatory power for negative attitudes toward fundamentalists than for the other three groups. Social and demographic explanations of anti-fundamentalism may be more powerful than for other types of animosities. However, it is also possible that we have not accounted for confounding variables that, if included in the model, would reduce the effect of these social and demographic variables. Future research should search for possible spurious relationships.

QUALITATIVE SAMPLE

We based our qualitative research on a questionnaire sent to respondents in a variety of groups noted for their opposition to the Christian Right. We located several groups on the Internet and through our own knowledge. We then contacted them about disseminating the survey.[2] We sent a link to a specific contact, who then sent the survey out to the members of his or her group.[3]

One of these groups, with a national scope, focuses on promoting atheism. Another group, also national, is known for progressive political activism. A third, regional group concentrates on education issues. Finally, we sent the link to a local activist group, which sent it out to other local groups. Although we do not have a probability sample, we did make efforts in selecting organizations to achieve some diversity in terms of respondents' religious ideology, level of political concern, and region of the country. We are certain that we did not succeed in varying the regional dimension due to the large number of respondents from the South.

Clearly all Christians did not elicit equal anger and hatred among our respondents. In our thermometer measure we included mainstream, or non-fundamentalist, Protestants and Catholics as possible groups to be evaluated by our respondents. Individuals with a great deal of animosity toward Christians may certainly display hostility toward individuals in those groups as well. However, our work indicates that in this sample, the level of animosity toward non-fundamentalist Christians was negligible. We found that less than 1 percent of respondents ranked non-fundamentalist Christians and less than 9 percent ranked Catholics a standard deviation lower than other religious and nonreligious groups. Cultural progressives' perception of conservative Protestants, and not other Christian groups, drives their animosity.

CODING SHORT ANSWERS

We entered the answers to the closed-ended questions into a statistical program. The coding of the questions was straightforward and allowed for a quantitative assessment of the group as a whole. Each open-ended response was coded by one researcher. Each attribute was coded as either "yes" or "no" with regard to that particular response. Each attribute was assessed on its own, and for many responses several attributes were coded as "yes." We did not code the same phrase or word in a response with more than one attribute. Thus a respondent who defined the Christian Right as "ignorant" would likely have that response coded as "defined as ignorant" but not as "against science." A respondent who hypothetically defined the Christian Right as "ignorant and does not care about science" could be coded as both "ignorant" and "against science" since different parts of the answer matched the two attributes. If the response did not match any particular code, then all of the attributes for that response were coded as "no." But because of the extensive nature of our coding system, this was uncommon. Table A.2 provides an explanation for each attribute linked to each question. In that table we limit ourselves to the attributes discussed in this book. For a complete list of all attributes, we refer readers to our earlier work (Yancey and Williamson 2012)

Table A.2. Selected Descriptions of Codes Used for Short-Answer Questions

The question "How would you define the Christian Right?" was coded with the following attributes in mind:

1. Defined as crazy: The respondent indicated that the Christian Right fosters some degree of mental instability or craziness. This is differentiated from stupidity as we looked for indications that the respondent indicated mental illness. The notion that the Christian Right is deluded is also coded as craziness.
2. Defined as politically undesirable: The respondent indicated that the Christian Right is involved politically in ways that are harmful to society or in ways that encourage political conservatism.
3. Defined as intolerant or bigoted: The respondent indicated that the Christian Right encourages intolerance or bigotry. Usually respondents used these terms directly, although at times they indicated that the Christian Right is not open to alternatives. In those cases we also coded the response with this attribute. Finally, we found that use of the term "bigotry" was almost never tied to racial bigotry. If it was, then this code was not used unless there was another reason to do so.
4. Defined as trying to takeover: The respondent indicated that the Christian Right is a threat to democracy and/or is trying to set up a theocracy. It was also used if the respondent indicated attempts to impose Christian values.

We considered the following attributes in coding the question "Please describe your general attitude toward the Christian Right":

1. Intolerance/bigotry creates attitude: The respondent indicated that intolerance and/or bigotry was responsible for his or her attitude toward the Christian Right.
2. Crazy creates attitude: The respondent indicated that craziness was responsible for his or her attitude toward the Christian Right.
3. Political aspects create attitude: The respondent indicated that political aspects of the Christian Right were partially responsible for his or her attitude toward the group. Generally, the respondent was reacting negatively to a political stance taken on a specific issue or in general.
4. Attempts to takeover society create attitude: The respondent indicated that concern about the Christian Right taking over society was responsible for his or her attitude.

The question "Is there any specific characteristic of members of the Christian Right or political issue that they support that drives this attitude?" was coded with the following attributes in mind:

1. Political difference: The respondent brought up political issues other than the issues stated below as the driving force behind his or her attitude.
2. Intolerance/bigotry: The respondent brought up intolerance/bigotry as the driving force behind his or her attitude.
3. Craziness: The respondent brought up craziness as the driving force behind his or her attitude.
4. Homophobia: The respondent brought up issues related to homosexuality or same-sex marriage as the driving force behind his or her attitude.
5. Takeover: The respondent brought up the attempts of the Christian Right to takeover society as the driving force behind his or her attitude.

The question "What is the most positive thing you can say about the Christian Right?" was coded with the following attributes in mind:

1. Nothing: The respondent indicated that there was nothing positive to be said about the Christian Right or merely listed another complaint about the Christian Right.
2. Well organized: The respondent admired the organization or community that the Christian Right has created.

The question "What is the most negative thing you can say about the Christian Right?" was coded with the following attributes in mind.

1. Intolerance/bigotry is negative: The respondent brought up intolerance and/or bigotry as an important negative of the Christian Right.
2. Bad politics is negative: The respondent brought up bad political solutions as an important negative of the Christian Right.
3. Craziness is negative: The respondent brought up craziness as an important negative of the Christian Right.
4. Takeover is negative: The respondent brought up the threat of the Christian Right taking over society as an important negative.

We considered the following attribute in coding the questions "What is your most memorable personal encounter with a member of the Christian Right?" and "What happened in that encounter, and how did you feel about that experience? Please list more than one such encounter if you so desire":

1. None: The respondent indicated no personal encounter that he or she remembered with a member of the Christian Right.

The question "Do you think that we should pass laws that would affect members of the Christian Right? If you do want to pass such laws, what would they be and why?" was coded with the following attributes in mind:

1. No laws: The respondent indicated that laws protect everybody and that no laws should be passed or amended to deal with Christian Right.

2. Enforcement of existing laws: The respondent indicated that the existing laws are sufficient. Sometimes he or she argued that the laws were not enforced strictly enough, such as in matters of the separation of church and state, but asserted that new laws were not needed.

3. Separation of law and religion: The respondent indicated that laws had to be kept out of religious concerns.

4. Freedom of speech: The respondent indicated that freedom of speech dictated that such laws can and/or should not be passed.

5. Not becoming like the Christian Right: The respondent indicated that support for passing such laws would make him or her like the Christian Right, which the respondent saw as trying to use laws to enforce its will. Those who feared that laws used against the Christian Right might one day be used against them were coded with this attribute.

6. Separation of church and state: The respondent indicated a desire to create laws that strengthen separation of church and state. Such laws might deal with aspects such as religious symbols, financial support for religious groups to do good works, and use of religion in governmental decisions.

7. Tax exemption for religious institutions: The respondent indicated a desire to create laws about tax exemption for religious institutions. He or she wanted the tax exemption removed either for all religious institutions or for those that engage too heavily in politics.

8. Homeschooling: The respondent indicated a desire to create laws limiting the rights of homeschoolers or getting rid of homeschooling altogether.

Once all of the answers had been coded, we created a series of master variables that combined some of these variables. For example, the measures "defined as trying to takeover," "attempts to takeover society creates attitude," "takeover," and "takeover as negative" were combined into a measure on which the respondent received a score ranging from

0 to 4. None of the respondents were coded as a 1 in all four measures, but six were coded in three of the categories and thus were scored as 3. This master variable assessed if, and how often, respondents remarked about a fear of the country being taken over by the Christian Right. This was used to create master variables for "takeover," "bad politics," "intolerance," and "crazy."

REGRESSION MODEL OF WHO HAS
ANTI-CHRISTIAN ANIMOSITY

Based on our quantitative findings, it is clear that cultural progressive activists (individuals who tend to be well educated, politically progressive, and not highly religious) are more likely to have animosity toward Christians than other individuals. It is possible that some with Christianophobia are not cultural progressives and are not represented in our qualitative sample. This is clearly a limitation of this particular qualitative project. However, with this current sample, we do have the ability to observe how Christianophobic cultural progressive activists differ from other cultural progressive activists, which would be difficult with a probability sample unless it was large enough to include enough cultural progressive activists to make such comparisons. To explore possible differences between Christianophobic respondents and other cultural progressive activists, we used logistic regression. Our dependent variable was whether the cultural progressive activist ranked fundamentalists a standard deviation lower than other groups. For independent variables we included male (dummy variable), age (a seven-point scale ranging from "18–25" to "over 75"), how many children the respondent had living with him or her, educational attainment, SES, white (dummy variable), married (dummy variable), whether the respondent had any belief in religion,[4] Christian (dummy variable), and the regional dummy variables of South, West, and North-Central. The results of this model can be seen in table A.3.

Five variables remain significant after the application of social and demographic controls. Males, younger individuals, the highly educated, those with no belief in religion, and non-Christians are more likely to have anti-fundamentalist antipathy. SES and region of the country the respondent lived in were no longer significant. Furthermore, race, hav-

Table A.3. Betas and Odds Ratios of Selected Variables' Impact on Whether a Cultural Progressive Has Anti-fundamentalist Attitudes

Variable	Beta (Odds Ratio)
Male	-0.281^b
	(.75)
Age	-0.067^a
	(.935)
Children	0.001
	(.988)
Education	0.151^c
	(1.163)
Income	-.013
	(.987)
White	0.27
	(1.309)
Married	0.047
	(1.048)
No belief in religion	-0.383^a
	(.682)
Christian	$.614^a$
	(1.848)
South	0.245
	(1.277)
West	-.212
	(.809)
North-Central	.154
	(1.167)
Nagelkerke R^2	2332
	(.06)

Note: Betas are entries; odds ratios are given in parentheses.

[a] p < .05

[b] p < .01

[c] p < .001

ing children, and being married also did not have significant effects. The regression models indicate that male, younger, highly educated, nonreligious cultural progressive activists have disaffection for Christian fundamentalists even after application of controls. Intrinsic elements in these qualities might help persuade a cultural progressive activist to develop disaffection for conservative Christians.

For the most part cultural progressive activists with anti-fundamentalist sympathies are not much different from other cultural progressive activists, providing further support for the notion that Christianophobia may develop within a cultural progressive subculture. This assertion is distorted a bit since our sample consists of only cultural progressive activists. However, our quantitative research, which utilized a national sample, confirms that those who have high antipathy toward fundamentalists tend to be highly educated and politically progressive, two hallmarks of cultural progressives.

Finally, it is possible that gender, education, age, and religious differences may account for the contrasts between those with Christianophobia and other cultural progressive activists. For example, the fact that those rejecting Christians worry that Christians are intolerant can stem from their being more educated and thus having been socialized to value tolerance. We wanted to test the differences documented in table 3.4 after controlling for sex, age, educational attainment, whether the respondent was an atheist or agnostic, and whether the respondent was a Christian. The results can be seen in table A.4.

We left out attributes as independent variables other than those significant in table A.3. Those variables basically retained their significant effects. Generally we found that the differences documented in table 3.4 remained after application of these demographic controls. All of the attributes linked to the differences between those with Christianophobia and other cultural progressive activists remain significant except for mentions of "bad politics" and having a personal encounter with the Christian Right. The overwhelming trend is that ideological contrasts between those with Christianophobia and other cultural progressives are not due to demographic and social differences. The differential attitudes they have in comparison to other respondents remain after controls, suggesting that dynamics embedded within an anti-Christian perspective, apart from religious and regional effects, likely account for its existence. Differences in age, religion, education, and

Table A.4. Betas and Standard Errors of Christians, Regional Variables Selected Descriptors Impact on Whether a Cultural Progressive Is Anti-Fundamentalist

Male	$-.278^b$	$-.264^b$	$-.229^a$	$-.276^b$
	(.757)	(.768)	(.795)	(.759)
Age	$-.065^a$	$-.067^a$	$-.074^a$	$-.066^a$
	(.937)	(.935)	(.929)	(.936)
Education	$.149^c$	$.145^c$	$.146^c$	$.146^c$
	(1.16)	(1.157)	(1.157)	(1.157)
Atheist/agnostic	$-.507^c$	$-.487^b$	$-.432^b$	$-.499c$
	$-.487^b$	(.563)	(.649)	(.607)
Christian	$.644^a$	$.584^a$	$.613^a$	$.613a$
	(1.905)	(1.793)	(1.845)	(1.846)
Mentions of "takeover"	$.157^b$			
	(1.17)			
Mentions of "crazy"		$-.424^c$		
		(.654)		
Mentions of "intolerance"			$.245^c$	
			(1.277)	
Mentions of "bad politics"				.076
				(1.079)
Nagelkerke R^2	.051	.06	.06	.048
N	2,482	2,480	2,481	2,482

Note: Betas are entries; odds ratios are given in parentheses.

[a] $p < .05$

[b] $p < .01$

[c] $p < .001$

gender do matter, but their importance should not be overestimated in attempts to discover the source of Christianophobia.

Table A.4 (cont.): Betas and Standard Errors of Christians, Regional Variables Selected Descriptors Impact on Whether a Cultural Progressive Is Anti-Fundamentalist

Male	$-.263^b$	$-.263^b$	$-.291^b$	$-.295^b$
	(.769)	(.769)	(.748)	(.745)
Age	$-.064^a$	$-.059$	$-.069^a$	$-.065$
	(.938)	(.943)	(.933)	(.937)
Education	$.143^c$	$.147^c$	$.152^c$	$.171^c$
	(1.154)	(1.158)	(1.164)	(1.186)
Atheist/agnostic	$-.506^c$	$-.513^c$	$-.505^c$	$-.501^b$
	(.603)	(.598)	(.603)	(.606)
Christian	$.606^a$	$.6^a$	$.606^a$	$.645^a$
	(1.833)	(1.821)	(1.832)	(1.906)
Belief that Christian right is well organized	$.36^a$			
	(1.433)			
Homophobia		$.258^a$		
		(1.295)		
Absence of personal encounters with Christian Right			$-.103$	
			(.902)	
Support for changing laws to deal with Christian Right				$-.269^b$
				(.764)
Nagelkerke R^2	.049	.05	.05	.056
N	2,488	2,511	2,362	2,092

Note: Betas are entries; odds ratios are given in parentheses.

[a] $p < .05$

[b] $p < .01$

[c] $p < .001$

APPENDIX B

QUESTIONNAIRE FOR ONLINE SURVEY OF CULTURAL PROGRESSIVE ACTIVISTS

1. We'd also like to get your feelings about some groups in American society. We'd like you to rate the group with what we call a feeling thermometer. Ratings between 50 degrees–100 degrees mean that you feel favorably and warm toward the group; ratings between 0 and 50 degrees mean that you don't feel favorably toward the group and that you don't care too much for that group. If you don't feel particularly warm or cold toward a group, you would rate them at 50 degrees. Also if you do not know anything about a group, you would rate them at 50 degrees.

Mormons
Atheists
Hindus
Fundamentalists
Non-Fundamentalist Protestants
Jews
Muslims
Catholics
Agnostics

2. Think back to a time when you were in high school. About what percentage (from 1 to 100) of your friends do you think were in the following religious groups?

Atheists or Agnostics
Born-Again Christians
Jews
Christians, but Not Born-Again
Spiritual, but Not Religious
Other

3. Now think back to a time when you were in college or just after high school. About what percentage (from 1 to 100) of your friends do you think were in the following religious groups?

Atheists or Agnostics
Born-Again Christians
Jews
Christians, but Not Born-Again
Spiritual, but Not Religious
Other

4. Finally, think about today. About what percentage (from 1 to 100) of your friends do you think are currently in the following religious groups? (If you are still in college, then please skip this question.)

Atheists or Agnostics
Born-Again Christians
Jews
Christians, but Not Born-Again
Spiritual, but Not Religious
Other

5. How would you define the Christian Right?

6. Please describe your general attitude toward the Christian Right.

7. Are there any specific characteristics of members of the Christian Right or political issue that they support that drives this attitude?

8. What is the most positive thing you can say about the Christian Right?

9. What is the most negative thing you can say about the Christian Right?

10. What is your most memorable personal encounter with a member of the Christian Right?

11. What happened in that encounter, and how did you feel about that experience? Please list more than one such encounter if you so desire.

12. Did that encounter alter how you perceived members of the Christian Right? If so, how did it do that?

13. Imagine that you choose who is going to be your neighbor. Please rate the desirability of having one of the following individuals as your neighbor.

A vocal Republican who is not a Christian
A vocal Christian who is apolitical

14. Which of the two hypothetical neighbors do you desire less, and why do you have a lower desire for the neighbor you ranked lower?

15. Would it bother you if most of your neighbors were members of the Christian Right, and if so then why?

16. Do you think that we should pass laws that would affect members of the Christian Right? If you do want to pass such laws, what would they be and why?

17. Are there any comments about the Christian Right you would like to add that you did not get a chance to in any of the other questions?

18. Sex

Male
Female

19. Age

18–25
26–35
36–45
46–55
56–65
66–75
Over 75

20. Race

White
Black
Hispanic
Asian
Native American
Middle Eastern
Multiracial

Other

21. Education Obtained

Not High School
High School Diploma
Some College
Bachelor's Degree
Some Graduate School
Master's Degree
Doctorate

22. Income

Under 30K
30K–75K
75K–125K
Over 125K

23. What region of the country do you live in?

East North-Central (Wisconsin, Illinois, Indiana, Michigan, Ohio)
Middle Atlantic (New York, New Jersey, Pennsylvania)
New England (Maine, Vermont, New Hampshire, Massachusetts, Connecticut, Rhode Island)
South Atlantic (Delaware, Maryland, West Virginia, Virginia, North Carolina, South Carolina, Georgia, Florida, District of Columbia)
West South Central (Arkansas, Oklahoma, Louisiana, Texas)
East South Central (Kentucky, Tennessee, Alabama, Mississippi)
Mountain (Montana, Idaho, Wyoming, Nevada, Utah, Colorado, Arizona, New Mexico)
Pacific (Washington, Oregon, California, Alaska, Hawaii)
West North-Central (Minnesota, Iowa, Missouri, North Dakota, South Dakota, Nebraska, Kansas)

24. How would you describe your own religious faith?

Non-Born-Again Christian
Born-Again Christian
Jewish
Muslim
Eastern Religion
Spiritual, but Not Religious

Agnostic
Atheist
Other

NOTES

1. INTRODUCTION

1. Stephanie Barry, "Pioneer Valley Performing Arts Public School Presses On with Gay Biblical Satire Despite Threats of Protests," *Republican*, March 7, 2013,http://www.masslive.com/news/index.ssf/2013/03/school_presses_on_with_gay_bib.html.

2. Barry, "Pioneer Valley Performing Arts Public School."

3. Steve Maltz, *The (Other) F-Word: Faith, the Last Taboo* (Ilford, UK: Saffron Planet, 2011); see also Philip Jenkins, *The New Anti-Catholicism: The Last Acceptable Prejudice* (New York: Oxford University Press, 2003).

4. Terry Sanderson, "How Many Times Can These Christian 'Victims' Cry Wolf before People Ignore Them," *National Secular Society*, August 5, 2011, http://www.secularism.org.uk/how-many-times-can-these-christi.html; see also Keith Parsons, *Persecution Myth* (Grand Rapids, MI: Grand Rapids Atheists and Freethinkers, 2013); Candida Moss, *The Myth of Persecution: How Early Christians Invented a Story of Martyrdom* (New York: Harper One, 2013).

5. Vianey A. Midgette, "The Relationship of Acculturative Stress, Machismo and Self-Esteem as Predictors to Aggression for Latino Males," PhD diss., University of Wisconsin, Madison, 2008.

6. At times we interchange the term "animosity," which Merriam-Webster has defined as "ill will or resentment tending toward active hostility," with the term "hostility." Technically one can argue that animosity is the emotional feeling one develops before actively engaging in hostile treatment of a rejected out-group; however, we envision both terms as somewhat passive since this work concerns itself with prejudicial attitudes rather than potentially discriminatory actions.

7. Leon Poliakov, *The History of Anti-Semitism: From Voltaire to Wagner* (Philadelphia: University of Pennsylvania Press, 2003); David Berger, *History and Hate: The Dimensions of Anti-Semitism* (Philadelphia: Jewish Publication Society, 1997); William Nicholls, *Christian Antisemitism: A History of Hate* (Lanham, MD: Rowman & Littlefield, 1993); Arthur Hertzberg, *The French Enlightenment and the Jews: The Origins of Modern Anti-Semitism* (New York: Columbia University Press, 1990); John G. Gager, *The Origins of Anti-Semitism: Attitudes toward Judaism in Pagan and Christian Antiquity* (New York: Oxford University Press, 1983); Jacob Katz, *From Prejudice to Destruction: Anti-Semitism, 1700–1933* (Cambridge, MA: Harvard University Press, 1980); Michael Checinski, *Poland: Communism, Nationalism, Anti-Semitism* (New York: Karz-Cohl Publishing, 1982); Lee Levinger, *A History of Jews in the United States* (Rockville, MD: Wildside Press, 2007).

8. Lorraine Sheridan, "Islamophobia Pre– and Post–September 11th, 2001," *Journal of Interpersonal Violence* 21, no. 3 (2006): 317–36; Pnina Werbner, "Islamophobia: Incitement to Religious Hatred—Legislating for a New Fear?" *Anthropology Today* 21, no. 1 (2005): 5–9; Barry, "Pioneer Valley Performing Arts Public School."

9. Whitney Anspach, Kevin Coe, and Crispin Thurlow, "The Other Closet? Atheists, Homosexuals and the Lateral Appropriation of Discursive Capital," *Critical Discourse Studies* 4, no. 1 (2007): 95–119; Lynne M. Jackson and Bruce Hunsberger, "An Intergroup Perspective on Religion and Prejudice," *Journal for the Scientific Study of Religion* 38, no. 4 (1999): 509–23; Penny Edgell, Joseph Gerteis, and Douglas Hartmann, "Atheists as 'Other': Moral Boundaries and Cultural Membership in American Society," *American Sociological Review* 71, no. 2 (2006): 211–34.

10. George Yancey, "Who Has Religious Prejudice? Differing Sources of Anti-religious Animosity in the United States," *Review of Religious Research* 52, no. 2 (December 2010): 159–71; Louis Bolce and Gerald De Maio, "A Prejudice for the Thinking Classes," *American Politics Research* 36, no. 2 (2008): 155–85; Lauri L. Hyers, "Everyday Discrimination Experienced by Conservative Christians at the Secular University," *Analyses of Social Issues and Public Policy* 8, no. 1 (2008): 113–37; Richard Revesz, "NYU Law School: No Conservative Christians Need Apply," *Catholic Online*, August 5, 2009, http://www.catholic.org/national/national_story.php?id=34204; Jonel Thaller, "Resilience and Resistance in Professional Identity Making: Gleanings from the Classroom Experiences of Devout Christian Social Workers," *Journal of Religion and Spirituality in Social Work* 30, no. 2 (2011): 144–63.

11. Hyers, "Everyday Discrimination"; Joseph K. Neumann, William Thompson, and Thomas W. Woolley, "Evangelical vs. Liberal Christianity: The Influence of Values on the Nonclinical Professional Decisions of Social Work-

ers," *Journal of Psychology and Christianity* 11, no. 1 (1992): 57–67; John D. Gartner, "Antireligious Prejudice in Admission to Doctoral Programs in Clinical Psychology," *Professional Psychology: Research and Practice* 17, no. 5 (1986): 473–75.

12. George Yancey and David Williamson, *What Motivates Cultural Progressives: Understanding Opposition to the Political and Christian Right* (Waco, TX: Baylor University Press, 2012); Yancey, "Who Has Religious Prejudice?"

13. It is not always clear that a group has to have lower economic and educational status to be considered a minority group. Research has documented that homosexuals have higher levels of education than heterosexuals (H. Antecol, A. Jong, and M. Steinberger, "The Sexual Orientation Wage Gap: The Role of Occupational Sorting and Human Capital," *Industrial and Labor Relations Review* 61, no. 4 [2008]: 518–43; Dan A. Black et al., *The Measurement of Same-Sex Unmarried Couples in the 2000 U.S. Census* [Los Angeles: California Center for Population Research, 2002]) and lesbians have higher levels of income than other women, although gays have lower levels of income than other men after controls are applied (Antecol, Jong, and Steinberger, "The Sexual Orientation Wage Gap"; Dan A. Black et al., "The Earning Effects of Sexual Orientation," *Industrial and Labor Relations Review* 56, no. 3 [2003]: 449–69). Yet, a great deal of work documents disadvantages faced by homosexuals relative to heterosexuals. Merely because a group has societal advantages in some dimensions does not mean that it universally enjoys those advantages. The majority group status of Christians as a religion may not spare some of them from suffering as a minority group in other societal realms.

14. This ability to affect the lives of conservative Christians is not necessarily limited to economic dimensions. Given the political activism of some with anti-Christian attitudes, it is fair to assert that those attitudes also likely shape the political reality for Christians. Furthermore, some with anti-Christian animosity may be located in opinion-shaping fields such as media and the arts, providing the opportunity to alter perceptions of conservative Christians.

15. These sentiments may be more popular than these few statements would imply, as we found that it is possible to purchase merchandise with the statement "So Many Christians, So Few Lions" (http://www.cafepress.com/+so-many-christians-so-few-lions+gifts).

16. Yancey, "Who Has Religious Prejudice?"

17. This data is publically available at http://www.thearda.com/Archive/Files/Descriptions/CHRSTRT.asp. Individuals who contend that we merely are cherry-picking our results have the ability to double-check our data.

18. Frank Mungeam, "Commenting on the News: How the Degree of Anonymity Affects Flaming Online" (thesis, Gonzaga University, 2011).

19. Selma Vonderwell, "An Examination of Asynchronous Communication Experiences and Perspectives of Students in an Online Course: A Case Study," *Internet and Higher Education* 6, no. 1 (2002): 77–90; see also Ally Ostrowski, "Texting Tolerance: Computer-Mediated Interfaith Dialogue," *Webology* 3, no. 4 (2006): http://www.webology.org/2006/v3n4/a34.html.

20. R. A. Ellis and R. A. Calvo, "Learning through Discussions in Blended Environments," *Educational Media International* 41, no. 3 (2004): 263–74; Noriko Hara, Cutis J. Bonk, and Charoula Angeli, "Content Analysis of Online Discussion in an Applied Educational Psychology Course," *Instructional Science* 28, no. 2 (1998): 115–52.

21. In fact, a few respondents even commented that they were glad to have a venue in which to express themselves. One stated, "Thanks for letting me sound off" (male, aged 66–75 with master's degree); another commented, "I so seldom get an opportunity to actually express my thoughts and feelings about these people and what they are doing to my life, I could probably go on and on" (female, aged 46–55 with master's degree). Statements like these reinforce our confidence that our respondents were honest and felt free to express themselves in a way they cannot in other social settings. Thus the hostility we picked up reflects reality and is not manufactured by our online methodology, which is merely an excellent vehicle for obtaining the respondents' honest perceptions and feelings.

22. Nick Haslam, "Dehumanization: An Integrative Review," *Personality and Social Psychology* 10, no. 3 (2006): 252–64.

2. A HISTORY OF ANTI-CHRISTIAN HOSTILITY IN THE UNITED STATES

1. Peter L. Berger, *Pyramids of Sacrifice: Political Ethics and Social Change* (Garden City, NY: Anchor Books, 1974).

2. Ian G. Barbour, *Religion and Science: Historical and Contemporary Issues* (San Francisco: Harper Publishers, 1997).

3. Irving M. Zeitlin, *The Religious Experience: Classical Philosophical and Social Theories* (Upper Saddle River, NJ: Pearson/Prentice Hall, 2004).

4. Barbour, *Religion and Science*.

5. J. D. Hunter, *Culture War: The Struggle to Define America* (New York: Basic Books, 1991).

6. Ronald Numbers, *Darwinism Comes to America* (Cambridge, MA: Harvard University Press, 1998), 62.

7. Robert K. Gustafson, *James Woodrow (1827–1907): Scientist, Theologian, Intellectual Leader* (Lewiston, NY: Mellen Press, 1995).

8. Numbers, *Darwinism Comes to America*.

9. Rodney Stark and Roger Finke, *Acts of Faith: Explaining the Human Side of Religion* (Berkeley: University of California Press, 2000).

10. Max Weber, *The Protestant Ethic and the Spirit of Capitalism* (London: Unwin Paperbacks, 1930); Richard Hofstadter, *Anti-intellectualism in American Life* (New York: Vintage, 1963).

11. Hofstadter, *Anti-intellectualism in American Life*.

12. James K. Wellman, *Evangelical vs. Liberal: The Clash of Christian Cultures in the Pacific Northwest* (New York: Oxford University Press, 2008).

13. Hofstadter, *Anti-intellectualism in American Life*; see also Michael Lienesch, *In the Beginning: Fundamentalism, the Scopes Trial, and the Making of the Antievolution Movement* (Chapel Hill: University of North Carolina Press, 2007).

14. It is worth noting that the word "fundamentalist" is often misused and applied to other religions or beliefs. As indicated in this section, the term "fundamentalist" developed among and belongs to a certain subgroup of Protestants. There are no fundamentalist Muslims, Mormons, or Jews. There are extremists in all of these groups, but that does not make them fundamentalists. At times our respondents use the term "fundamentalist" to describe non-Protestants. We argue that the best explanation for such usage is an attempt to co-opt the term so that "fundamentalist" is used to indicate extremism instead of beliefs within a certain Protestant sect.

15. Hofstadter, *Anti-intellectualism in American Life*.

16. John J. Redekop, *The American Far Right* (Grand Rapids, MI: William B. Eerdmans Publishing Co., 1968).

17. Jack P. Gibbs, *Control: Sociology's Central Notion* (Urbana-Champaign: University of Illinois Press, 1989).

18. Emile Durkheim, *The Elementary Forms of the Religious Life* (New York: Allen and Unwin, 1915).

19. Stephen L. Carter, *The Culture of Disbelief: How American Law and Politics Trivialize Religious Devotion* (New York: Basic Books, 1993).

20. Matthew C. Moen, *The Transformation of the Christian Right* (Tuscaloosa: University of Alabama Press, 1992); Clyde Wilcox, *God's Warriors: The Christian Right in Twentieth-Century America* (Baltimore: Johns Hopkins University Press, 1992); William Martin, *With God on Our Side: The Rise of the Religious Right in America* (New York: Broadway, 2005).

3. WHO ARE THOSE WITH
ANTI-CHRISTIAN ANIMOSITY?

1. George Yancey, "Who Has Religious Prejudice? Differing Sources of Anti-religious Animosity in the United States," *Review of Religious Research* 52, no. 2 (December 2010): 159–71.

2. One reason why we did not simply use the actual thermometer measure is that individuals have differing propensities to give higher overall scores, and these differences vary by social and demographic characteristics (Clyde Wilcox, Lee Sigelman, and Elizabeth Cook, "Some Like It Hot: Individual Differences in Responses to Group Feeling Thermometers," *Public Opinion Quarterly* 53, no. 2 [1989]: 246–57). Therefore it is important to standardize thermometer findings to make sure that differences in the thermometer measures of a particular group do not stem from one individual's propensity to rate all groups relatively high. Using an average of all groups and seeing if a group is rated a standard deviation lower than that average is a way to standardize the thermometer ratings.

3. William A. Barnard and Mark S. Benn, "Belief Congruence and Prejudice and Ethnic Relations," *Journal of Social Psychology* 128 (February 1988): 125–34; Harold D. Fishbein, *Peer Prejudice and Discrimination: The Origins of Prejudice* (Mahwah, NJ: Lawrence Erlbaum Associates, 2002); Richard T. Schaefer, "Education and Prejudice: Unraveling the Relationship," *Sociological Quarterly* 37 (1996): 1–16; Alan N. Wright and Jan Tolan, "Prejudice Reduction through Shared Adventure: A Qualitative Outcome Assessment of a Multicultural Education Class," *Journal of Experiential Education* 32, no. 2 (2009): 137–54; C. Daniel Batson and E. L. Stocks, "Religion and Prejudice," in *On the Nature of Prejudice: Fifty Years after Allport*, ed. John F. Dovidio, Peter Glick, and Laurie A. Rudman, 413–28 (Malden, MA: Blackwell Publishing, 2005).

4. Lilia I. Bartolome and Donaldo P. Macedo, "Dancing with Bigotry: The Poisoning of Racial and Ethnic Identities," *Harvard Educational Review* 67, no. 2 (2009): 222–47; Joleen Kirschenman and Kathryn M. Neckerman, "'We'd Love to Hire Them, but . . . ': The Meaning of Race for Employers," in *The Urban Underclass*, ed. Christopher Jencks and Paul Peterson, 203–34 (Washington, DC: Brookings Institution, 1991); Tomás Almaguer, *Racial Fault Lines: The Historical Origins of White Supremacy in California* (Berkeley: University of California Press, 2009); Howard Schuman et al., *Racial Attitudes in America: Trends and Interpretations* (Cambridge, MA: Harvard University Press, 1997); Eduardo Bonilla-Silva, *Racism without Racists: Color-Blind Racism and the Persistence of Racial Inequality in the United States* (Lanham, MD: Rowman & Littlefield, 2006); Michael Omi and Howard Winant, *Racial Formation*

in the United States: From the 1960s to the 1990s, 2nd ed. (New York: Routledge, 1994).

5. Of course, this does not mean that racial animosity is exactly the same as religious animosity. Hartmann et al. ("How Americans Understand Racial and Religious Differences," *Sociological Quarterly* 52 [2011]: 323–45) argue that race and religion can be understood in contrasting ways. Racial identity is seen as a social problem, whereas religion is envisioned as the choice of an individual and part of the collective good. Respondents generally perceived religious differences as more meaningful, socially useful, positive, and less troublesome than racial differences, but these contrasting ways of understanding religious and racial differences were not as great as one might expect, given the distinct ways that racial and religious dynamics play out in the United States. Thus it is reasonable to create a scale with both racial and religious groups, which will provide a wider context for our assessment of anti-Christian attitudes.

6. Paul M. Sniderman and Thomas Piazza, *The Scar of Race* (Cambridge, MA: Harvard University Press, 1993); Marcel Coenders and Peer Scheepers, "The Effect of Education on Nationalism and Ethnic Exclusionism: An International Comparison," *Political Psychology* 24, no. 2 (2003): 313–43; J. Eric Oliver and Tali Mendelberg, "Reconsidering the Environmental Determinants of White Racial Attitudes," *American Journal of Political Science* 44, no. 3 (2000): 574–89.

7. Jim Sidanius, Felicia Pratto, and Lawrence Bobo, "Racism, Conservatism, Affirmative Action, and Intellectual Sophistication: A Matter of Principled Conservatism of Group Dominance?" *Interpersonal Relations and Group Processes* 70, no. 3 (1996): 476–90; Bob Altemeyer, *The Authoritarians* (Manitoba, Canada: Bob Altemeyer, 2007).

8. James H. Kuklinski and Michael D. Cobb, "Racial Attitudes and the 'New South.'" *Journal of Politics* 59, no. 2 (1997): 323–49; Oliver and Mendelberg, "Reconsidering the Environmental Determinants."

9. Thomas C. Wilson, "Cohort and Prejudice: Whites' Attitudes toward Blacks, Hispanics, Jews, and Asians," *Public Opinion Quarterly* 60, no. 2 (1996): 253–74; Brandon D. Stewart, William von Hippel, and Gabriel A. Radvansky, "Age, Race, and Implicit Prejudice: Using Process Dissociation to Separate the Underlying Components," *Psychological Science* 20, no. 2 (2009): 164–68.

10. Kerem Ozan Kalkan, Geoffrey Layman, and Eric M. Uslaner, "'Band of Others'? Attitudes towards Muslims in Contemporary American Society," *Journal of Politics* 71, no. 3 (2009): 1–16; Penny Edgell, Joseph Gerteis, and Douglas Hartmann, "Atheists as 'Other': Moral Boundaries and Cultural Membership in American Society," *American Sociological Review* 71, no. 2 (2006): 211–34.

11. Kalkan, Layman, and Uslaner, "'Band of Others'?"; Will M. Gervais, *Do You Believe in Atheists? Trust and Anti-atheist Prejudice* (master's thesis, University of British Columbia, Vancouver, 2008).

12. Jamie B. Luguri, Jaime L. Napier, and John F. Dovidio, "Reconstruing Intolerance: Abstract Thinking Reduces Conservatives' Prejudice against Nonnormative Groups," *Psychological Science* 24, no. 7 (2012): 756–63; Altemeyer, *The Authoritarians*.

13. Edgell, Gerteis, and Hartmann, "Atheists as 'Other'"; Zan Strabac and Ola Listhaug, "Anti-Muslim Prejudice in Europe: A Multilevel Analysis of Survey Data from 30 Countries," *Social Science Research* 37, no. 1 (2008): 268–86.

14. Yancey, "Who Has Religious Prejudice?"; Louis Bolce and Gerald De Maio, "A Prejudice for the Thinking Classes," *American Politics Research* 36, no. 2 (2008): 155–85.

15. For example, education is positively correlated to the average ranking of the groups (r = .056; p < .05); the highly educated, who are more likely to have anti-fundamentalist animosity, can in theory rank fundamentalists as high as other respondents without being labeled as having religious animosity.

16. We used the data weighted for the full postelection sample.

17. To make sure that this was not an artifact of selecting racial and religious groups, we also ran this analysis and included all of the social groups in the survey (twenty-seven in total). The basic order of the religious and racial groups remained the same, and fundamentalists ranked twenty-second among these groups, with only the federal government, Congress, Tea Party, illegal immigrants, and atheists ranked below them.

18. We talk about Protestants since our data indicates that Catholics do not face the same level of animosity as Christian fundamentalists. However, we are mindful of our nation's history of anti-Catholicism. We suspect that Catholics are less likely to be seen as challenging the type of political, social, and cultural visions those with anti-Christian perspectives are likely to possess. However, if a perception of Catholics develops that is similar to that held by many of our respondents regarding conservative Protestants, Catholics will quite likely experience the same resentment and animosity as their conservative Protestant peers.

19. As argued in chapter 1, anti-Christian perspectives are more relevant for conservative Christians than for moderate or progressive Christians. To this end, although the ANES data only allows us to assess attitudes toward Christian fundamentalists, it is reasonable to assert that most survey respondents link Christian fundamentalism to some form of conservative Christianity. Indeed, one of us recently presented a paper for which the research team asked teachers on college campuses how they would define Christian fundamental-

ism (George Yancey, Sam Reimer, and Jake O'Connell, "Science Defines Religion: How U.S. Scholars Define and Perceive Fundamentalist, Evangelical and Mainline Protestants," paper presented at the Society for the Scientific Study of Religion Annual Meeting, Boston, Massachusetts, November 8–10, 2013). The respondents' answers indicated that Christian fundamentalists are usually seen as conservative Christians who accept a literal interpretation of the Bible. Although this paper focuses only on how one subculture defines fundamentalism, we assert that most definitions of fundamentalism will include an element of conservative Christianity.

20. To construct the variables for this table, we used the one-to-seven scale provided in the survey. If respondents indicated that they were either extremely liberal, liberal, or slightly liberal, then we labeled them as liberal. We did the same for the conservative labels in the question. Those who marked themselves as moderate were not included in either the liberal or conservative category.

21. In a model where we used Hispanic as the reference group, the whites group was significant at p = .027.

22. According to the odds ratios, an increase in an income category resulted in an increased probability of having an anti-Christian attitude by 2.9 percent. An increase in an educational category resulted in an increased probability of having an anti-Christian attitude by 48.5 percent. The income variable contained twenty-eight categories, whereas the education variable contained only five categories, so the lack of variability in the educational category helps to explain some of this difference in percentage change. But it still appears that education may have slightly more explanatory value than income.

23. This variable includes three categories: (1) Bible is word of God, (2) Bible is God's Word but not literal, and (3) Bible is man-made. Thus higher numbers indicates less reverence for the Bible.

24. In our sample, 57.9 percent of the white respondents with at least a bachelor's degree and making at least $100,000 a year were anti-fundamentalist. Among those with these characteristics who identified themselves as politically liberal instead of conservative or middle-of-the-road, the percentage rose to 88.1 percent.

25. George Yancey and David Williamson, *What Motivates Cultural Progressives: Understanding Opposition to the Political and Christian Right* (Waco, TX: Baylor University Press, 2012).

26. There is an exception to this tendency. We found that some individuals connected to the Christian Right joined these organizations in an effort to monitor them. We eliminated several of our surveys when it became clear that the individuals filling them out were quite sympathetic to the Christian Right.

It is possible that a couple of "plants" got through our screening; however, one or two individuals are unlikely to skew our very powerful results.

27. The organization's focus attracted far more atheists and agnostics than the other organizations we surveyed. Among our respondents the correlation between belonging to this organization and being either an atheist or agnostic was quite strong (r = .509). Members of this organization were actually slightly more likely to have anti-Christian attitudes than other respondents, but this difference disappeared once we controlled for whether the respondent was an atheist or agnostic. We also found members of this organization were more likely to be male, younger, and less educated. Since we do not have a probability sample, the overrepresentation of this organization is not troubling and is perhaps even helpful since it produces a higher percentage of individuals with anti-Christian animosity than the rest of the sample. Having more such individuals provides us with more opportunities to gather qualitative data about them.

28. It can be argued that agnostics and atheists are not religious groups and should not be included in this list. Several respondents made such a point, and some preferred the word "humanist" to describe themselves. But the terms "atheist" and "agnostic" indicate a certain set of assertions about the nature of religious reality. Since we are measuring the feelings of respondents toward those with conservative Christian beliefs as opposed to those with other assertions about religion, including these groups is appropriate.

29. Even though academically the term "fundamentalist" should be limited to Protestants, it is technically possible that some respondents link the term to other religious extremists. This is not a concern in the ANES data since that thermometer question specifically asked about "Christian fundamentalists." Although we only use the term "fundamentalist," we are not concerned about our respondents attaching the concept to other religious groups for two reasons. First, they would most likely attach this term to Muslims, and we specifically ask about Muslims in another thermometer question. Second, the premise of the online survey was an exploration of the Christian Right. In this context, respondents could logically assume that "fundamentalist" referred to conservative Christians.

30. Our score likely would have been different if we had also asked the respondents about racial groups and included them in our measure. We believe that including such groups would have increased the percentage of individuals scored with anti-Christian animosity. We make this argument since individuals in the ANES sample generally ranked racial groups higher than religious groups. This would raise the mean of the respondent and create more distance between that mean and a potentially lower thermometer score for fundamentalists.

31. One key difference in the reaction to Christian conservatives between the population collected with the neighborhood measure and the larger sample is that the former group is more likely to complain that Christians are anti-science. The perception of Christians as anti-scientific is common among cultural progressive activists, but it is possible that those with a more emotional distaste for Christians are more likely to hold on to such an image. Future research may be able to further investigate such a possibility.

32. Christian Smith, David Sikkink, and Jason Bailey, "Devotion in Dixie and Beyond: A Test of the 'Shibley Thesis' on the Effect of Regional Origin and Migration on Individual Religiosity," *Journal for the Scientific Study of Religion* 37, no. 3 (1998): 494–506; Larry L. Hunt and Matthew O. Hunt, "Race, Region, and Religious Involvement: A Comparison Study of Whites and African Americans," *Social Forces* 80, no. 2 (2001): 605–31; Christian Smith et al., "Mapping American Adolescent Religious Participation," *Journal for the Scientific Study of Religion* 41, no. 4 (2002): 597–612.

33. This measure responds to a question about what the respondent did not like about the Christian Right. We noted how many times respondents mentioned a concern about homophobia or any gay-related issue to create this variable.

34. Of course, "bad politics" is a relative term. Given the type of political issues these respondents tend to endorse, it is reasonable to assert that their idea of bad politics would be political activism that supports conservative causes, especially as it pertains to cultural or social issues. Thus a fair interpretation is that cultural progressive activists with anti-Christian animosity exhibit stronger concern than other cultural progressive activists over the political goals and actions of conservative Christians that promote political conservatism.

35. This is linked to a question about what society should do to deal with the Christian Right. If respondents discussed a way of changing laws to deal with the Christian Right, they were coded as 1 in this measure. If they did not mention altering laws, they were coded as 0. We explore this question in more depth in chapter 6.

36. D. Michael Lindsay, *Faith in the Halls of Power* (New York: Oxford University Press, 2007).

4. HOW ANTI-CHRISTIAN HOSTILITY
SHAPES PERCEPTIONS OF CHRISTIANS

1. George Yancey and David Williamson, *What Motivates Cultural Progressives: Understanding Opposition to the Political and Christian Right* (Waco, TX: Baylor University Press, 2012).

2. r = 349; p < .01.

3. r = .187; p < .01.

4. r = .226; p < .01.

5. We used the same independent variables used in table A.2. The results are available from the authors upon request.

6. W. W. Wilkinson, "Religiosity, Authoritarianism and Homophobia: A Multidimensional Approach," *International Journal for the Psychology of Religion* 14, no. 1 (2004): 55–67; Peer Scheepers, Manfred T. Grotenhuis, and Frans Van Der Slik, "Education, Religiosity and Moral Attitudes: Explaining Cross-National Effect Differences," *Sociology of Religion* 63, no. 2 (2002): 157–76.

7. P. Bain et al., "Attributing Human Uniqueness and Human Nature to Cultural Groups: Distinct Forms of Subtle Dehumanization," *Group Processes and Intergroup Relations* 12, no. 6 (2009): 789–805; J. Hagan and W. Rymond-Richmond, "The Collective Dynamics of Racial Dehumanization and Genocidal Victimization in Darfur," *American Sociological Review* 73, no. 6 (2008): 875–902; D. Moshman, "Us and Them: Identity and Genocide," *Identity: An International Journal of Theory and Research* 7, no. 2 (2007): 115–35.

5. DEHUMANIZING AND HATING CHRISTIANS

1. J. Hagan and W. Rymond-Richmond, "The Collective Dynamics of Racial Dehumanization and Genocidal Victimization in Darfur," *American Sociological Review* 73, no. 6 (2008): 875–902; H. C. Kelman, "Violence without Restraint: Reflections on the Dehumanization of Victims and Victimizers," in *Varieties of Psychohistory*, ed. G. M. Kren and L. H. Rappoport, 282–314 (New York: Springer, 1976); Cristian Tileaga, "Ideologies of Moral Exclusion: A Critical Discursive Reframing of Depersonalization, Delegitimization and Dehumanization," *British Journal of Social Psychology* 46, no. 4 (2007): 717–37; Nick Haslam, "Dehumanization: An Integrative Review," *Personality and Social Psychology* 10, no. 3 (2006): 252–64; F. Chalk and K. Jonassohn, *The History and Sociology of Genocide: Analyses and Case Studies* (New

Haven, CT: Yale University Press, 1990); Susan Opotow, "Moral Exclusion and Injustice: An Introduction," *Journal of Social Issues* 46, no. 1 (1990): 1–20.

2. Tileaga, "Ideologies of Moral Exclusion"; Chalk and Jonassohn, *The History and Sociology of Genocide*; Kelman, "Violence without Restraint."

3. Opotow, "Moral Exclusion and Injustice."

4. Lasana T. Harris and Susan T. Fiske, "Dehumanizing the Lowest of the Low: Neuroimaging Responses to Extreme Out-Groups," *Psychological Science* 17 (2006): 847–53.

5. Haslam, "Dehumanization."

6. Jan Nederveen Pieterse, *White on Black: Images of Africa and Blacks in Western Popular Culture* (New Haven, CT: Yale University Press, 1995); Tomás Almaguer, *Racial Fault Lines: The Historical Origins of White Supremacy in California* (Berkeley: University of California Press, 2009); Etta R. Hollins, *Transforming Curriculum for a Culturally Diverse Society* (Mahwah, NJ: Lawrence Erlbaum Associates, 1996); James W. Messerschmidt, "'We Must Protect Our Southern Women': On Whiteness, Masculinities, and Lynching," in *Race, Gender, and Punishment: From Colonialism to the War on Terror*, ed. Mary Bosworth and Jeanne Flavin, 77–94 (Piscataway, NJ: Rutgers University Press, 2007); Patrick B. Shape, *Savage Perils: Racial Frontiers and Nuclear Apocalypse in American Culture* (Norman: University of Oklahoma Press, 2007); S. Plous and Tyrone Williams, "Racial Stereotypes from the Days of American Slavery: A Continuing Legacy," *Journal of Applied Social Psychology* 25, no. 9 (1995): 795–817.

7. Shape, *Savage Perils*; Theodore W. Allen, *The Invention of the White Race: The Origin of Racial Oppression in Anglo-America*, edited by Ernest Cashmore and James Jennings (New York: Verso, 1997); Luana Ross, *Inventing the Savage: The Social Construction of Native American Criminality* (Austin: University of Texas Press, 1998); Joe R. Feagin, *Systemic Racism: A Theory of Oppression* (New York: Taylor & Francis Group, 2006).

8. Joshua Harris, *Sex Is Not the Problem (Lust Is): Sexual Purity in a Lust-Saturated World* (Colorado Springs, CO: Multnomah Publishers, 2005); Daniel R. Heimbach, *True Sexual Morality: Recovering Biblical Standards for a Culture in Crisis* (Wheaton, IL: Crossway Books, 2004); Erwin W. Lutzer, *The Truth about Same Sex Marriage: 6 Things You Need to Know about What's Really at Stake* (Chicago: Moody Publishers, 2010).

9. Daniel G. Solorzano, "Images and Words That Wound: Critical Race Theory, Racial Stereotyping, and Teacher Education," *Teacher Education Quarterly* (summer 1997): 5–20; Hugh Pearson, "Developing the Rage to Win," in *The Bell Curve Wars: Race, Intelligence and the Future of America*, ed. Steve Fraser, 164–71 (New York: Basic Books, 1995); Plous and Williams,

"Racial Stereotypes"; Irving L. Allen, *Unkind Words: Ethnic Labeling from Redskin to WASP* (New York: Bergin & Garvey, 1990).

10. Carlos Zubaran, "Human Nomenclature: From Race to Racism," *World Health and Population* 11, no. 2 (2009): 43–52; Thomas F. Gossett, *Race* (New York: Schocken Books, 1965).

11. Dora Capozza et al., "Categorization of Ambiguous Human/Ape Faces: Protection of Ingroup but Not Outgroup Humanity," *Group Processes and Intergroup Relations* 12, no. 6 (2009): 777–87; Haslam, "Dehumanization"; Abby L. Ferber, "The Construction of Black Masculinity: White Supremacy Now and Then," *Sport and Social Issues* 34, no. 3 (2007): 11–24; Otto S. Ana, "Like an Animal I Was Treated: Anti-immigrant Metaphor in U.S. Public Discourse," *Discourse and Society* 10 (1994): 191–224.

12. Chalk and Jonassohn, *The History and Sociology of Genocide*; G. V. O'Brien, "People with Cognitive Disabilities: The Argument from Marginal Cases and Social Work Ethics," *Social Work* 48 (2003): 331–37; Haslam, "Dehumanization"; Opotow, "Moral Exclusion and Injustice."

13. George Yancey and David Williamson, *What Motivates Cultural Progressives: Understanding Opposition to the Political and Christian Right* (Waco, TX: Baylor University Press, 2012).

14. Edward B. Royzman, Clark McCauley, and Paul Rosin, "From Plato to Putnam: Four Ways to Think about Hate," in *The Psychology of Hate*, ed. Robert J. Strenberg (Washington, DC: American Psychological Association, 2005).

15. Eran Halperin, "Group-Based Hatred in Intractable Conflict in Israel," *Journal of Conflict Resolution* 52, no. 5 (2008): 713–36.

16. Aaron Ben-Zeev, "Anger and Hate," *Journal of Social Philosophy* 2 (1992): 85–110.

17. Jon Elster, *Alchemies of the Mind: Rationality and the Emotions* (Cambridge: Cambridge University Press, 1999).

18. Ralph K. White, "Why the Serbs Fought: Motives and Misperceptions," *Peace and Conflict: Journal of Peace Psychology* 2, no. 2 (1996): 109–28.

19. Halperin, "Group-Based Hatred," 718.

20. Halperin, "Group-Based Hatred," 729.

21. Gordon Allport, *The Nature of Prejudice* (New York: Anchor, 1958).

22. Harold D. Fishbein, *Peer Prejudice and Discrimination: The Origins of Prejudice* (Mahwah, NJ: Lawrence Erlbaum Associates, 2002).

23. Aubyn S. Fulton, Richard L. Gorsuch, and Elizabeth A. Maynard, "Religious Orientation, Antihomosexual Sentiment, and Fundamentalism among Christians," *Journal for the Scientific Study of Religion* 38, no. 1 (1999): 14–22.

24. P. Holtz and W. Wagner, "Essentialism and Attribution of Monstrosity in Racist Discourse: Right-Wing Internet Postings about Africans and Jews,"

Journal of Community and Applied Social Psychology 19, no. 6 (2009): 411–25; I. D. Kalmar, "Anti-Semitism and Islamophobia: The Formation of a Secret," *Human Architecture: Journal of the Sociology of Self-Knowledge* 7, no. 2 (2009): 135–44; Penny Edgell, Joseph Gerteis, and Douglas Hartmann, "Atheists as 'Other': Moral Boundaries and Cultural Membership in American Society," *American Sociological Review* 71, no. 2 (2006): 211–34.

25. Political progressives may argue that the conservative policies of Christian are tied to oppressive governmental regimes. However, conservative politicians are just as likely to argue that progressive policies lead to governmental oppression. We take no sides in this debate other than to argue that Christian politicians do not appear to exhibit a desire for a Nazi- or Taliban-style government any more than non-Christian politicians. Some may look at research into right-wing authoritarianism to argue that religious individuals have a higher willingness to misuse authoritative power (Bob Altemeyer, *The Authoritarians* [Manitoba, Canada: Bob Altemeyer, 2007]; Robert J. Duck and Bruce Hunsberger, "Religious Orientation and Prejudice: The Role of Religious Proscription, Right-Wing Authoritarianism, and Social Desirability," *International Journal for the Psychology of Religion* 9, no. 3 [1999]: 157–79; Bruce Hunsberger, "Religious Fundamentalism, Right-Wing Authoritarianism, and Hostility towards Homosexuals in Non-Christian Religious Groups," *International Journal for the Psychology of Religion* 6, no. 1 [1996]: 39–49), but one of us has conducted research showing that political and religious progressives show a similar proclivity to misuse authoritative power (George Yancey, *Dehumanizing Christians* [Piscataway, NJ: Transaction Publishers, 2013]).

26. Simon McCormack, "Dan Savage Speech Controversy: 'It Gets Better' Creator Offends Christian Students," *Huffington Post*, April 28, 2012, http://www.huffingtonpost.com/2012/04/28/dan-savage-speech-controversy_n_1461863.html; Byron R. Johnson, *More God, Less Crime* (West Conshohocken, PA: Templeton Press, 2012); Colin Baier and Bradley R. E. Wright, "'If You Love Me, Keep My Commandments': A Meta Analysis of the Effect of Religion on Crime," *Journal of Research in Crime and Delinquency* 38 (2001): 3–21; Byron Johnson et al., "A Systematic Review of the Religiosity and Delinquency Literature: A Research Note," *Journal of Contemporary Criminal Justice* 16, no. 1 (2000): 32–52; T. D. Evans et al., "Religion and Crime Reexamined: The Impact of Religion, Secular Controls, and Social Ecology on Adult Criminality," *Criminology* 33 (1995): 195–224.

27. There is debate as to whether Christian beliefs correlate with racism. Keith A. Roberts and David Yamane (*Religion in Sociological Perspective*, 5th ed. [Los Angeles, CA: Sage, 2012]) point out that early research confirmed a positive relationship between Christian beliefs and racism. However later work found that only extrinsic, rather than intrinsic, Christianity was tied to racist

beliefs (Gordon Allport, "The Religious Context of Prejudice," *Journal for the Scientific Study of Religion* [fall 1966]: 447–57; Lee A. Kirkpatrick, "Fundamentalism, Christian Orthodoxy, and Intrinsic Religious Orientation as Predictors of Discriminatory Attitudes," *Journal for the Scientific Study of Religion* [March 1993]: 256–68; Richard L. Gorsuch and Daniel Aleshire, "Christian Faith and Ethnic Prejudice: A Review and Interpretation of Research," *Journal for the Scientific Study of Religion* [September 1974]: 281–307). There is some research casting doubt on whether such a distinction still matters (Lynne M. Jackson and Bruce Hunsberger, "An Intergroup Perspective on Religion and Prejudice," *Journal for the Scientific Study of Religion* 38, no. 4 [1999]: 509–23; C. Daniel Batson, "Religion as Prosocial: Agent or Double Agent," *Journal for the Scientific Study of Religion* [March 1976]: 29–45; Glenn A. E. Griffin, Richard L. Gorsuch, and Andrea-Lee Davis, "A Cross-Cultural Investigation of Religious Orientation, Social Norms, and Prejudice," *Journal for the Scientific Study of Religion* [September 1987]: 358–65) but not enough empirical work to define an easy positive relationship between Christian beliefs and racism. Furthermore, recent discussions of a quest Christian religiosity and racism suggest that certain Christians may be less racist than the general public (Duck and Hunsberger, "Religious Orientation and Prejudice"; Deborah L. Hall, David C. Matz, and Wendy Wood, "Why Don't We Practice What We Preach? A Meta-analytic Review of Religious Racism," *Personality and Social Psychology Review* 14, no. 1 [2010]: 126–39).

28. Gregory B. Lewis, "Black-White Differences in Attitudes towards Homosexuality and Gay Rights," *Public Opinion Quarterly* 67, no. 1 (2003): 59–78; Louis Bonilla and Judith Porter, "A Comparison of Latino, Black, and Non-Hispanic White Attitudes towards Homosexuality," *Hispanic Journal of Behavioral Sciences* 12, no. 4 (1990): 437–52; Linda M. Chatters et al., "Spirituality and Subjective Religiosity among African Americans, Caribbean Blacks, and Non-Hispanic Whites," *Journal for the Scientific Study of Religion* 47, no. 4 (2008): 725–37; Christopher Ellison, Samuel Echevarria, and Brad Smith, "Religion and Abortion Attitudes among U.S. Hispanics: Findings from the 1990 Latino National Political Survey," *Social Science Quarterly* 86, no. 1 (2005): 192–208; Emily W. Kane, "Racial and Ethnic Variation in Gender-Related Attitudes," *Annual Review of Sociology* 26 (2000): 419–39; George H. Gallup and D. Michael Lindsay, *Surveying the Religious Landscape: Trends in U.S. Belief* (Harrisburg, PA: Morehouse, 1999).

29. George Yancey, *Compromising Scholarship: Religious and Political Bias in American Higher Education* (Waco, TX: Baylor University Press, 2011).

30. George E. Haggerty, "Teaching Tolerance: Introduction," *ADFL Bulletin* 31, no. 1 (1999): 36–37.

31. Ali Unsal, "Religious Tolerance (Tolerance in Islam)," paper presented at the 4th International Conference of the Asian Philosophical Association, Depok, Indonesia, November 4–6, 2009.

32. Lilia I. Bartolome and Donaldo P. Macedo, "Dancing with Bigotry: The Poisoning of Racial and Ethnic Identities," *Harvard Educational Review* 67, no. 2 (2009): 222–47; Hans Oberdiek, *Tolerance: Between Forbearance and Acceptance* (Lanham, MD: Rowman & Littlefield, 2001); Charles E. Bailey, "A General Theory of Psychological Relativity and Cognitive Evolution," *ETC: A Review of General Semantics* 63, no. 3 (2006): 278–89.

33. Joseph K. Neumann, William Thompson, and Thomas W. Woolley, "Evangelical vs. Liberal Christianity: The Influence of Values on the Nonclinical Professional Decisions of Social Workers," *Journal of Psychology and Christianity* 11, no. 1 (1992): 57–67; Louis Bolce and Gerald De Maio, "A Prejudice for the Thinking Classes," *American Politics Research* 36, no. 2 (2008): 155–85; George Yancey, "Who Has Religious Prejudice? Differing Sources of Antireligious Animosity in the United States," *Review of Religious Research* 52, no. 2 (December 2010): 159–71; John D. Gartner, "Antireligious Prejudice in Admission to Doctoral Programs in Clinical Psychology," *Professional Psychology: Research and Practice* 17, no. 5 (1986): 473–75.

6. WHAT DO PEOPLE WITH
ANTI-CHRISTIAN ANIMOSITY WANT?

1. Susan Opotow, "Moral Exclusion and Injustice: An Introduction," *Journal of Social Issues* 46, no. 1 (1990): 1–20; F. Chalk and K. Jonassohn, *The History and Sociology of Genocide: Analyses and Case Studies* (New Haven, CT: Yale University Press, 1990); H. C. Kelman, "Violence without Restraint: Reflections on the Dehumanization of Victims and Victimizers," in *Varieties of Psychohistory*, ed. G. M. Kren and L. H. Rappoport, 282–314 (New York: Springer, 1976).

2. It is not clear whether conservative Christians do outnumber those with anti-Christian antipathy. As we saw in our ANES data, a little under a third of all Americans technically have disaffection toward conservative Christians. Given that the percentage of individuals who state that they are born-again, according to the weighted 2012 ANES data, is 33.1, we can argue that the groups are roughly equal in size. However, we are not sure of the percentage of those individuals having the type of hostility exhibited in our qualitative research. Thus, ultimately, the relative numbers of born-again individuals, who may be thought of as conservative Christians, and individuals with the type of anti-Christian hostilities exhibited in this book are uncertain.

3. Lawrence Bobo, "White Opposition to Busing: Symbolic Racism or Realistic Group Conflict," *Journal of Personality and Social Psychology* 45, no. 6 (1983): 1196–210; David O. Sears, "Symbolic Racism," in *Eliminating Racism: Profiles in Controversy*, ed. Phyllis A. Katz and Dalams A. Taylor, 55–58 (Plenum Press: New York, 1988); John B. McConahay, "Modern Racism," in *Prejudice, Discrimination and Racism*, ed. John F. Dovidio and Samuel L. Gaertner (Orlando, FL: Academic, 1986).

4. Samuel L. Gaertner and John F. Dovidio, "Prejudice, Discrimination, and Racism: Problems, Progress, and Promise," in *Prejudice, Discrimination and Racism: Theory and Research*, ed. Samuel L. Gaertner (New York: Academic Press, 1986); Maria Krysan, "Privacy and the Expression of White Racial Attitudes: A Comparison across Three Contexts," *Public Opinion Quarterly* 62 (1998): 506–44; Sears, "Symbolic Racism."

5. George Yancey, *Compromising Scholarship: Religious and Political Bias in American Higher Education* (Waco, TX: Baylor University Press, 2011).

6. Matt Recla, "Anti-Christian Bias in Academia Is Responsible for Religious Bigotry. Part Two . . . ," *Even the Bravest* . . . , June 26, 2013, http://www.mattrecla.com/2013/06/26/anti-christian-bias-in-academia-is-responsible-for-religious-bigotry-part-two.

7. It should be noted that although it is true that Christians may bring biases into their work, the same can be said for members of other social groups (e.g., Southerners, feminists, Catholics, environmentalists). The focus on the potential of conservative Christians to exhibit bias, to the exclusion of other social groups, may be an important way anti-Christian sentiment manifests itself.

8. Exactly 170 respondents (15.3 percent) who exhibited anti-Christian animosity discussed a desire to limit the tax-exempt status of Christian churches.

9. Stephen L. Carter, *The Culture of Disbelief: How American Law and Politics Trivialize Religious Devotion* (New York: Basic Books, 1993).

10. J. Richardson, "A Critique of 'Brainwashing' Claims about New Religious Movements," in *Cults and New Religious Movements: A Reader*, ed. Lorne L. Dawson (Malden, MA: Blackwell Publishing, 2007); Dick Anthony and Thomas Robbins, "Conversion and 'Brainwashing' in New Religion Movements," in *The Oxford Handbook of New Religious Movements*, ed. James R. Lewis (New York: Oxford University Press, 2004).

11. Many with anti-Christian animosity have a desire to escape all religious influence. Their focus on Christianity may be the natural consequence of the fact that they currently dwell in a society where Christianity is the dominant religion.

12. Paul W. Vogt, *Tolerance and Education: Learning to Live with Diversity and Difference* (Thousand Oaks, CA: Sage, 1997); Marcel Coenders and Peer Scheepers, "The Effect of Education on Nationalism and Ethnic Exclusionism: An International Comparison," *Political Psychology* 24, no. 2 (2003): 313–43; Lawrence Bobo and Frederick C. Licari, "Education and Political Tolerance: Testing the Effects of Cognitive Sophistication and Target Groups Affect," *Public Opinion Quarterly* 53 (1989): 285–308.

13. Michael O. Emerson and David Sikkink, "School Choice and Racial Residential Segregation in U.S. Schools: The Role of Parent's Education," *Ethnic and Racial Studies* 31, no. 2 (2008): 267–93; see also Richard T. Schaefer, "Education and Prejudice: Unraveling the Relationship," *Sociological Quarterly* 37 (1996): 1–16.

14. Sears, "Symbolic Racism"; David R. Kinder and Lynn M. Sanders, *Divided by Color: Racial Politics and Democratic Ideals* (Chicago: University of Chicago Press, 1996); John B. McConahay and Joseph C. Hough Jr., "Symbolic Racism," *Journal of Social Issues* 32, no. 2 (1976): 23–45.

7. CHRISTIANOPHOBIA IN THE UNITED STATES

1. Malcolm Evans, "Advancing Freedom of Religion or Belief: Agendas for Change," *Oxford Journal of Law and Religion* 1, no. 1 (2012): 5–14; Ekmeleddin Ihsanoglu, "Islamophobia and Terrorism: Impediments to the Culture of Peace," *Arches Quarterly* 4, no. 7 (2010): 11–13; Natan Lerner, "Do Religion and Human Rights Interact," *International Journal on Minority and Group Rights* 15, no. 2–3 (2008): 403–11; Nazila Ghanea, "'Phobias' and 'Isms': Recognition of Difference or the Slippery Slope of Particularism?" in *Does God Believe in Human Rights?* edited by Nazila Ghanea, Alan Stephens, and Raphael Walden, 211–32 (Boston: Brill, 2007).

2. Rupert Shortt, *Christianophobia: A Faith under Attack* (Grand Rapids, MI: William B. Eerdmans Publishing Co., 2013).

3. This reinforces our speculation in chapter 1 that animosity to conservative Christians may serve to blunt possible animosity toward other Christians since the conservative Christians are seen as the immediate threat. Clearly the number of respondents who dismissed all Christians is lower than the number of those who dismissed only conservative Christians. Yet individuals with animosity toward Christians in general do exist, and it is beyond the scope of this current research to assess how closely the features of that hostility parallel the hostility expressed toward conservative Christians.

4. It may be better to talk about a racialized society instead of racism (Michael Omi and Howard Winant, *Racial Formation in the United States: From the 1960s to the 1990s*, 2nd ed. [New York: Routledge, 1994]; Eduardo Bonilla-Silva, *Racism without Racists: Color-Blind Racism and the Persistence of Racial Inequality in the United States* [Lanham, MD: Rowman & Littlefield, 2006]). Some tend to dismiss a charge of racism unless it is accompanied by pictures of the Ku Klux Klan. However, few people deny that our society is racialized and that race plays a role in shaping our lives. But whether we talk about racism or a racialized society, our basic argument is still that certain aspects of our society cannot be fully understood without acknowledging the importance of racial effects.

5. It should be noted that academics are more likely to fall victim to other types of bigotry than Christianophobia. For example, a female scholar may still experience sexism regardless of her academic success. Thus she may become motivated to conduct research on sexism. However, it is well established that conservative Christians are highly underrepresented in academia (Elaine H. Ecklund, Jerry Z. Park, and Phil T. Veliz, "Secularization and Religious Change among Elite Scientists," *Social Forces* 86, no. 4 [2008]: 1805–40; Edward J. Larson and Larry Witham, "Leading Scientists Still Reject God," *Nature* 394, no, 6691 [1998]: 313). Thus, relatively few academics have experienced Christianophobia relative to other forms of bigotry.

6. David H. Weaver et al., *The American Journalist in the 21st Century: U.S. News People at the Dawn of a New Millennium* (Mahwah, NJ: Taylor & Francis, 2007).

7. Since Christianophobia appears to be tied to higher levels of education, we could have searched the Internet to locate comments from professors and others in higher education, like the ones from Timothy Shortell, sociology professor at Brooklyn College, who stated, "It is no wonder, then, that those who are religious are incapable of moral action, just as children are. To be moral requires that one accept full responsibility for one's self. Morality is based on scientific rationality." We have chosen the media personality route for two reasons. First, readers are more likely to have heard about the media personalities and to appreciate the impact of their sentiments. Second, previous work by one of us has already documented religious biases among those in academia (George Yancey, *Compromising Scholarship: Religious and Political Bias in American Higher Education* [Waco, TX: Baylor University Press, 2011]). Those interested in investigating the Christianophobia in that arena would do well to look to Yancey's *Compromising Scholarship* for a more systematic study of this problem.

8. A good case of this can be seen in the anti-Semitic comments of Mel Gibson, which were just as hateful as some of the comments here. Note how

quickly his comments were denounced and Gibson was forced to apologize. The different treatment of Gibson's comments and the comments of these media figures helps explain why it is so much easier to find Christianophobia than anti-Semitism expressed by media personalities and pop culture figures.

9. Rachel B. Duke, "Lawsuit Claims School Bias on Christian Views," *Washington Times*, July 26, 2010, http://www.washingtontimes.com/news/2010/jul/26/lawsuit-claims-school-bias-on-christian-views.

10. Simon McCormack, "Dan Savage Speech Controversy: 'It Gets Better' Creator Offends Christian Students," *Huffington Post*, April 28, 2012, http://www.huffingtonpost.com/2012/04/28/dan-savage-speech-controversy_n_1461863.html.

11. Meredith Skrzypczak, "Should It Be Illegal to Post Ad Seeking Christian Roommate?" *Grand Rapids Press*, October 22, 2010, http://www.mlive.com/news/grand-rapids/index.ssf/2010/10/should_it_be_illegal_to_post_a.html.

12. Peter Hegarty, "Christian Students Sue Peralta College District, Saying They Were Disciplined for Praying," *Alameda Journal*, April 9, 2009, http://www.insidebayarea.com/news/ci_12110179.

13. As professors we consider what would embolden us to intervene in the conversation one professor was having with his or her student in his or her office. For example, if we overheard sexual or racial harassment, then we would likely intervene. Verbal abuse of the student by the professor or vice versa might also require intervention. This professor's actions suggest that the action of students praying for a professor is elevated to the level of harassment or abuse. Such a perspective is clearly tied to notions of Christianophobia.

14. Justin Miller, "EMU Sued for Booting Student over Views on Gays," *Michigan Messenger*, April 9. 2009, available at http://www.alliancealert.org/2009/04/09/emu-sued-for-booting-student-over-views-on-gays.

15. Other issues may come into play here. For example, some may argue that teachers' unions have a vested interest in fighting a voucher system since it may decrease the institutional power of their unions. On the other hand, it can also be argued that corporate interests might support such a system for their own materialist desires since it will open up new markets. We consider these to be side issues to the main question about whether saving the public school system warrants the lack of educational choice parents currently have.

16. This is similar to our previous example of how symbolic racism helps to account for potential hostile attitudes toward immigration. If individuals from Central and South American countries were not more likely to enter the country illegally than individuals from Europe, then it would be difficult to argue that there is a racialized component to issues of immigration. Likewise, if there were few or no Christian schools, then it would be difficult to assert that there is a potential Christianophobic aspect to the question of school choice.

17. All of these are issues some respondents brought up in their statements.

18. Ruy Teixeira and Alan Abramowitz, "The Decline of the White Working Class and the Rise of a Mass Upper Middle Class," in *Red, Blue and Purple America: The Future of Election Demographics*, ed. Ruy Teixeira, 109–43 (Washington, DC: Brookings Institute Press, 2008).

19. Clyde Wilcox, "Sources of Support for the Old Right: A Comparison of the John Birch Society and the Christian Anti-communism Crusade," *Social Science History* 12, no. 4 (1988): 429–49; John R. Petrocik, "Party Coalitions, Issue Agendas, and Morality Politics: The 2004 Presidential Election," paper read at *The State of the Parties: 2004 and Beyond*, Akron, Ohio, October 2–5, 2005.

20. Thomas Frank, *What's the Matter with Kansas? How Conservatives Won the Heart of America* (New York: Metropolitan Books, 2004); see also William G. Mayer, *The Changing American Mind: How and Why American Public Opinion Changed between 1960 and 1988* (Ann Arbor: University of Michigan Press, 1992).

21. Amy Adamczyk, "Understanding the Effects of Personal and School Religiosity on the Decision to Abort a Premarital Pregnancy," *Journal of Health and Social Behavior* 50, no. 2 (2009): 180–95; Steven Brint and Seth Abrutyn, "Who's Right about the Right? Comparing Competing Explanations of the Link between White Evangelicals and Conservative Politics in the United States," *Journal for the Scientific Study of Religion* 49, no. 2 (2010): 328–50.

22. Peter Gottschalk and Gabriel Greenberg, *Islamophobia: Making Muslims the Enemy* (Lanham, MD: Rowman & Littlefield, 2008); Jack Bass and Walter De Vries, *The Transformation of Southern Politics: Social Change and Political Consequence since 1945* (Athens: University of Georgia Press, 1995); Frank Brown, "Nixon's 'Southern Strategy' and Forces against Brown," *Journal of Negro Education* 73, no. 3 (2004): 191–208.

23. Ironically, several respondents in our entire sample indicated dismay at what they perceived as conservative Christianity influencing poorer individuals to vote against their own economic interest due to their adherence to their religious and cultural beliefs. If political conservatism provides more economic opportunities for those with higher SES, then many wealthy cultural progressives also vote against their own economic interest. They do so either due to the cultural issues connected to the culture war or because of their antipathy toward conservative Christians. Either way, they may be engaging in the same type of self-defeating economic behavior they perceive in lower-SES Christians.

24. Our explanation illustrates not only why highly educated, wealthy individuals move toward the Democratic Party but also why more Republicans take an uncompromising conservative stance on social issues. Because conser-

vative Christians have become an important constituency within the Republican Party, Republicans can ill afford to insult them with Christianophobia. Christianophobia may be energizing some highly educated, wealthy individuals to engage in political activism. Thus moderate Republicans have to balance the need to attract highly educated and wealthy individuals who exhibit Christianophobia with the need not to alienate conservative Christians who may vote for them. Since white conservative Christians are relatively unlikely to support a Democrat, that candidate does not have to perform such a balancing act and is free to espouse implicit or explicit Christianophobia.

25. Matt A. Batterto, Stephen A. Nuno, and Gabriel R. Sanchez, "Voter ID Requirements and the Disenfranchisements of Latino, Black and Asian Voters," paper presented at the annual meeting of the American Political Science Association, Hyatt Regency Chicago and the Sheraton Chicago Hotel and Towers, Chicago, Illinois, August 30, 2007, http://citation.allacademic.com/meta/p209601_index.html; Rachael V. Cobb, James D. Greiner, and Kevin M. Quinn, "Can Voter ID Laws Be Administered in a Race-Neutral Manner? Evidence from the City of Boston in 2008," *Quarterly Journal of Political Science* 7 (2012): 1–33.

26. Batterto, Nuno, and Sanchez, "Voter ID Requirements"; Jeremiah Goulka, "Playing the Voter ID Card," *Nation*, October 15, 2012, http://www.thenation.com/article/170562/playing-voter-id-card; Jim Rice, "Are Voter-ID Laws Racist?" *Sojourners*, April 2012, http://sojo.net/magazine/2012/04/are-voter-id-laws-racist.

27. Vilna Bashi, "Racial Categories Matter Because Racial Hierarchies Matter: A Commentary," *Ethnic and Racial Studies* 21, no. 5 (1998): 959–68; Eduardo Bonilla-Silva, "Rethinking Racism: Toward a Structural Interpretation," *American Sociological Review* 62, no. 3 (1997): 465–80.

28. Leonard Dinnerstein, *Antisemitism in America* (New York: Oxford University Press, 1994).

29. Yancey, *Compromising Scholarship*.

30. Lauri L. Hyers, "Everyday Discrimination Experienced by Conservative Christians at the Secular University," *Analyses of Social Issues and Public Policy* 8, no. 1 (2008): 113–37; John D. Gartner, "Antireligious Prejudice in Admission to Doctoral Programs in Clinical Psychology," *Professional Psychology: Research and Practice* 17, no. 5 (1986): 473–75.

31. G. Bergenhenegouwen, "Hidden Curriculum in the University," *Higher Education* 16 (1987): 535–43; Margaret LeCompte, "Learning to Work: The Hidden Curriculum of the Classroom," *Anthropology and Education Quarterly* 9, no. 1 (1978): 22–37; John Taylor Gatto, *Dumbing Us Down: The Hidden Curriculum of Compulsory Schooling* (Philadelphia: New Society Publisher,

2005); Wendy Titman, *Special Places, Special People: The Hidden Curriculum of School Grounds* (Toronto, Ontario: Green Brick Road, 1994).

32. Jonel Thaller, "Resilience and Resistance in Professional Identity Making: Gleanings from the Classroom Experiences of Devout Christian Social Workers," *Journal of Religion and Spirituality in Social Work* 30, no. 2 (2011): 144–63; David R. Hodge, "Does Social Work Oppress Evangelical Christians: A 'New Class' Analysis of Society and Social Work," *Social Work* 47 (2002): 401–14.

33. David R. Hodge, "Secular Privilege: Deconstructing the Invisible Rose-Tinted Sunglasses," *Journal of Religion and Spirituality in Social Work* 28, no. 1–2 (2008): 8–34.

34. This is not blind speculation but based on data. Researchers who have talked about symbolic racism have generally done so without direct evidence of a great deal of overt anger or fear directed at African Americans. If our respondents were European Americans talking about African Americans and their communities, we believe, such researchers would eagerly accept the evidence of emotional anger and fear in our qualitative data as evidence of the hostile attitudes some whites have toward blacks, since we document this hostility with straightforward questions. If these researchers could establish this level of hostility on racial issues, then they would likely argue that such hostility expresses itself in symbolic resistance to what African Americans desire. Our speculation is not that anger and fear directed at conservative Christians exist. We have established those sentiments with arguably as least as much evidence as proponents of symbolic racism have adduced to establish emotional anger or fear directed at African Americans. We speculate only about how such anger and fear are manifested in our larger society. We contend that we are farther toward establishing the presence of symbolic actions against conservative Christians than proponents of symbolic racism are toward establishing the existence of this phenomenon in our racialized society due to the level of overt hostility we document relative to the level of overt racial hostility documented in contemporary research.

35. Matthew C. Moen, *The Transformation of the Christian Right* (Tuscaloosa: University of Alabama Press, 1992); Clyde Wilcox, *God's Warriors: The Christian Right in Twentieth-Century America* (Baltimore: Johns Hopkins University Press, 1992); Clyde Wilcox and Carin Larson, *Onward Christian Soldiers? The Religious Right in American Politics* (Boulder, CO: Westview Press, 2006).

36. George Yancey and David Williamson, *What Motivates Cultural Progressives: Understanding Opposition to the Political and Christian Right* (Waco, TX: Baylor University Press, 2012).

37. Mitch Berbrier, "Assimilation and Pluralism as Cultural Tools," *Sociological Forum* 19, no. 1 (2004): 29–61; Thomas B. Edsall, *Building Red America: The New Conservative Coalition and the Drive for Permanent Power* (New York: Basic Books, 2006); Allan J. Lichtman, *White Protestant Nation: The Rise of the American Conservative Movement* (New York: Grove Press, 2009); H. Michael Crowson, "Are All Conservatives Alike? A Study of the Psychological Correlates of Cultural and Economic Conservatism," *Journal of Psychology: Interdisciplinary and Applied* 143, no. 5 (2009): 449–63.

8. CONCLUSION

1. For more information on that situation, see Annalisa Musarra, "Vanderbilt Christian Groups, Citing Religious Freedom, Follow Catholics Off Campus," *Huffington Post*, April 10, 2012, http://www.huffingtonpost.com/2012/04/10/vanderbilt-religious-groups_n_1416561.html; Michael Paulson, "Colleges and Evangelicals Collide on Bias Policy," *New York Times*, June 9, 2014, http://www.nytimes.com/2014/06/10/us/colleges-and-evangelicals-collide-on-bias-policy.html?_r=0.

2. Research done by one of us, which shows through a hypothetical case that individuals with a propensity to dehumanize Christians are also likely to recommend harsh punishment for a Christian couple accused of homophobia, strengthens this point (George Yancey, *Dehumanizing Christians* [Piscataway, NJ: Transaction Publishers, 2013]). While the operationalization of dehumanization used in that research is different from the operationalization of Christianophobia in this research, the politically progressive non-Christians who scored high in the dehumanization scale would be relatively likely to be found to be Christianophobic using this research design.

3. Keith A. Roberts, "Sociology in the General Education Curriculum: A Cognitive Structuralist Perspective," *Teaching Sociology* 14, no. 4 (1986): 207–16; see also Christian M. Itin, "Reasserting the Philosophy of Experiential Education as a Vehicle for Change in the 21st Century," *Journal of Distance Education* 22, no. 2 (1999): 91–98; Maurianne Adams, "Charting Cognitive and Moral Development in Diversity Classes," *Diversity Digest* 6, no. 1/2 (2002): 21–23.

4. David Gillman, *Racism and Antiracism in Real Schools* (Bristol, PA: Open University Press, 1995); Kim A. Case, "Raising Male Privilege Awareness and Reducing Sexism: An Evaluation of Diversity Courses," *Psychology of Women Quarterly* 31, no. 4 (2007): 426–35; Lester W. Wright, Henry E. Adams, and Jeffery A. Bernat, "The Homophobia Scale: Development and Validation," *Journal of Psychopathology and Behavioral Assessment* 21 (1999):

337–47; Daniel K. Cho, "Adorno on Education or, Can Critical Self-Reflection Prevent the Next Auschwitz?" *Historical Materialism* 17, no. 1 (2009): 74–97; Marcel Coenders and Peer Scheepers, "The Effect of Education on Nationalism and Ethnic Exclusionism: An International Comparison," *Political Psychology* 24, no. 2 (2003): 313–43; Stuart Oskamp, *Reducing Prejudice and Discrimination* (Mahwah, NJ: Lawrence Erlbaum Associates, 2000).

5. Michael O. Emerson and David Sikkink, "School Choice and Racial Residential Segregation in U.S. Schools: The Role of Parent's Education," *Ethnic and Racial Studies* 31, no. 2 (2008): 267–93.

6. N. Daneshvary, C. J. Waddoups, and B. S. Wimmer, "Educational Attainment and the Lesbian Wage Premium," *Journal of Labor Research* 29, no. 4 (2008): 365–79; William Sander, "Religious Background and Educational Attainment: The Effects of Buddhism, Islam, and Judaism," *Economics of Education Review* 29, no. 3 (2009): 489–93; Ali M. Ahmed and Mats Hammarstedt, "Sexual Orientation and Earnings: A Register Data-Based Approach to Identify Homosexuals," *Journal of Population Economics* 23, no. 3 (2010): 835–49.

7. One of us used these findings to construct and test an index of Christian dehumanization (Yancey, *Dehumanizing Christians*). We envision this as an initial step in what we hope will be continuing research into the nature of Christianophobia.

8. Such speculation is not limited to assertions about Christianophobia. Paul M. Sniderman and Philip E. Tetlock ("Symbolic Racism: Problems of Motive Attribution in Political Analysis," *Journal of Social Issues* 42 [1986]: 129–50) have pointed out the difficulty of attributing racist motivation to the attitudes of European Americans. Likewise, we can only speculate about Christianophobic motivations. However, in our qualitative research some respondents have spoken freely of their hatred of conservative Protestants, giving us more confidence that Christianophobia forms part of the motivation behind the examples in the last chapter.

9. For example, Carols A. Ball, "Is It Possible to Be against Same-Sex Marriage without Being Homophobic?" *Huffington Post*, November 9, 2010, http://www.huffingtonpost.com/carlos-a-ball/is-it-possible-to-be-again_b_692187.html; Ladoris Cordell, "Proposition 8 vs. Black Homophobia," *Salon*, October 30, 2008, http://www.salon.com/2008/10/30/proposition_8_2; Christopher Lisotta, "Homophobia of All Hues: The Marriage-Equality Movement Confronts Antigay Sentiment among Blacks," *Nation*, May 17, 2004, 15–17.

10. Jong Hyun Jung ("Islamophobia? Religion, Contact with Muslims, and the Respect for Islam," *Review of Religious Research* 54, no. 1 [2012]: 113–26) conducts research with a national probability sample but focuses on respect for

Islam, which may be influenced by Islamophobia, rather than Islamophobia itself.

11. However, this does not mean that violence against Christians for their religious beliefs never occurs in the United States. The mass killings at Wedgwood Baptist Church in 1999 illustrate this possibility.

12. Keith Gunnar Bentele et al., "Breaking Down the Wall between Church and State: Adoption of Religious Inclusion Legislation, 1995–2009," *Church and State* 55, no. 3 (2013): http://jcs.oxfordjournals.org/content/early/2013/01/28/jcs.css145.full; D. Michael Lindsay, *Faith in the Halls of Power* (New York: Oxford University Press, 2007).

13. John D. Gartner, "Antireligious Prejudice in Admission to Doctoral Programs in Clinical Psychology," *Professional Psychology: Research and Practice* 17, no. 5 (1986): 473–75; Lauri L. Hyers, "Everyday Discrimination Experienced by Conservative Christians at the Secular University," *Analyses of Social Issues and Public Policy* 8, no. 1 (2008): 113–37; George Yancey, *Compromising Scholarship: Religious and Political Bias in American Higher Education* (Waco, TX: Baylor University Press, 2011).

APPENDIX A

1. However, it should be noted that those who did not fill out all of the thermometer questions tended to be younger, less educated, poorer, male, white, and less likely to believe the Bible is the word of God than the other respondents. We also found that those who did not fill out all of the thermometer questions were more likely to rank religious groups lower than other respondents with the exception of atheists. These respondents rated Asians higher than average but blacks lower than average and were not significantly different from other respondents in their ratings of whites and Hispanics. If we had been able to include them in our sample, their presence would have likely depressed the percentage of anti-atheists but not necessarily of anti-fundamentalists, anti-Muslims, or anti-Mormons. In fact, it is possible that their inclusion would have increased the percentage of the sample in the latter three groups.

2. We did not tell the leaders about our own religious preferences. This reduced possible social-desirability biases among respondents attempting to placate our personal religious beliefs.

3. We allowed the organizations to send the survey out to their members. That helped the organizations ensure the privacy of the contact information of their members. However, that also meant that we could not completely control how they introduced the survey to respondents. We asked them to inform respondents that we were two researchers interested in studying cultural pro-

gressives, and we have little reason to believe that they did not basically introduce the survey in this way. But we have no way of confirming that.

　　4. This is a dummy variable where respondents who indicated that they were atheist or agnostic were coded as 1.

REFERENCES

Adamczyk, Amy. 2009. "Understanding the Effects of Personal and School Religiosity on the Decision to Abort a Premarital Pregnancy." *Journal of Health and Social Behavior* 50, no. 2: 180–95.

Adams, Maurianne. 2002. "Charting Cognitive and Moral Development in Diversity Classes." *Diversity Digest* 6, no. 1/2: 21–23.

Ahmed, Ali M., and Mats Hammarstedt. 2010. "Sexual Orientation and Earnings: A Register Data-Based Approach to Identify Homosexuals." *Journal of Population Economics* 23, no. 3: 835–49.

Allen, Irving L. 1990. *Unkind Words: Ethnic Labeling from Redskin to WASP*. New York: Bergin & Garvey.

Allen, Theodore W. 1997. *The Invention of the White Race: The Origin of Racial Oppression in Anglo-America*. Edited by Ernest Cashmore and James Jennings. New York: Verso.

Allport, Gordon. 1958. *The Nature of Prejudice*. New York: Anchor.

———. 1966. "The Religious Context of Prejudice." *Journal for the Scientific Study of Religion* (fall): 447–57.

Almaguer, Tomás. 2009. *Racial Fault Lines: The Historical Origins of White Supremacy in California*. Berkeley: University of California Press.

Altemeyer, Bob. 2007. *The Authoritarians*. Manitoba, Canada: Bob Altemeyer.

Ana, Otto S. 1994. "Like an Animal I Was Treated: Anti-immigrant Metaphor in U.S. Public Discourse." *Discourse and Society* 10: 191–224.

Anspach, Whitney, Kevin Coe, and Crispin Thurlow. 2007. "The Other Closet? Atheists, Homosexuals and the Lateral Appropriation of Discursive Capital." *Critical Discourse Studies* 4, no. 1: 95–119.

Antecol, H., A. Jong, and M. Steinberger. 2008. "The Sexual Orientation Wage Gap: The Role of Occupational Sorting and Human Capital." *Industrial and Labor Relations Review* 61, no. 4: 518–43.

Anthony, Dick, and Thomas Robbins. 2004. "Conversion and 'Brainwashing' in New Religion Movements." In *The Oxford Handbook of New Religious Movements*, edited by James R. Lewis, 243–97. New York: Oxford University Press.

Baier, Colin, and Bradley R. E. Wright. 2001. "'If You Love Me, Keep My Commandments': A Meta Analysis of the Effect of Religion on Crime." *Journal of Research in Crime and Delinquency* 38: 3–21.

Bailey, Charles E. 2006. "A General Theory of Psychological Relativity and Cognitive Evolution." *ETC: A Review of General Semantics* 63, no. 3: 278–89.

Bain, P., J. Park, C. Kwok, and N. Haslam. 2009. "Attributing Human Uniqueness and Human Nature to Cultural Groups: Distinct Forms of Subtle Dehumanization." *Group Processes and Intergroup Relations* 12, no. 6: 789–805.

Ball, Carols A. 2010. "Is It Possible to Be against Same-Sex Marriage without Being Homophobic?" *Huffington Post*, November 9, http://www.huffingtonpost.com/carlos-a-ball/is-it-possible-to-be-again_b_692187.html.

Barbour, Ian G. 1997. *Religion and Science: Historical and Contemporary Issues*. San Francisco: Harper Publishers.

Barnard, William A., and Mark S. Benn. 1988. "Belief Congruence and Prejudice and Ethnic Relations." *Journal of Social Psychology* 128 (February): 125–34.

Barry, Stephanie. 2013. "Pioneer Valley Performing Arts Public School Presses On with Gay Biblical Satire Despite Threats of Protests." *Republican*, March 7, http://www.masslive.com/news/index.ssf/2013/03/school_presses_on_with_gay_bib.html.

Bartolome, Lilia I., and Donaldo P. Macedo. 2009. "Dancing with Bigotry: The Poisoning of Racial and Ethnic Identities." *Harvard Educational Review* 67, no. 2: 222–47.

Bashi, Vilna. 1998. "Racial Categories Matter Because Racial Hierarchies Matter: A Commentary." *Ethnic and Racial Studies* 21, no. 5: 959–68.

Bass, Jack, and Walter De Vries. 1995. *The Transformation of Southern Politics: Social Change and Political Consequence since 1945*. Athens: University of Georgia Press.

Batson, C. Daniel. 1976. "Religion as Prosocial: Agent or Double Agent." *Journal for the Scientific Study of Religion* (March): 29–45.

Batson, C. Daniel, and E. L. Stocks. 2005. "Religion and Prejudice." In *On the Nature of Prejudice: Fifty Years after Allport*, edited by John F. Dovidio, Peter Glick, and Laurie A. Rudman, 413–28. Malden, MA: Blackwell Publishing.

Batterto, Matt A., Stephen A. Nuno, and Gabriel R. Sanchez. 2007. "Voter ID Requirements and the Disenfranchisements of Latino, Black and Asian Voters." Paper presented at the annual meeting of the American Political Science Association, Hyatt Regency Chicago and the Sheraton Chicago Hotel and Towers, Chicago, Illinois, August 30, http://citation.allacademic.com/meta/p209601_index.html.

Ben-Zeev, Aaron. 1992. "Anger and Hate." *Journal of Social Philosophy* 2: 85–110.

Bentele, Keith Gunnar, Rebecca Sager, Sarah A. Soule, and Gary Adler Jr. 2013. "Breaking Down the Wall between Church and State: Adoption of Religious Inclusion Legislation, 1995–2009." *Church and State* 55, no. 3: http://jcs.oxfordjournals.org/content/early/2013/01/28/jcs.css145.full.

Berbrier, Mitch. 2004. "Assimilation and Pluralism as Cultural Tools." *Sociological Forum* 19, no. 1: 29–61.

Bergenhenegouwen, G. 1987. "Hidden Curriculum in the University." *Higher Education* 16: 535–43.

Berger, David. 1997. *History and Hate: The Dimensions of Anti-Semitism*. Philadelphia: Jewish Publication Society.

Berger, Peter L. 1974. *Pyramids of Sacrifice: Political Ethics and Social Change*. Garden City, NY: Anchor Books.

Black, Dan A., Gary Gates, Seth G. Sanders, and Lowell J. Taylor. 2002. *The Measurement of Same-Sex Unmarried Couples in the 2000 U.S. Census*. Los Angeles: California Center for Population Research.

Black, Dan A., Hoda R. Makar, Seth G. Sanders, and Lowell J. Taylor. 2003. "The Earning Effects of Sexual Orientation." *Industrial and Labor Relations Review* 56, no. 3: 449–69.

Bobo, Lawrence. 1983. "White Opposition to Busing: Symbolic Racism or Realistic Group Conflict." *Journal of Personality and Social Psychology* 45, no. 6: 1196–210.

Bobo, Lawrence, and Frederick C. Licari. 1989. "Education and Political Tolerance: Testing the Effects of Cognitive Sophistication and Target Groups Affect." *Public Opinion Quarterly* 53: 285–308.

Bolce, Louis, and Gerald De Maio. 2008. "A Prejudice for the Thinking Classes." *American Politics Research* 36, no. 2: 155–85.

Bonilla, Louis, and Judith Porter. 1990. "A Comparison of Latino, Black, and Non-Hispanic White Attitudes towards Homosexuality." *Hispanic Journal of Behavioral Sciences* 12, no. 4: 437–52.

Bonilla-Silva, Eduardo. 1997. "Rethinking Racism: Toward a Structural Interpretation." *American Sociological Review* 62, no. 3: 465–80.

————. 2006. *Racism without Racists: Color-Blind Racism and the Persistence of Racial Inequality in the United States.* Lanham, MD: Rowman & Littlefield.

Brint, Steven, and Seth Abrutyn. 2010. "Who's Right about the Right? Comparing Competing Explanations of the Link between White Evangelicals and Conservative Politics in the United States." *Journal for the Scientific Study of Religion* 49, no. 2: 328–50.

Brown, Frank. 2004. "Nixon's 'Southern Strategy' and Forces against Brown." *Journal of Negro Education* 73, no. 3: 191–208.

Capozza, Dora, Giulio Boccato, Luca Andrighetto, and Rossella Falvo. 2009. "Categorization of Ambiguous Human/Ape Faces: Protection of Ingroup but Not Outgroup Humanity." *Group Processes and Intergroup Relations* 12, no. 6: 777–87.

Carter, Stephen L. 1993. *The Culture of Disbelief: How American Law and Politics Trivialize Religious Devotion.* New York: Basic Books.

Case, Kim A. 2007. "Raising Male Privilege Awareness and Reducing Sexim: An Evaluation of Diversity Courses." *Psychology of Women Quarterly* 31, no. 4: 426–35.

Chalk, F., and K. Jonassohn. 1990. *The History and Sociology of Genocide: Analyses and Case Studies.* New Haven, CT: Yale University Press.

Chatters, Linda M., Robert J. Taylor, Kai M. Bullard, and James S. Jackson. 2008. "Spirituality and Subjective Religiosity among African Americans, Caribbean Blacks, and Non-Hispanic Whites." *Journal for the Scientific Study of Religion* 47, no. 4: 725–37.

Checinski, Michael. 1982. *Poland: Communism, Nationalism, Anti-Semitism.* New York: Karz-Cohl Publishing.

Cho, Daniel K. 2009. "Adorno on Education or, Can Critical Self-Reflection Prevent the Next Auschwitz?" *Historical Materialism* 17, no. 1: 74–97.

Cobb, Rachael V., James D. Greiner, and Kevin M. Quinn. 2012. "Can Voter ID Laws Be Administered in a Race-Neutral Manner? Evidence from the City of Boston in 2008." *Quarterly Journal of Political Science* 7: 1–33.

Coenders, Marcel, and Peer Scheepers. 2003. "The Effect of Education on Nationalism and Ethnic Exclusionism: An International Comparison." *Political Psychology* 24, no. 2: 313–43.

Cordell, Ladoris. 2008. "Proposition 8 vs. Black Homophobia." *Salon*, October 30, http://www.salon.com/2008/10/30/proposition_8_2.

Crowson, H. Michael. 2009. "Are All Conservatives Alike? A Study of the Psychological Correlates of Cultural and Economic Conservatism." *Journal of Psychology: Interdisciplinary and Applied* 143, no. 5: 449–63.

Daneshvary, N., C. J. Waddoups, and B. S. Wimmer. 2008. "Educational Attainment and the Lebian Wage Premium." *Journal of Labor Research* 29, no. 4: 365–79.

Dinnerstein, Leonard. 1994. *Antisemitism in America.* New York: Oxford University Press.

Duck, Robert J., and Bruce Hunsberger. 1999. "Religious Orientation and Prejudice: The Role of Religious Proscription, Right-Wing Authoritarianism, and Social Desirability." *International Journal for the Pscyhology of Religion* 9, no. 3: 157–79.

Duke, Rachel B. 2010. "Lawsuit Claims School Bias on Christian Views." *Washington Times*, July 26, http://www.washingtontimes.com/news/2010/jul/26/lawsuit-claims-school-bias-on-christian-views.

Durkheim, Emile. 1915. *The Elementary Forms of the Religious Life.* New York: Allen and Unwin.

Ecklund, Elaine H., Jerry Z. Park, and Phil T. Veliz. 2008. "Secularization and Religious Change among Elite Scientists." *Social Forces* 86, no. 4: 1805–40.

Edgell, Penny, Joseph Gerteis, and Douglas Hartmann. 2006. "Atheists as 'Other': Moral Boundaries and Cultural Membership in American Society." *American Sociological Review* 71, no. 2: 211–34.

Edsall, Thomas B. 2006. *Building Red America: The New Conservative Coalition and the Drive for Permanent Power*. New York: Basic Books.

Ellis, R. A., and R. A. Calvo. 2004. "Learning through Discussions in Blended Environments." *Educational Media International* 41, no. 3: 263–74.

Ellison, Christopher, Samuel Echevarria, and Brad Smith. 2005. "Religion and Abortion Attitudes among U.S. Hispanics: Findings from the 1990 Latino National Political Survey." *Social Science Quarterly* 86, no. 1: 192–208.

Elster, Jon. 1999. *Alchemies of the Mind: Rationality and the Emotions*. Cambridge: Cambridge University Press.

Emerson, Michael O., and David Sikkink. 2008. "School Choice and Racial Residential Segregation in U.S. Schools: The Role of Parent's Education." *Ethnic and Racial Studies* 31, no. 2: 267–93.

Evans, Malcolm. 2012. "Advancing Freedom of Religion or Belief: Agendas for Change." *Oxford Journal of Law and Religion* 1, no. 1: 5–14.

Evans, T. D., Francis T. Cullen, R. Gregory Dunaway, and Velmer S. Burton. 1995. "Religion and Crime Reexamined: The Impact of Religion, Secular Controls, and Social Ecology on Adult Criminality." *Criminology* 33: 195–224.

Feagin, Joe R. 2006. *Systemic Racism: A Theory of Oppression*. New York: Taylor & Francis Group.

Ferber, Abby L. 2007. "The Construction of Black Masculinity: White Supremacy Now and Then." *Sport and Social Issues* 34, no. 3: 11–24.

Fishbein, Harold D. 2002. *Peer Prejudice and Discrimination: The Origins of Prejudice*. Mahwah, NJ: Lawrence Erlbaum Associates.

Frank, Thomas. 2004. *What's the Matter with Kansas? How Conservatives Won the Heart of America*. New York: Metropolitan Books.

Fulton, Aubyn S., Richard L. Gorsuch, and Elizabeth A. Maynard. 1999. "Religious Orientation, Antihomosexual Sentiment, and Fundamentalism among Christians." *Journal for the Scientific Study of Religion* 38, no. 1: 14–22.

Gaertner, Samuel L., and John F. Dovidio. 1986. "Prejudice, Discrimination, and Racism: Problems, Progress, and Promise." In *Prejudice, Discrimination and Racism: Theory and Research*, edited by John F. Dovidio and Samuel L. Gaertner, 315–32. New York: Academic Press.

Gager, John G. 1983. *The Origins of Anti-Semitism: Attitudes toward Judaism in Pagan and Christian Antiquity*. New York: Oxford University Press.

Gallup, George H., and D. Michael Lindsay. 1999. *Surveying the Religious Landscape: Trends in U.S. Belief*. Harrisburg, PA: Morehouse.

Gartner, John D. 1986. "Antireligious Prejudice in Admission to Doctoral Programs in Clinical Psychology." *Professional Psychology: Research and Practice* 17, no. 5: 473–75.

Gatto, John Taylor. 2005. *Dumbing Us Down: The Hidden Curriculum of Compulsory Schooling*. Philadelphia: New Society Publisher.

Gervais, Will M. 2008. *Do You Believe in Atheists? Trust and Anti-atheist Prejudice*. Master's thesis, University of British Columbia, Vancouver.

Ghanea, Nazila. 2007. "'Phobias' and 'Isms': Recognition of Difference or the Slippery Slope of Particularism?" In *Does God Believe in Human Rights?* edited by Nazila Ghanea, Alan Stephens, and Raphael Walden, 211–32. Boston: Brill.

Gibbs, Jack P. 1989. *Control: Sociology's Central Notion*. Urbana-Champaign: University of Illinois Press.

Gillman, David. 1995. *Racism and Antiracism in Real Schools*. Bristol, PA: Open University Press.

Gorsuch, Richard L., and Daniel Aleshire. 1974. "Christian Faith and Ethnic Prejudice: A Review and Interpretation of Research." *Journal for the Scientific Study of Religion* (September): 281–307.

Gossett, Thomas F. 1965. *Race*. New York: Schocken Books.

Gottschalk, Peter, and Gabriel Greenberg. 2008. *Islamophobia: Making Muslims the Enemy*. Lanham, MD: Rowman & Littlefield.

Goulka, Jeremiah. 2012. "Playing the Voter ID Card." *Nation*, October 15, http://www.thenation.com/article/170562/playing-voter-id-card.

Griffin, Glenn A. E., Richard L. Gorsuch, and Andrea-Lee Davis. 1987. "A Cross-Cultural Investigation of Religious Orientation, Social Norms, and Prejudice." *Journal for the Scientific Study of Religion* (September): 358–65.

Gustafson, Robert K. 1995. *James Woodrow (1827–1907): Scientist, Theologian, Intellectual Leader*. Lewiston, NY: Mellen Press.

Hagan, J., and W. Rymond-Richmond. 2008. "The Collective Dynamics of Racial Dehumanization and Genocidal Victimization in Darfur." *American Sociological Review* 73, no. 6: 875–902.

Haggerty, George E. 1999. "Teaching Tolerance: Introduction." *ADFL Bulletin* 31, no. 1: 36–37.

Hall, Deborah L., David C. Matz, and Wendy Wood. 2010. "Why Don't We Practice What We Preach? A Meta-analytic Review of Religious Racism." *Personality and Social Psychology Review* 14, no. 1: 126–39.

Halperin, Eran. 2008. "Group-Based Hatred in Intractable Conflict in Israel." *Journal of Conflict Resolution* 52, no. 5: 713–36.

Hara, Noriko, Cutis J. Bonk, and Charoula Angeli. 1998. "Content Analysis of Online Discussion in an Applied Educational Psychology Course." *Instructional Science* 28, no. 2: 115–52.

Harris, Joshua. 2005. *Sex Is Not the Problem (Lust Is): Sexual Purity in a Lust-Saturated World*. Colorado Springs, CO: Multnomah Publishers.

Harris, Lasana T., and Susan T. Fiske. 2006. "Dehumanizing the Lowest of the Low: Neuroimaging Responses to Extreme Out-Groups." *Psychological Science* 17: 847–53.

Hartmann, Douglas, Daniel Winchester, Penny Edgell, and Joseph Gerteis. 2011. "How Americans Understand Racial and Religious Differences." *Sociological Quarterly* 52: 323–45.

Haslam, Nick. 2006. "Dehumanization: An Integrative Review." *Personality and Social Psychology Review* 10, no. 3: 252–64.

Hegarty, Peter. 2009. "Christian Students Sue Peralta College District, Saying They Were Disciplined for Praying." *Alameda Journal*, April 9, http://www.insidebayarea.com/news/ci_12110179.

Heimbach, Daniel R. 2004. *True Sexual Morality: Recovering Biblical Standards for a Culture in Crisis*. Wheaton, IL: Crossway Books.

Hertzberg, Arthur. 1990. *The French Enlightenment and the Jews: The Origins of Modern Anti-Semitism*. New York: Columbia University Press.

Hodge, David R. 2002. "Does Social Work Oppress Evangelical Christians: A 'New Class' Analysis of Society and Social Work." *Social Work* 47: 401–14.

———. 2008. "Secular Privilege: Deconstructing the Invisible Rose-Tinted Sunglasses." *Journal of Religion and Spirituality in Social Work* 28, no. 1–2: 8–34.

Hofstadter, Richard. 1963. *Anti-intellectualism in American Life*. New York: Vintage.

Hollins, Etta R. 1996. *Transforming Curriculum for a Culturally Diverse Society*. Mahwah, NJ: Lawrence Erlbaum Associates.

Holtz, P., and W. Wagner. 2009. "Essentialism and Attribution of Monstrosity in Racist Discourse: Right-Wing Internet Postings about Africans and Jews." *Journal of Community and Applied Social Psychology* 19, no. 6: 411–25.

Hunsberger, Bruce. 1996. "Religious Fundamentalism, Right-Wing Authoritarianism, and Hostility towards Homosexuals in Non-Christian Religious Groups." *International Journal for the Psychology of Religion* 6, no. 1: 39–49.

Hunt, Larry L., and Matthew O. Hunt. 2001. "Race, Region, and Religious Involvement: A Comparison Study of Whites and African Americans." *Social Forces* 80, no. 2: 605–31.

Hunter, J. D. 1991. *Culture War: The Struggle to Define America*. New York: Basic Books.

Hyers, Lauri L. 2008. "Everyday Discrimination Experienced by Conservative Christians at the Secular University." *Analyses of Social Issues and Public Policy* 8, no. 1: 113–37.

Ihsanoglu, Ekmeleddin. 2010. "Islamophobia and Terrorism: Impediments to the Culture of Peace." *Arches Quarterly* 4, no. 7: 11–13.

Itin, Christian M. 1999. "Reasserting the Philosophy of Experiential Education as a Vehicle for Change in the 21st Century." *Journal of Distance Education* 22, no. 2: 91–98.

Jackson, Lynne M., and Bruce Hunsberger. 1999. "An Intergroup Perspective on Religion and Prejudice." *Journal for the Scientific Study of Religion* 38, no. 4: 509–23.

Jenkins, Philip. 2003. *The New Anti-Catholicism: The Last Acceptable Prejudice*. New York: Oxford University Press.

Johnson, Byron R. 2012. *More God, Less Crime*. West Conshohocken, PA: Templeton Press.

Johnson, Byron, Spencer D. Li, David B. Larson, and Michael McCullough. 2000. "A Systematic Review of the Religiosity and Delinquency Literature: A Research Note." *Journal of Contemporary Criminal Justice* 16, no. 1: 32–52.

Jung, Jong Hyun. 2012. "Islamophobia? Religion, Contact with Muslims, and the Respect for Islam." *Review of Religious Research* 54, no. 1: 113–26.

Kalkan, Kerem Ozan, Geoffrey Layman, and Eric M. Uslaner. 2009. "'Band of Others'? Attitudes towards Muslims in Contemporary American Society." *Journal of Politics* 71, no. 3: 1–16.

Kalmar, I. D. 2009. "Anti-Semitism and Islamophobia: The Formation of a Secret." *Human Architecture: Journal of the Sociology of Self-Knowledge* 7, no. 2: 135–44.

Kane, Emily W. 2000. "Racial and Ethnic Variation in Gender-Related Attitudes." *Annual Review of Sociology* 26: 419–39.

Katz, Jacob. 1980. *From Prejudice to Destruction: Anti-Semitism, 1700–1933*. Cambridge, MA: Harvard University Press.

Kelman, H. C. 1976. "Violence without Restraint: Reflections on the Dehumanization of Victims and Victimizers." In *Varieties of psychohistory*, edited by G. M. Kren and L. H. Rappoport, 282–314. New York: Springer.

Kinder, David R., and Lynn M. Sanders. 1996. *Divided by Color: Racial Politics and Democratic Ideals*. Chicago: University of Chicago Press.

Kirkpatrick, Lee A. 1993. "Fundamentalism, Christian Orthodoxy, and Intrinsic Religious Orientation as Predictors of Discriminatory Attitudes." *Journal for the Scientific Study of Religion* (March): 256–68.

Kirschenman, Joleen, and Kathryn M. Neckerman. 1991. "'We'd Love to Hire Them, but . . . ': The Meaning of Race for Employers." In *The Urban Underclass*, edited by Christopher Jencks and Paul Peterson, 203–34. Washington, DC: Brookings Institution.

Krysan, Maria. 1998. "Privacy and the Expression of White Racial Attitudes: A Comparison across Three Contexts." *Public Opinion Quarterly* 62: 506–44.

Kuklinski, James H., and Michael D. Cobb. 1997. "Racial Attitudes and the 'New South.'" *Journal of Politics* 59, no. 2: 323–49.

Larson, Edward J., and Larry Witham. 1998. "Leading Scientists Still Reject God." *Nature* 394, no. 6691: 313.

LeCompte, Margaret. 1978. "Learning to Work: The Hidden Curriculum of the Classroom." *Anthropology and Education Quarterly* 9, no. 1: 22–37.

Lerner, Natan. 2008. "Do Religion and Human Rights Interact." *International Journal on Minority and Group Rights* 15, no. 2–3: 403–11.

Levinger, Lee. 2007. *A History of Jews in the United States*. Rockville, MD: Wildside Press.

Lewis, Gregory B. 2003. "Black-White Differences in Attitudes towards Homosexuality and Gay Rights." *Public Opinion Quarterly* 67, no. 1: 59–78.

Lichtman, Allan J. 2009. *White Protestant Nation: The Rise of the American Conservative Movement*. New York: Grove Press.

Lienesch, Michael. 2007. *In the Beginning: Fundamentalism, the Scopes Trial, and the Making of the Antievolution Movement*. Chapel Hill: University of North Carolina Press.

Lindsay, D. Michael. 2007. *Faith in the Halls of Power*. New York: Oxford University Press.

Lisotta, Christopher. 2004. "Homophobia of All Hues: The Marriage-Equality Movement Confronts Antigay Sentiment among Blacks." *Nation*, May 17, 15–17.

Luguri, Jamie B., Jaime L. Napier, and John F. Dovidio. 2012. "Reconstruing Intolerance: Abstract Thinking Reduces Conservatives' Prejudice against Nonnormative Groups." *Psychological Science* 24, no. 7: 756–63.

Lutzer, Erwin W. 2010. *The Truth about Same Sex Marriage: 6 Things You Need to Know about What's Really at Stake.* Chicago: Moody Publishers.

Maltz, Steve. 2011. *The (Other) F-Word: Faith, the Last Taboo.* Ilford, UK: Saffron Planet.

Martin, William. 2005. *With God on Our Side: The Rise of the Religious Right in America.* New York: Broadway.

Mayer, William G. 1992. *The Changing American Mind: How and Why American Public Opinion Changed between 1960 and 1988.* Ann Arbor: University of Michigan Press.

McConahay, John B. 1986. "Modern Racism, Ambivalence, and the Modern Racism Scale." In *Prejudice, Discrimination and Racism,* edited by John F. Dovidio and Samuel L. Gaertner, 91–125. Orlando, FL: Academic.

McConahay, John B., and Joseph C. Hough Jr. 1976. "Symbolic Racism." *Journal of Social Issues* 32, no. 2: 23–45.

McCormack, Simon. 2012. "Dan Savage Speech Controversy: 'It Gets Better' Creator Offends Christian Students." *Huffington Post,* April 28, http://www.huffingtonpost.com/2012/04/28/dan-savage-speech-controversy_n_1461863.html.

Messerschmidt, James W. 2007. "'We Must Protect Our Southern Women': On Whiteness, Masculinities, and Lynching." In *Race, Gender, and Punishment: From Colonialism to the War on Terror,* edited by Mary Bosworth and Jeanne Flavin, 77–94. Piscataway, NJ: Rutgers University Press.

Midgette, Vianey A. 2008. "The Relationship of Acculturative Stress, Machismo and Self-Esteem as Predictors to Aggression for Latino Males." PhD diss., University of Wisconsin, Madison.

Miller, Justin. 2009. "EMU Sued for Booting Student over Views on Gays." *Michigan Messenger,* April 9. Available at http://www.alliancealert.org/2009/04/09/emu-sued-for-booting-student-over-views-on-gays.

Moen, Matthew C. 1992. *The Transformation of the Christian Right.* Tuscaloosa: University of Alabama Press.

Moshman, D. 2007. "Us and Them: Identity and Genocide." *Identity: An International Journal of Theory and Research* 7, no. 2: 115–35.

Moss, Candida. 2013. *The Myth of Persecution: How Early Christians Invented a Story of Martyrdom.* New York: Harper One.

Mungeam, Frank. 2011. "Commenting on the News: How the Degree of Anonymity Affects Flaming Online." Thesis, Gonzaga University.

Musarra, Annalisa. 2012. "Vanderbilt Christian Groups, Citing Religious Freedom, Follow Catholics Off Campus." *Huffington Post,* April 10, http://www.huffingtonpost.com/2012/04/10/vanderbilt-religious-groups_n_1416561.html.

Neumann, Joseph K., William Thompson, and Thomas W. Woolley. 1992. "Evangelical vs. Liberal Christianity: The Influence of Values on the Nonclinical Professional Decisions of Social Workers." *Journal of Psychology and Christianity* 11, no. 1: 57–67.

Nicholls, William. 1993. *Christian Antisemitism: A History of Hate.* Lanham, MD: Rowman & Littlefield.

Numbers, Ronald. 1998. *Darwinism Comes to America.* Cambridge, MA: Harvard University Press.

O'Brien, G. V. 2003. "People with Cognitive Disabilities: The Argument from Marginal Cases and Social Work Ethics." *Social Work* 48: 331–37.

Oberdiek, Hans. 2001. *Tolerance: Between Forbearance and Acceptance.* Lanham, MD: Rowman & Littlefield.

Oliver, J. Eric, and Tali Mendelberg. 2000. "Reconsidering the Environmental Determinants of White Racial Attitudes." *American Journal of Political Science* 44, no. 3: 574–89.

Omi, Michael, and Howard Winant. 1994. *Racial Formation in the United States: From the 1960s to the 1990s.* 2nd ed. New York: Routledge.

Opotow, Susan. 1990. "Moral Exclusion and Injustice: An Introduction." *Journal of Social Issues* 46, no. 1: 1–20.

Oskamp, Stuart. 2000. *Reducing Prejudice and Discrimination.* Mahwah, NJ: Lawrence Erlbaum Associates.

Ostrowski, Ally. 2006. "Texting Tolerance: Computer-Mediated Interfaith Dialogue." *Webology* 3, no. 4, article 34.

Parsons, Keith. 2013. *Persecution Myth*. Grand Rapids, MI: Grand Rapids Atheists and Freethinkers.

Paulson, Michael. 2014. "Colleges and Evangelicals Collide on Bias Policy." *New York Times*, June 9, http://www.nytimes.com/2014/06/10/us/colleges-and-evangelicals-collide-on-bias-policy.html?_r=0.

Pearson, Hugh. 1995. "Developing the Rage to Win." In *The Bell Curve Wars: Race, Intelligence and the Future of America*, edited by Steve Fraser, 164–71. New York: Basic Books.

Petrocik, John R. 2005. "Party Coalitions, Issue Agendas, and Morality Politics: The 2004 Presidential Election." Paper read at *The State of the Parties: 2004 and Beyond*, Akron, Ohio, October 2–5.

Pieterse, Jan Nederveen. 1995. *White on Black: Images of Africa and Blacks in Western Popular Culture*. New Haven, CT: Yale University Press.

Plous, S., and Tyrone Williams. 1995. "Racial Stereotypes from the Days of American Slavery: A Continuing Legacy." *Journal of Applied Social Psychology* 25, no. 9: 795–817.

Poliakov, Leon. 2003. *The History of Anti-Semitism: From Voltaire to Wagner*. Philadelphia: University of Pennsylvania Press.

Redekop, John J. 1968. *The American Far Right*. Grand Rapids, MI: William B. Eerdmans Publishing Co.

Revesz, Richard. 2009. "NYU Law School: No Conservative Christians Need Apply." *Catholic Online*, August 5, http://www.catholic.org/national/national_story.php?id=34204.

Rice, Jim. 2012. "Are Voter-ID Laws Racist?" *Sojourners*, April, http://sojo.net/magazine/2012/04/are-voter-id-laws-racist.

Richardson, J. 2007. "A Critique of 'Brainwashing' Claims about New Religious Movements." In *Cults and New Religious Movements: A Reader*, edited by Lorne L. Dawson, 160–66. Malden, MA: Blackwell Publishing.

Roberts, Keith A. 1986. "Sociology in the General Education Curriculum: A Cognitive Structuralist Perspective." *Teaching Sociology* 14, no. 4: 207–16.

Roberts, Keith A., and David Yamane. 2012. *Religion in Sociological Perspective*. 5th ed. Los Angeles, CA: Sage.

Ross, Luana. 1998. *Inventing the Savage: The Social Construction of Native American Criminality*. Austin: University of Texas Press.

Royzman, Edward B., Clark McCauley, and Paul Rosin. 2005. "From Plato to Putnam: Four Ways to Think about Hate." In *The Psychology of Hate*, edited by Robert J. Strenberg, 3–35. Washington, DC: American Psychological Association.

Sander, William. 2009. "Religious Background and Educational Attainment: The Effects of Buddhism, Islam, and Judaism." *Economics of Education Review* 29, no. 3: 489–93.

Sanderson, Terry. 2011. "How Many Times Can These Christian 'Victims' Cry Wolf before People Ignore Them." *National Secular Society*, August 5, http://www.secularism.org.uk/how-many-times-can-these-christi.html.

Schaefer, Richard T. 1996. "Education and Prejudice: Unraveling the Relationship." *Sociological Quarterly* 37: 1–16.

Scheepers, Peer, Manfred T. Grotenhuis, and Frans Van Der Slik. 2002. "Education, Religiosity and Moral Attitudes: Explaining Cross-National Effect Differences." *Sociology of Religion* 63, no. 2: 157–76.

Schuman, Howard, Charlotte Steeh, Lawrence Bobo, and Maria Krysan. 1997. *Racial Attitudes in America: Trends and Interpretations*. Cambridge, MA: Harvard University Press.

Sears, David O. 1988. "Symbolic Racism." In *Eliminating Racism: Profiles in Controversy*, edited by Phyllis A. Katz and Dalams A. Taylor, 55–58. Plenum Press: New York.

Shape, Patrick B. 2007. *Savage Perils: Racial Frontiers and Nuclear Apocalypse in American Culture*. Norman: University of Oklahoma Press.

Sheridan, Lorraine. 2006. "Islamophobia Pre– and Post–September 11th, 2001." *Journal of Interpersonal Violence* 21, no. 3: 317–36.

Shortt, Rupert. 2013. *Christianophobia: A Faith under Attack*. Grand Rapids, MI: William B. Eerdmans Publishing Co.

Sidanius, Jim, Felicia Pratto, and Lawrence Bobo. 1996. "Racism, Conservatism, Affirmative Action, and Intellectual Sophistication: A Matter of Principled Conservatism of Group Dominance?" *Interpersonal Relations and Group Processes* 70, no. 3: 476–90.

Skrzypczak, Meredith. 2010. "Should It Be Illegal to Post Ad Seeking Christian Roommate?" *Grand Rapids Press*, October 22, http://www.mlive.com/news/grand-rapids/index.ssf/2010/10/should_it_be_illegal_to_post_a.html.

Smith, Christian, Melinda Lundquist Denton, Robert Faris, and Mark Regnerus. 2002. "Mapping American Adolescent Religious Participation." *Journal for the Scientific Study of Religion* 41, no. 4: 597–612.

Smith, Christian, David Sikkink, and Jason Bailey. 1998. "Devotion in Dixie and Beyond: A Test of the 'Shibley Thesis' on the Effect of Regional Origin and Migration on Individual Religiosity." *Journal for the Scientific Study of Religion* 37, no. 3: 494–506.

Sniderman, Paul M., and Thomas Piazza. 1993. *The Scar of Race*. Cambridge, MA: Harvard University Press.

Sniderman, Paul M., and Philip E. Tetlock. 1986. "Symbolic Racism: Problems of Motive Attribution in Political Analysis." *Journal of Social Issues* 42: 129–50.

Solorzano, Daniel G. 1997. "Images and Words That Wound: Critical Race Theory, Racial Stereotyping, and Teacher Education." *Teacher Education Quarterly* (summer): 5–20.

Stark, Rodney, and Roger Finke. 2000. *Acts of Faith: Explaining the Human Side of Religion*. Berkeley: University of California Press.

Stewart, Brandon D., William von Hippel, and Gabriel A. Radvansky. 2009. "Age, Race, and Implicit Prejudice: Using Process Dissociation to Separate the Underlying Components." *Psychological Science* 20, no. 2: 164–68.

Strabac, Zan, and Ola Listhaug. 2008. "Anti-Muslim Prejudice in Europe: A Multilevel Analysis of Survey Data from 30 Countries." *Social Science Research* 37, no. 1: 268–86.

Teixeira, Ruy, and Alan Abramowitz. 2008. "The Decline of the White Working Class and the Rise of a Mass Upper Middle Class." In *Red, Blue and Purple America: The Future of Election Demographics*, edited by Ruy Teixeira, 109–43. Washington, DC: Brookings Institute Press.

Thaller, Jonel. 2011. "Resilience and Resistance in Professional Identity Making: Gleanings from the Classroom Experiences of Devout Christian Social Workers." *Journal of Religion and Spirituality in Social Work* 30, no. 2: 144–63.

Tileaga, Cristian. 2007. "Ideologies of Moral Exclusion: A Critical Discursive Reframing of Depersonalization, Delegitimization and Dehumanization." *British Journal of Social Psychology* 46, no. 4: 717–37.

Titman, Wendy. 1994. *Special Places, Special People: The Hidden Curriculum of School Grounds*. Toronto, Ontario: Green Brick Road.

Unsal, Ali. 2009. "Religious Tolerance (Tolerance in Islam)." Paper presented at the 4th International Conference of the Asian Philosophical Association, Depok, Indonesia, November 4–6.

Vogt, Paul W. 1997. *Tolerance and Education: Learning to Live with Diversity and Difference*. Thousand Oaks, CA: Sage.

Vonderwell, Selma. 2002. "An Examination of Asynchronous Communication Experiences and Perspectives of Students in an Online Course: A Case Study." *Internet and Higher Education* 6, no. 1: 77–90.

Weaver, David H., Randal A. Beam, Bonnie J. Brownlee, Paul S. Voakes, and G. Cleveland Wilhoit. 2007. *The American Journalist in the 21st Century: U.S. News People at the Dawn of a New Millennium*. Mahwah, NJ: Taylor & Francis.

Weber, Max. 1930. *The Protestant Ethic and the Spirit of Capitalism*. London: Unwin Paperbacks.

Wellman, James K. 2008. *Evangelical vs. Liberal: The Clash of Christian Cultures in the Pacific Northwest*. New York: Oxford University Press.

Werbner, Pnina. 2005. "Islamophobia: Incitement to Religious Hatred—Legislating for a New Fear?" *Anthropology Today* 21, no. 1: 5–9.

White, Ralph K. 1996. "Why the Serbs Fought: Motives and Misperceptions." *Peace and Conflict: Journal of Peace Psychology* 2, no. 2: 109–28.

Wilcox, Clyde. 1988. "Sources of Support for the Old Right: A Comparison of the John Birch Society and the Christian Anti-communism Crusade." *Social Science History* 12, no. 4: 429–49.

———. 1992. *God's Warriors: The Christian Right in Twentieth-Century America.* Baltimore: Johns Hopkins University Press.

Wilcox, Clyde, and Carin Larson. 2006. *Onward Christian Soldiers? The Religious Right in American Politics.* Boulder, CO: Westview Press.

Wilcox, Clyde, Lee Sigelman, and Elizabeth Cook. 1989. "Some Like It Hot: Individual Differences in Responses to Group Feeling Thermometers." *Public Opinion Quarterly* 53, no. 2: 246–57.

Wilkinson, W. W. 2004. "Religiosity, Authoritarianism and Homophobia: A Multidimensional Approach." *International Journal for the Psychology of Religion* 14, no. 1: 55–67.

Wilson, Thomas C. 1996. "Cohort and Prejudice: Whites' Attitudes toward Blacks, Hispanics, Jews, and Asians." *Public Opinion Quarterly* 60, no. 2: 253–74.

Wright, Alan N., and Jan Tolan. 2009. "Prejudice Reduction through Shared Adventure: A Qualitative Outcome Assessment of a Multicultural Education Class." *Journal of Experiential Education* 32, no. 2: 137–54.

Wright, Lester W., Henry E. Adams, and Jeffery A. Bernat. 1999. "The Homophobia Scale: Development and Validation." *Journal of Psychopathology and Behavioral Assessment* 21: 337–47.

Yancey, George. 2010. "Who Has Religious Prejudice? Differing Sources of Anti-religious Animosity in the United States." *Review of Religious Research* 52, no. 2 (December): 159–71.

———. 2011. *Compromising Scholarship: Religious and Political Bias in American Higher Education.* Waco, TX: Baylor University Press.

———. 2013. *Dehumanizing Christians.* Piscataway, NJ: Transaction Publishers.

Yancey, George, Sam Reimer, and Jake O'Connell. 2013. "Science Defines Religion: How U.S. Scholars Define and Perceive Fundamentalist, Evangelical and Mainline Protestants." Paper presented at the Society for the Scientific Study of Religion Annual Meeting, Boston, Massachusetts, November 8–10.

Yancey, George, and David Williamson. 2012. *What Motivates Cultural Progressives: Understanding Opposition to the Political and Christian Right.* Waco, TX: Baylor University Press.

Zeitlin, Irving M. 2004. *The Religious Experience: Classical Philosophical and Social Theories.* Upper Saddle River, NJ: Pearson/Prentice Hall.

Zubaran, Carlos. 2009. "Human Nomenclature: From Race to Racism." *World Health and Population* 11, no. 2: 43–52.

INDEX

ABOUT THE AUTHORS

George Yancey is professor of sociology at the University of North Texas. He is author of numerous books, including *Compromising Scholarship: Religious and Political Bias in American Higher Education* and *Dehumanizing Christians: Cultural Competition in a Multicultural World*. His teaching and research have focused on issues of race and religion.

David A. Williamson is associate professor of sociology at the University of North Texas and is author with George Yancey of *What Motivates Cultural Progressives?* and *There Is No God: Atheists in America*. He has taught extensively and conducted research for more than twenty years in Israel and throughout Africa.